D1475108

ADJUSTING THE BALANCE

**Recent Titles in
Contributions in Political Science
Series Editor: Bernard K. Johnpoll**

ADJUSTING THE BALANCE

Federal Policy and Victim Services

STEVEN RATHGEB SMITH and
SUSAN FREINKEL

Foreword by Laurence E. Lynn, Jr.

CONTRIBUTIONS IN POLITICAL SCIENCE,
NUMBER 194

GREENWOOD PRESS

New York
Westport, Connecticut
London

Library of Congress Cataloging-in-Publication Data

Smith, Steven Rathgeb, 1951–
  Adjusting the balance.

  (Contributions in political science,
ISSN 0147-1066 ; no. 194)
  Bibliography: p.
  Includes index.
    1. Victims of crimes—Government policy—United
States. 2. Victims of crimes—Services for—
Government policy—United States. I. Freinkel,
Susan, 1957–   II. Title. III. Series.
HV6250.3.U5S58 1988   362.89'8   87-15027
ISBN 0-313-25305-6 (lib. bdg. : alk. paper)

British Library Cataloguing in Publication Data is available.

Library of Congress Catalog Card Number: 87-15027
ISBN: 0-313-25305-6
ISSN: 0147-1066

First published in 1988

Greenwood Press, Inc.
88 Post Road West, Westport, Connecticut 06881

Printed in the United States of America

The paper used in this book complies with the
Permanent Paper Standard issued by the National
Information Standards Organization (Z39.48-1984).

10 9 8 7 6 5 4 3 2 1

CONTENTS

FOREWORD

Studies of social policy formation often reflect a normative perspective. The actions of public officials and the outcomes of governmental activity as they affect needy or dependent groups are, often in implicit, subtle ways, compared to idealized actions and outcomes, thought to be morally and ethically appropriate. To evaluate public policy formation in this manner is invariably to see policymaking in an unfavorable light: Public policies are viewed as a resultant of unfortunate compromises between our noblest impulses and our baser, more selfish desires. While conclusions of this sort may produce in a reader a determination to engage in more effective advocacy, they are just as likely to create or deepen cynicism about government. In the end, we may gain little insight into how a heterogeneous society collectively confronts controversial, morally charged issues.

In this study of federal policy toward the victims of rape, spouse abuse, child abuse, and crimes against the elderly, Steven Rathgeb Smith and Susan Freinkel have avoided such ideologic traps. Though moved by sympathy for these and other victims of violence, their primary goal is deeper understanding of how public policies are formed and implemented. In particular, they seek evidence bearing on their conjecture, supported by a number of other policy studies, that the way in which a social problem is defined—the particular linguistic forms, images, or symbols by which the concerns of policymakers are aroused—has enduring influence on the development of policy. Their careful and detailed examination of the initiation and evolution of public policies and services toward four distinctive groups of victims provides the basis for conclusions concerning the processes of policy formation which are both insightful to students of public policy and useful to those concerned with the availability and quality of victims' services.

In its conceptual orientation and respect for empirical detail, *Adjusting the Balance: Federal Policy and Victim Services* clearly reflects the influence of political scientists such as Hugh Heclo, John Kingdon, Charles E. Lindblom, and Michael Lipsky. Smith and Freinkel view policy formation as ongoing, fluid, spontaneous, and multivariate. It is shaped in subtle but powerful ways by those factors that shape policymakers' affective responses. Their responses in turn influence the choices of agencies, professional groups, and administrative forms through which funds are channeled into the service delivery system. Subsequent policy adjustment and change occurs within the context created by these affect-influenced choices. While avoiding reductionist generalizations, Smith and Freinkel nonetheless are able to note that the different groups of victims tended to be viewed similarly: as "helpless, frail, vulnerable, and trauma stricken," and as victims of crime rather than as victims of gender-, age-, class-, or wealth-based inequities. Because victims' issues were framed this way, policymakers were able to avoid divisive ideologic controversies that might have stymied action.

In another sense, this book is about the evolution of the American Welfare State in the latter half of the twentieth century. Thus, it is a useful addition to the rapidly growing literature devoted to the critical reexamination of social welfare policies and programs. In tracing the development of policies toward victims from their initiation in accordance with the liberal premises of the 1960s and 1970s into the Reagan era, Smith and Freinkel provide a rich body of evidence concerning the programmatic and administrative consequences of the shift to more conservative policy premises. They invite us to speculate on the future implications for public policy of viewing victims as "a class of injured citizens with shared problems and experiences, rather than as separate categories of unfortunates, which was the implicit view that prevailed in the 1970s." Their sympathies for victims candidly revealed, they are not optimistic. By illuminating the policymaking process in an insightful way, however, *Adjusting the Balance* can only heighten awareness of the policy issues affecting criminal victims and make possible more enlightened and informed policy analysis and advocacy.

—Laurence E. Lynn, Jr.

ACKNOWLEDGMENTS

This book reflects the contributions of countless people who provided research assistance, advice, criticism, and moral support to us during the course of our research and writing.

Financial support for the initial research that forms the basis for this book was generously provided by the National Institute of Mental Health (NIMH); we are deeply indebted to Susan Salasin of NIMH for her support of the project.

We are especially thankful to Laurence E. Lynn, Jr., who provided us with the opportunity to conduct our research at the Kennedy School of Government at Harvard University. His counsel throughout the project was invaluable. His continued interest during subsequent research and rewriting has also been deeply appreciated.

At the Kennedy School, our research was aided by the insights and assistance of David Samuel Kruse, Ruth Rose, and Carol Joy Gordon. David worked on the initial stages of the project, developing key theories to guide the research. Ruth researched and wrote a bibliography on federal involvement in victim services that helped us organize our research strategy, and Joy investigated congressional deliberations on victim services.

Ultimately, though, our work depended upon the graciousness and good will of dozens of people working in the field of victim services who gave of their time to answer our questions and provide written information on their programs. Needless to say, without their cooperation, this book would not have been written. We have tried to mention each person we interviewed in our notes at the end of each chapter.

A few additional people deserve mention. Fay Lomax Cook of Northwestern University was an early supporter of our research; her contributions throughout our project have improved our final product in important and substantial ways. Likewise, Michael Lipsky of the Massachusetts Institute of Technology encouraged our project and commented usefully on several chapters. Deborah A. Stone of Brandeis University and Martha Wagner Weinberg of Brown University also provided advice and criticism.

Finally, Penny Smith deserves our thanks and gratitude. Her support of both of us and her toleration of the countless hours her husband spent at the word processor have made this project possible. She also served as a thoughtful critic throughout the project.

Of course, the authors take full responsibility for any errors, mistakes, or misinterpretations.

1

INTRODUCTION

On 28 September 1981, in a speech to the International Association of Chiefs of Police, President Ronald Reagan announced that his administration was declaring a war on crime.

Such announcements from new presidents are not unusual; nearly every recent administration has sworn to do something about this issue, which preoccupies so many Americans. But Reagan added a twist. Pledging to overhaul the federal criminal code, he promised an effort to "redress the imbalance between the rights of the accused and the rights of the innocent."[1]

Reagan's statement was testimony to just how far the movement to advance the rights of victims of crime had come. Earlier in the year, he had declared a National Victims' Rights Week to draw attention to the problems of crime victims. In 1982, he formed a President's Task Force on Victims of Crime to examine victims' treatment by the criminal justice system and to recommend ways to "redress the imbalance." In Reagan, victims' advocates had at last found a national spokesman for their cause.

It was the capstone to a movement that has been slowly escalating over the last 30 years.

Interest in the problem of criminal victimization comes from many quarters—academia, the legal and social service system, special interest groups, and politicians. There has been a surge of attention to the psychological trauma of victimization and to the emotional and material hardships crime exacts of its victims. And as Reagan's speech suggests, there is increased interest in the legal status of victims and their position in the justice system, which victims' advocates say is sacrificed through excessive attention to the rights of criminal defendants.

In short, over the past three decades, the status of crime victims has been transformed from that of a random group of unlucky individuals into a class whose common misfortune renders them especially deserving of governmental attention.

Every state has passed dozens of laws to address victims' grievances—from rewriting certain criminal laws to creating programs to reimburse victims for crime-related losses. And in 1984, Congress passed the Victims of Crime Act (VOCA), which will distribute millions collected from fines on federal crimes to victims' assistance groups.[2] As of early 1986, there were at least 5,000 grassroots groups across the country devoted to the rights of victims.[3] "It's the civil rights movement of the 80s," the head of a Maryland victims' organization told *The Wall Street Journal.*[4]

The new interest in victims arose out of the confluence of several social streams. One, not surprisingly, was the wellspring of public anxiety about crime. Social scientist Fay Lomax Cook has observed, "Although there have been other times in our history when the issue of crime aroused greater anxiety, the reaction to crime which began during the 1960s and continued into the 1970s was unprecedented."[5] As Cook notes, the crime issue occupied a central place in both the public mind and the formal policy agenda—that is, the list of issues constituting the focus of policy at any given time. The importance of the crime issue was signified by the creation in 1968 of the Law Enforcement Assistance Administration (LEAA), established with the ambitious mandate to eliminate crime.

The mandate was, in a sense, the last gasp of a two-decade-long effort at criminal justice reform. Throughout the 1950s and 1960s, public policy revolved around efforts to redress social and class prejudices in the prosecution of criminals and to deter crime through the rehabilitation of criminals.

Philosophically, these efforts were predicated on the belief that crime was an outgrowth of social and economic inequalities, rather than the result of an innate or immutable criminal deviance. Thus, policy tried to provide opportunities to offenders, through jail-based prisoner counseling programs, diversion programs, or community-based correctional services. The rehabilitative approach always had its opponents, but by the early 1970s, it was drawing heavy fire.

Opponents argued that rehabilitation was ineffective, that reform efforts had left the justice system too heavily weighted toward protecting the rights of defendants to the neglect of those of victims, and that the implementation of rehabilitation programs was discriminatory and inequitable.[6] It was a short philosophical step from a rejection of the concept of rehabilitation to an embrace of the idea of retribution—readjusting the system to ensure that criminals got their just deserts. Advocates of retribution argued that if society could not prevent crime, at least it should ensure the punishment of those who commit crime.

Support for a retributive approach came from disparate quarters, cutting across traditional political lines. One reason was that, increasingly, the old retribution argument was being couched in a new civil liberties language. Victims were described as a forgotten minority, one whose rights had been lost in the criminal justice process.[7]

That victims' issues should be framed in such terms is understandable: since the civil rights movement, "rights language" has provided the vocabulary for groups seeking governmental attention. In addition, the victims' movement is a grandchild of the civil rights movement, born from the social movements that arose in the 1970s, in the wake of the civil rights struggle. Issues of criminal victimization emerged as subsets of larger issues of social victimization that had galvanized such groups as women, senior citizens, and children's advocates into political action.

Thus, feminists articulated and publicized such issues as rape and spouse abuse, senior citizens called attention to crime against the elderly, and children's advocates sought publicity on child abuse. While these groups generally hovered near the liberal end of the political spectrum, they often worked with more conservative allies when it came to pressing for a policy response to issues of criminal victimization. Indeed, this liberal-conservative alliance has strengthened in the 1980s, as the notion of victims' rights has gained wider acceptance in political circles and among the general public.[8]

Trends in the social sciences also lent weight to victims' issues. The field of victimology dates back to the 1940s, when several criminologists rebelled against their discipline's focus on offenders and began to study the long-neglected victim. The field attracted academics and practitioners from a variety of backgrounds, who spent many years on the margins of collegial credibility. But by the 1970s, victimology had gained sufficient stature and sophistication to exert influence on policy. Further, as the political popularity of victims' issues increased, the number of academicians and researchers involved in victimology grew. Thus, the circle of people and institutions with a stake in continued governmental attention to the issues widened.

These kinds of factors coalesced in "a ripe issue climate": a political, cultural, and social readiness to address crime-related problems from the victim's standpoint.[9] Not only did these factors facilitate recognition of victims' issues; they also influenced how the issues were introduced, defined, and ultimately acted upon.

Throughout the 1960s and 1970s, a succession of victims' issues assumed a major place on social policy agendas. Child abuse was brought to public attention by pediatricians and child advocates in the early 1960s, and it remains the most firmly established of all victims' issues. In the early 1970s, the issue of rape and the problem of insensitive treatment of rape victims by medical, legal, and social institutions achieved prominence through the efforts of the women's movement. Attention shifted in the mid-1970s to the problem of crime against the elderly, an issue initiated by senior citizens' organizations and their legislative allies. And the issue of battered women, or domestic violence, dominated victims' policy in the late 1970s—a product of the women's movement and the research of social scientists. Each victims' issue was the object of initial enthusiasm: a number of federal agencies became involved in activities aimed at a specific type of victimization, and the field of service programs expanded. Over time, interest in each issue receded, its policy salience diminished, and service programs found it increasingly difficult to muster the support they had once enjoyed, especially at the federal level.

During the last ten years, important and pioneering research has been done on the emergence of some of these victims' issues as public policy problems. For example, Barbara Nelson has written extensively about the rise of child abuse onto the public policy agenda.[10] Similarly, Fay Lomax Cook has analyzed the public policy toward elderly crime victims in the 1970s.[11] Other scholars have investigated the development of programs for rape victims,[12] battered women,[13] and crime victims in general.[14]

Our study of public policy for victims of crime is a departure from earlier work on crime victims in two key respects: (1) it is a comparative analysis of the evolution of four separate, albeit related issues; and (2) it examines the implementation of victims' programs and services at the local level, with a focus on the impact of federal policy on those service organizations.

The conception of public policy that guided our analysis challenges many conventional definitions of policy. Rather than viewing policy as a particular piece of legislation or agency directive, we see it as an ongoing process extending from issue definition through implementation.[15] Therefore, in analyzing the development of policy at the federal level the examination reaches beyond agency and congressional action to account for the role of interest groups, professionals, and academics, as well as the general ideational and political currents that exert both formal and informal influence on the shaping of an issue. A particular emphasis is on the agenda-building process: the ways in which issues vie for and receive the attention of policymakers.[16] The manner in which the policy agenda is established—and the definition of the issues that become the focus of policy—often has enduring impact on later policy developments.

Analysis of developments at the local level is considered equally important to an understanding of policy. Because legislation and agency directives are often vague and fraught with political exigencies, there is enormous potential for differences between stated objectives and subsequent outcomes. Thus the process of implementation has tremendous impact on what the record of a particular policy will look like.[17] If the programs and services created or sponsored by the federal government represent policy implementation, then factors such as the types of service programs that predominate, the professional and community groups involved, the background of service providers, and the kinds of services and organizations that endure are all relevant in analyzing policy implementation. Most important is how funding was distributed. For funding can be considered the most tangible link between policy conceptualization and implementation; thus, it is essential to examine the patterns of funding and its effects.

Accordingly, one goal of this book is to show the ways in which various stages of the policy process are crucially linked: how the initial definition of an issue affects its political fate, the articulated policy and policy implementation; how the course of implementation is a crucial determinant of policy, and how the interaction among federal, state, and local administrations influences the creation and implementation of policy.

A second objective of our study is to provide a developmental history of categorical victims' programs. Despite the copious articles and books specifically addressed to the issues of rape, child abuse, spouse abuse, and crimes against the elderly, there is surprisingly little detailed discussion and analysis of services or programs for these four victims groups. Even fewer works are concerned with critical analysis of the policymaking process for these issues either separately or as a whole.

Analyzing victims' policy involved a three-part research process. The initial phase of the research was a review of the relevant literature, to gain an overview of the varied programmatic responses to victims' issues and the intellectual influences upon them. This effort included an examination of academic work such as studies investigating causality, rates of frequency, offenders' and victims' traits, and the psychological, socioeconomic, and cultural factors associated with victimization. Also covered were debates pertaining to the experience of practitioners: the development of ideas about service delivery, the various models proposed for victims' assistance, and the way victims' needs have been conceptualized by different professional groups.

The second phase of the research was an effort to locate federally funded programs delivering services to victims of rape, child abuse, spouse abuse, and crimes against the elderly. Ideally, the programs chosen for study were to be representative of the constellation of services available in each category. However, the development of this group of representative programs was difficult. There is a surprising paucity of literature describing, comparing, or evaluating existing programs or services for victims. And most of the work that exists has an academic orientation—tending toward theoretical debate, rather than evaluation of practice. The level of organization in a given field also affected the process of locating programs. When strong organizational contacts or networks existed, identifying programs was relatively easy. But when these contacts were lacking, the problems multiplied. For example, because rape crisis centers operated more or less independently of one another, it was very difficult to locate centers, much less gain a sense of the various types or number in existence at any one time. By contrast, programs for elderly crime victims were easily located and cataloged, in large measure because of the existence of well-developed, powerful senior citizens organizations that monitored programs and shepherded the issue at all levels of government. This difficulty in identifying victims' programs was exacerbated by the general instability of the programs. Programs for all four categories of victims' services were, and are, notoriously short-lived. Indeed, a common lament among service providers was that by the time program directories could be published, they were already out of date.

The last stage of the research involved gathering information on specific programs. While some of this data was available through primary and secondary sources, the majority of the information was gained through interviews with the staff of particular programs. Questions focused upon service components and delivery, program administration, and funding. Information was requested on the types of services available, the historical events that led to the development of the services, and the factors influencing the choice of particular service models.

The investigation also focused on the organizational structure of service programs and how these changed over time. Thus, staffing patterns and the role of professionals, paraprofessionals, and volunteers in the operation and delivery of services were examined. The decision-making structure of programs—how lines of authority and accountability were drawn—was also relevant to the analysis. Other aspects of service delivery studied included budget size, the sources of support, and the kinds of conflicts engendered by various types of funding. The overriding interest, however, was in the effects of federal funding: How had federal grants influenced the service or organizational policy of a local program?

Most of the interviews were conducted in the period 1980–82.

However, archival research and selected interviews have been used to track the developments in the victims' programs in the study during the last five years.

The research addressed the four victims' issues separately, as distinct foci of policy attention. Yet a major question underlying the research was whether for analytical or political purposes rape, spouse abuse, child abuse, and crimes against the elderly were best understood as discrete and unrelated. Or could they be seen as parts of a generic package: the victims' issue? Thus, the research was undertaken not only to evaluate policy for the individual issues but also with an eye to discerning underlying patterns attending victimization policy as a whole.

An analysis of victims' programs is particularly apropos at this juncture. The policies of the Reagan administration represent a sharp turning point for the federal government's role in social policy, including victims' issues. The administration has expressed a determination to strengthen the ability of the criminal justice system to respond to the crime problem and to improve the status of the victim within the justice system. Yet the administration's commitment to block grant funding, fiscal retrenchment, and program deregulation has meant a dramatic shift in responsibility for social programs from the federal government to the states.

These two developments have produced a major transition period for American social policy in general and victimization policy in particular. Thus, an assessment of past experiences can be both useful and illuminating. An analysis of the past federal response to the problems of child abuse, spouse abuse, rape, and crimes against the elderly can clarify present policy developments and provide guidance for the future of victims' issues.

NOTES

1. *Facts on File*, 1981.
2. The Victims of Crime Act of 1984 is P. L. 98–473.
3. National Organization for Victims' Assistance, quoted by Cynthia Crossen, "Crime Victims Are Winning Share of Fines, Role in Judicial Process," *The Wall Street Journal*, 18 April 1986, p. 37.
4. Ibid.
5. Fay Lomax Cook, "Criminal Victimization of the Elderly: The Role of Social Science Knowledge in Moving the Issue onto and off the Policy

Agenda" (paper presented at A Conference on Knowledge Use, Pittsburgh, Pa., 18–20 March 1981), p. 4.

6. For a good discussion of the decline of faith in rehabilitation, see Martin R. Gardner, "The Renaissance of Retribution—An Examination of Doing Justice," *Wisconsin Law Review* (1976):781–814. More recently, see Roger Starr, "Crime: How It Destroys, What Can Be Done," *The New York Times Magazine*, 27 January 1985, pp. 19–60.

7. See, for example, Morton Bard and Dawn Sangrey, *The Crime Victim's Book* (New York: Basic Books, 1979); Robert Reiff, *The Invisible Victim: The Criminal Justice System's Forgotten Responsibility* (New York: Basic Books, 1979).

8. Examples of the growing strength and appeal of the victims' movement in the 1980s are contained in the following articles: Molly Ivins, "Victims Say Lives Echo with Grief," *The New York Times*, 21 April 1981, p. B1; Richard Higgins, "Help for the Victim," *The Boston Globe Magazine*, 11 January 1981, pp. 12–13, 22–30; John Heinz, "On Justice to Victims," *The New York Times*, 7 July 1982, p. A19; Barbara Kaplan, "A Survivor's Story," *The Boston Globe Magazine*, 16 March 1983, pp. 8, 57–63; "Panel Urges New Laws to Aid Crime Victims," *The New York Times*, 28 January 1983, p. B7; Jeffrey Schmalz, "Crime Victims Seeking Voice in Legal System," *The New York Times*, 6 March 1985, p. B2; Crossen, "Crime Victims Are Winning Share of Fines."

9. The concept of a "ripe issue climate" is discussed by Cook, "Criminal Victimization of the Elderly," p. 4. For further discussion of the factors responsible for the adoption of issues by policymakers, see John W. Kingdon, *Agendas, Alternatives, and Public Policies* (Boston: Little, Brown and Co., 1984), esp. chap. 8; Barbara J. Nelson, *Making an Issue of Child Abuse: Political Agenda Setting for Social Problems* (Chicago: University of Chicago Press, 1984), esp. chap. 7; Jack L. Walker, "The Diffusion of Innovations among the American States," *American Political Science Review* 63, 3 (September 1969):880–99; Virginia Gray, "Innovation in the States: A Diffusion Study," *American Political Science Review* 67, 4 (December 1973):1174–85.

10. Nelson, *Making an Issue of Child Abuse.*

11. See Cook, "Criminal Victimization of the Elderly."

12. See Elizabeth O'Sullivan, "What Has Happened to Rape Crisis Centers? A Look at Their Structure, Members and Funding," *Victimology: An International Journal* 3, 1–2 (1978):45–62.

13. See Susan Schechter, *Women and Male Violence: The Visions and Struggles of the Battered Women's Movement* (Boston: South End Press, 1982).

14. See Bard and Sangrey, *The Crime Victim's Book*; Reiff, *The Invisible Victim.*

15. For further discussion of conceptions of public policy as a process extending from issue definition through implementation, consult Hugh Heclo, "Review Article: Policy Analysis," *British Journal of Political Science* 2 (1971):83–108. Also see Donald C. Baumer and Carl E. Van Horn, *The Politics of Unemployment* (Washington, D. C.: CQ Press, 1985), esp. pp. 33–57.

16. Important studies of the agenda-building process include Roger W. Cobb and Charles D. Elder, *Participation in American Politics: The Dynamics of Agenda-Building* (Baltimore: Johns Hopkins University Press, 1972); Nelson, *Making an Issue of Child Abuse*; Kingdon, *Agendas, Alternatives, and Public Policies.*

17. The studies that discuss the important role of the implementation phase of the policymaking process on policy outcomes are, by now, very numerous. For a few representative studies, consult Jeffrey L. Pressman and Aaron Wildavsky, *Implementation*, 3rd ed. (Berkeley: The University of California Press, 1984); Michael Lipsky, "Standing the Study of Public Policy Implementation on Its Head," in *American Politics and Public Policy*, ed. by Walter Dean Burnham and Martha Wagner Weinberg (Cambridge, Mass.: MIT Press, 1978); Daniel A. Mazmanian and Paul A. Sabatier, *Implementation and Public Policy* (Glenview, Ill.: Scott, Foresman and Co., 1983).

2

THE VICTIM IN
PERSPECTIVE

Underlying the recent emergence of programs for victims of crime is a widespread dissatisfaction with the existing relationship between the criminal justice system and the victim. To many people, the victim has been the neglected party in criminal cases, treated with indifference and callousness by judges, lawyers, and the police. To exacerbate the situation, the legal system provides few legal avenues for the victim to seek redress beyond the trial. Victim compensation and restitution programs, for example, remain very restricted despite the efforts of victims' advocates. This, as many writers have noted, was not always the case; in earlier times the victim had a far more prominent, prestigious status within the administration of justice.[1]

In primitive cultures, victims were allowed to seek private revenge and retaliation. As these cultures became more organized, private vengeance was replaced by a collective retribution—"blood feuds" regulated by clans or tribes. But as communities grew and stabilized, collective vengeance also proved unsatisfactory, since it frequently led to unmanageable, disruptive levels of violence. Thus, there gradually arose a new procedure, composition: a formalized negotiation process between the families of the offender and victim to provide "indemnification to the victim through the payment of goods and money."[2]

Generally, composition applied in cases of "personal wrongs, not public crimes."[3] In practice, this distinction was difficult to determine; however, personal wrongs usually were cases of personal bodily injury or property crimes. Public crimes, by contrast, were offenses against the entire community such as theft or destruction of community property. (These crimes were simply punished, often quite severely.) In its most elaborate forms, the composition process occurred within a structured framework; specific amounts of compensation were prescribed, depending upon the nature of the crime and the "age, rank, sex, and prestige of the injured party."[4] Since the communities in these societies established these compensation schedules, composition was the first significant intrusion of the community into the relationship between victim and criminal.

Composition was an important development in a number of respects. It was the first formal restitution arrangement for victims. It provided an opportunity for the victim to influence the restitution decision. And in retrospect, it was a bridge between the chaotic early blood feuds and the monopolization of punishment by the state in the Middle Ages and thereafter, which undermined composition and greatly reduced the ability of the victim to seek redress from the criminal. Thus, the relationship of the victim to the criminal was bound up with the relationship of the state to its citizens: as the state grew in power, crime was redefined as an offense against the state rather than the individual, and the victim became an incidental observer of the administration of justice.

As the state grew, composition was gradually replaced by a system of fines paid by the offender to the state, underscoring that the offender had wronged not merely the individual victim but the state. This arrangement was formalized within Anglo-Saxon law during the late Middle Ages. As the state gained control over criminal punishment, the practice of obliging offenders to pay damages directly to their victims—the composition system—became the basis of a separate, special field of law: civil law.[5]

The primacy of the state-offender relationship persisted until the mid-twentieth century, although through the intervening centuries a number of prominent individuals continued to advocate restitution. Sir Thomas More, for example, urged that offenders should be obligated to make restitution to their victims and that they should earn the money through forced public works projects. Jeremy Bentham advocated mandatory restitution, paid by a state compensation system, in cases of property crime.[6] Bentham's idea went largely unnoticed and unsupported until the late nineteenth century, when a number of noted criminologists of the day once again urged the adoption of a restitution program for crime victims.[7] The Fifth International Prison Congress, a convocation of criminologists and legal experts in 1895 in Paris, officially resolved that "penal legislation ought to take more account than it has hitherto done of the necessity of assuring reparation to the injured party."[8] Despite this formal recommendation, efforts to initiate victim compensation and restitution remained moribund.

Ironically, this same Paris Congress also recommended that countries adopt indeterminate sentencing, parole, and probation, measures that today are opposed by many victims' advocates. As a noted criminologist later observed, these policy recommendations represented the "individualization of punishment."[9] By fitting the punishment to the criminal rather than to the crime, supporters of these measures hoped to use sentencing as a tool of rehabilitation. Their hopes for rehabilitative sentencing were staked on the perceived effectiveness of the new fields of psychology and psychiatry in understanding and altering human behavior. Crime was considered to be a dynamic phenomenon whose etiology varied depending upon the individual in question. Thus, by employing the knowledge provided by these nascent behavioral sciences, judges, lawyers, and prison officials would be able to discern the familial, cultural, and psychological factors that had led the individual to the criminal act. This information would then be used to rehabilitate the criminal and prevent future crime. As in the earlier schemes, the victim was still relegated to the sidelines.

Given this offender orientation in criminology in the early twentieth century, it is not surprising that the first American scholar to call attention to the crime victim was one who was primarily interested in the psychology of the criminal.[10] Hans von Hentig believed that criminologists had overlooked the most important dynamic relationship affecting criminal behavior: the criminal-victim relationship. As he noted, "Many criminal deeds are more indicative of a subject-object relation than of the perpetrator alone."[11] Von Hentig's analysis of the criminal-victim relationship showed little sympathy for the victim. Indeed, to von Hentig, the victim, in many instances, shared the culpability for his or her victimization. In a high percentage of criminal cases, he postulated, "the victim shapes and moulds the criminal."[12] For example, the greedy, he contended, were ripe for victimization. "They can be hooked by all sorts of devices which hold out bait to their cupidity."[13]

Further, he argued that just as a variety of interacting forces shaped the criminal, the victim was the product of a set of forces that facilitated victimization: "The suggestion is offered herewith that slums attract both potential victims and potential criminals, the preyer and the prey, and that out of their contact originates what we call crime, or vice, or unlabeled exploitation."[14]

Independent of von Hentig, a Romanian lawyer, Beniamin Mendelsohn, published a series of articles in the early post–World War II period examining the crime victim from "a bio-psycho-social point of view" in an attempt to explain how specific criminal-victim relationships may have precipitated a criminal act.[15] But, departing from von Hentig, he dubbed the new field "victimology," to highlight that the new science's structure and aims were separate from the traditional study of crime—criminology.[16]

But throughout the 1950s and early 1960s, von Hentig's view predominated, and victims remained the province of criminology. Typical of the prevailing thinking was a book published in 1954 by a psychoanalyst, Dr. Henri Ellenberger, entitled *Relations psychologiques entre le criminel et sa victims*. He observed, "The idea of criminal-victim needs to be put in its proper place. This means, among other things, that in criminological practice one should think much more often of examining the victim. . . . Criminologists should give to victimogenesis as much attention as to criminogenesis."[17] Concurring with Ellenberger was Dr. W. H. Nagel, who wrote that because modern criminology now recognized the importance of the "victimological situation" there was no longer any need for a separate science of victimology.[18]

A variant of the "victimogenesis" thesis offered by Ellenberger, victim precipitation, was put forth in a 1957 article by the American criminologist Marvin E. Wolfgang. As a result of his study of criminal homicide in Philadelphia, he concluded that in many homicides "the victim may be one of the major precipitating causes of his own demise."[19]

The types of examples Wolfgang cited were: (1) "In an argument over a business transaction, the victim fired several shots at his adversary, who in turn fatally returned the fire," (2) "A drunken victim with knife in hand approached his slayer during a quarrel. The slayer showed a gun, and the victim dared him to shoot. He did," and (3) "A drunken husband, beating his wife in their kitchen, gave her a butcher knife and dared her to use it on him." After further physical abuse, "she fatally stabbed him."[20]

As noted, many individuals prior to the twentieth century had offered an alternative reason for public and private interest in the victim: that victims were entitled, because of their misfortune, to public and private assistance. The resurrection of this entitlement principle in the mid-twentieth century was led by the English social reformer Margery Fry, who published a series of articles urging the adoption of victim compensation proposals. Her original interest in the victim, like that of many of her contemporaries, was motivated by a desire to understand criminal behavior and help the criminal. "Compensation," she wrote in 1951, "cannot undo the wrong, but it will often assuage the injury, and it has a real educative value for the offender, whether adult or child."[21] By 1957, her views had shifted, and she began to emphasize that the injury the victim had suffered was in itself legitimate rationale for victim compensation programs. Her argument rested on two major assumptions. First, she believed that the state had an obligation to help its injured citizens, an argument that to her was made more compelling by England's extensive workman's compensation programs. Second, she argued that the state was obligated to compensate the victim since it was the state's responsibility to protect its citizens. A crime was a "failure to protect" on the part of the state, which entitled the victim to receive monetary damages from the state.[22]

At the time, Fry's proposal was met with scattered opposition. Fred E. Inbau, a professor of law at Northwestern University, observed, "to compensate victims of violent crimes is to indulge in the kind of thinking that could lead us into an abandonment of all notions of individual responsibility and a resort to complete dependence upon governmental paternalism."[23] Henry Weihofen, also a professor of law, thought the precipitating role of many victims could create numerous legal obstacles and investigative problems for any victims' compensation program.[24]

Like other critics of Fry, both Inbau and Weihofen believed that the victim's culpability in many crimes should preclude the development of a government compensation program for crime victims. Others, criminologists who believed that victims were inherently entitled to governmental assistance, recognized that their focus on offenders and offender rehabilitation was unpopular with the public. The prevalence of this thinking was evident in a 1959 British white paper entitled *Penal Practice in a Changing Society.* The authors of the report observed: ,

The assumption that the claims of the victim are sufficiently satisfied if the offender is punished by society becomes less persuasive as society in its dealings with offenders increasingly emphasizes the reformative aspects of punishment. Indeed, in the public mind the interests of the offender may not infrequently seem to be placed before those of the victim. This is certainly not the correct emphasis. It may well be that our penal system would not only provide a more effective deterrent to crime, but would also find a greater moral value, if the concept of personal reparation to the victim were added to the concepts of deterrence by punishment and of reformation by training.[25]

Reformative policies were unpopular because, according to two prominent criminologists, Harry Elmer Barnes and Negley K. Teeters, most laymen regarded probation and parole as overly lenient sentences that were "a sop thrown to the criminal and a slap at society." Barnes and Teeters, who were advocates of rehabilitation programs, countered with the observation that the prejudices against probation and parole were based upon inadequate information and inappropriate, negative generalizations drawn from a few cases of ineffective or injudicious implementation.[26]

The elevation of victims as appropriate clients of government social policy coincided with the dramatic expansion of the welfare state in the 1960s. For example, it was from an overall sense of social justice that the liberal Supreme Court justice Arthur J. Goldberg urged in a 1964 article that the "serious consideration" of government compensation for victims of crime was "long overdue."[27] In a similar vein, Robert Childres, a New York University law professor, asked rhetorically, "If each year 160,000 people are violently attacked, is it the more enlightened policy to share their losses in common or to leave the injured to do as they can? Should we all suffer unnoticeable losses or should a few meet disaster?"[28] Echoing Fry's argument of seven years earlier, Childres wrote that a society which "tolerates havens of violence is responsible for the damage their inmates inflict" upon the citizenry.[29] Yet Childres, like many criminologists and laymen, was troubled that the failure-to-protect argument could justify deterministic arguments that placed the responsibility for all crime upon society, denying freedom of will and individual responsibility.[30]

Notwithstanding these doubts, the failure-to-protect argument, coupled with the widespread sentiment for an enhanced government role on behalf of the disadvantaged, provided theoretical justification for a growing political movement to enact victims' compensation legislation. At the federal level, Senator Ralph W. Yarborough (D-Tex.) in 1965 introduced in the U.S. Senate a bill proposing a federal victims' compensation program. Senator Yarborough's bill deliberately defined the jurisdiction of the proposed program as "the limited areas of general federal police power and responsibility" because the "right of the victim to compensation from the state arises from the failure of the state to protect from crime."[31]

Although Yarborough's proposal died in committee, the movement to enact victims' compensation programs continued to gain strength. Shortly before Yarborough's bill was introduced in Congress, California enacted the nation's first victims' compensation program. New York (1967), Hawaii (1967), Maryland (1968), and Massachusetts (1968) soon followed with their own victims' compensation programs.

A predominant view among many state legislators at the time was that the criminal justice system was tilted too far in favor of the criminal: the criminal was entitled to numerous rights and services, while the victim was ignored and neglected. In this spirit, the sponsor of California's victims' compensation legislation, State Senator J. Eugene McAteer, observed, "What the legislature had in mind was seeing to it that innocent victims of crime get the same kind of treatment from society that the criminal gets—medical treatment, plastic surgery, rehabilitation, everything that we provide for the wrongdoer."[32]

The flip side of this entitlement principle was a reemphasis on retribution, although in the late 1960s, the arguments that society had "gone soft" on criminals were not as strident as they would become in the 1970s and 1980s. Rehabilitation-based criminal law, it was believed, not only was ineffective but also discriminated against victims by being too lenient toward criminals. Thus, rehabilitation-based programs, such as parole, probation, and offender counseling, prevented the victim from achieving satisfaction—exacting retribution—by mitigating or preventing long prison sentences.

The potential for crime prevention also drew support to victims' compensation programs. In response to a rising crime rate in the late 1960s, many legislators reasoned that victims' compensation programs would encourage cooperation with the police. In an environment where reporting was encouraged, it was hoped that the conviction rate would increase and crime prevention would improve through a more vigilant citizenry.[33]

The entitlement principle, the call for retribution, the failure-to-protect argument, and the social welfare argument provided the intellectual impetus for the passage of victims' compensation proposals during the late 1960s. However, an enduring ambivalence about the victim's responsibility for his or her plight and the fiscal conservatism of state legislatures conspired to restrict and limit victims' compensation programs. Without exception, the state victims' compensation programs enacted in this period were underfunded, considering the potential need, and excluded large numbers of victims through restrictive regulations.

California's program was typical of the severe underfunding problem. In its first year of operation, the program was appropriated only $100,000 by the state legislature. With a ceiling of $5,000 on compensation awards, it was estimated that only 40 families a year would receive aid.[34]

The exclusionary regulations related primarily to the type of victim covered and the kind of recoverable expenses. Regarding the former, every state program but one limited compensation eligibility to victims of violent crime; only Hawaii allowed recovery for property crime. In addition, most states limited the applicant pool by disqualifying many victims of violent crime from eligibility, including victims who were related to the offender, victims who had a prior "intimate contact" with the offender, and victims who were culpable for their victimization.[35] California and

New York initially required a needs test for their programs, limiting compensation to people with low incomes. Also, most states restricted compensation to concrete expenses such as medical costs and loss of earnings; only Hawaii allowed recovery for pain and suffering. Moreover, recovery for allowable expenses was rarely awarded in full, and most states deducted any public or private insurance reimbursement from the amount of the compensation award.[36] The number of victims likely to apply for compensation was also limited by the lack of publicity about the programs and the detailed, time-consuming process required for application.

Since the late 1960s, victims' compensation programs have experienced dramatic growth. Forty-four states and the District of Columbia currently have victims' compensation programs. Nearly all still limit eligible expenses to medical costs and lost wages. Property losses and recovery for pain and suffering are still not covered in most states.[37]

At the federal level, several unsuccessful attempts were made in the 1970s to pass a federal victims' compensation law. In 1984, though, Congress passed the Victims of Crime Act (VOCA), which channels funds collected from federal criminal penalties and fines to victims' groups across the country. During fiscal year 1986, approximately $68 million was raised for victims' programs through this collection system; roughly one-third of this amount is being devoted to victims' compensation programs, with the remaining two-thirds for victims' services. Consistent with the Reagan administration philosophy of social program decentralization, the disbursement and administration of the VOCA funds reside with the states. However, three priority groups have been identified by the federal government: victims of sexual assault, spouse abuse, and child abuse.[38]

The passage of VOCA and the continued proliferation of victims' compensation programs are symptoms of three important developments in American social policy during the last 15 years: the continued decline of public and professional support for rehabilitation of the criminal, the progressive expansion of the welfare state to include victims, and the rise of self-help groups and social movements as alternatives to traditional political parties and interest groups.

The attack on rehabilitation programs in the 1970s and 1980s has been led by conservatives who are highly critical of the claims of psychiatrists, sociologists, and liberal penologists that rehabilitation programs worked and could reduce crime.[39] But in a new development, conservative critics of rehabilitation have been joined by many liberals, who historically were outspoken champions of these programs. A notable example of this shift in liberal thinking was the final report of the Committee for the Study of Incarceration, a distinguished group of lawyers and scholars brought together through the financial support of a national foundation. The report, entitled *Doing Justice: The Choice of Punishment*, was published in 1976. Its major conclusions were that (1) the character of the penal institution had little or no effect on recidivism rates; (2) probation appeared to have little rehabilitative utility; and (3) vocational training, educational programs, and psychiatrically oriented counseling had a marginal impact on the ability of prison inmates to refrain from criminal activity upon release.[40]

An underlying theme of the report was the view that the benevolent intentions of professionals can be oppressive and discriminatory in practice. Indeterminate sentences, the authors argued, often led to the long confinement of poor and minority offenders for minor offenses. In the view of the report's authors, punishment based upon the principle of rehabilitation was inequitable and discriminatory in practice. As an alternative to rehabilitation and the individualization of punishment, the authors proposed "just deserts": the idea that "the offender may be justly subjected to certain deprivations because he deserves it."[41] In other words, society has the right to impose a prison sentence because society is entitled to exact retribution for the offenses committed by the criminal. By endorsing this view, the report's authors signaled a break with the idea popular in the 1960s that mitigating psychological and environmental factors could exculpate or diminish the responsibility of an individual criminal for his or her offense.

This greater faith in individual responsibility for criminal activity has contributed to the proliferation of restitution programs for victims of crime.[42] Restitution programs vary substantially: some programs use restitution as a way of avoiding prison sentences; other programs use it to reduce prison sentences or to demonstrate good behavior in order to evaluate a prisoner's suitability for parole. There is also variation in the extent to which the criminal is required to contact and meet his or her victim. But the disparate programs all emphasize that the criminal should repay the victim for damages through monetary payment or repay society through community service work.

Restitution is gaining popularity, for it appeals to both conservatives and liberals, although for different reasons. Conservatives tend to support it because it is an additional punishment that gives the victim an added measure of satisfaction that justice has been done; liberals offer support because it can be used as a "non-punitive alternative to other more restrictive sanctions such as fines or imprisonment."[43] Other arguments advanced by proponents are that restitution avoids the expense and deleterious influences of incarceration; reduces the burgeoning prison population; offers, at least theoretically, the opportunity to place minor offenders in community service or public sector jobs that would otherwise go unfilled; and aids the rehabilitation of criminals by making them vividly aware of the consequences of their action on the victim.[44]

While there has been a renewed philosophical emphasis on the individual responsibility of the criminal, the reverse has been the case for the victim. The growing successes of the victims' movement indicate that the crime victim is no longer considered solely responsible for the consequences of victimization. During the 1960s and 1970s, a number of government programs were developed to "socialize the risk" of disease, injury, and old age by using public funds and programs to reduce the potentially catastrophic effects of such conditions on an individual. The victims' rights movement represents an effort to "socialize the risk" of victimization by using social services, monetary compensation, and changes in the legal system—such as the right to be heard at a criminal sentencing, or protections against intrusive, prying legal strategies by defense attorneys—to minimize the emotional and monetary toll that crime exacts from a victim.[45]

The victims' rights movement is partly the stepchild of self-help groups and larger social movements in American politics. Since the early 1970s, self-help groups have been established as a way for individuals with shared problems and objectives to develop solutions outside of traditional helping systems. Thus, abusive parents joined up to form Parents Anonymous; ex–mental patients formed the Alliance for the Mentally Ill; a mother whose daughter was killed by a drunk driver created MADD (Mothers against Drunk Driving); and women who felt oppressed by sexist practices and institutions created consciousness-raising groups, as well as alternative service programs for women. But these groups and movements also stood as alternatives and sometimes as challenges to conventional politics and policies.[46] Each of the four victims' service programs in our study was established through the efforts of individuals and groups that were dissatisfied with the prevailing public policy toward a specific subcategory of victim. Major intervention programs for child abuse were proposed in the 1960s by reform-minded physicians who were outraged at the neglect of abused children by the social welfare service system at the time. Service programs for elderly victims of crime were urged in the 1970s as a way of remedying the neglect of elderly crime by the criminal justice system. And rape crisis centers and battered women's shelters were developed as alternatives to the conventional medical and social service establishment, which feminists believed was insensitive to victims' needs and perpetuated the dependent status of women, thus encouraging continued victimization.

The movement to develop services for specific categories of victims owed an intellectual debt to a number of psychiatrists and other mental health professionals who pioneered a generic approach to victims. They argued that individuals and families in personal crisis all proceed through similar identifiable stages of emotional reaction; thus, a trained professional can intervene successfully with a person in crisis, regardless of the precipitating event.[47]

As the various programs for specific categories of victims proliferated in the 1970s, they focused widespread attention to the needs and concerns of all victims. Also, the advocates of service programs for victims of child abuse, rape, elderly crime, and spouse abuse helped generate support for the victims' rights movement. This support, in turn, spurred the growth of generic service programs for victims.

Although a few one-stop, generic victims' service agencies have been established in the last 15 years,[48] the most common type of generic program is the victim/witness program, which is usually lodged in a district attorney's office. Typically, these programs provide crisis intervention counseling, assistance in filing criminal

charges and testifying in court, information, and referral to medical and social service agencies, if necessary, for any crime victim. Usually, the staff of these programs are involved in advocacy efforts to change criminal justice procedures in a direction that is more sensitive to victims' concerns and needs.[49]
The proliferation of generic programs, as well as the new VOCA funding, indicates that victims' services may be entering a new phase of development in which victims are increasingly treated as a class of injured citizens with shared emotional and legal needs. Yet this turn for victims' services is by no means assured. The Reagan administration, despite the VOCA monies, remains committed to shrinking the federal role in social policy. State, municipal, and private sources of funds are faced with greater and greater demands on their limited resources. And with many multiservice social service and health agencies developing the capability of assisting crime victims, there is the risk that special victims' concerns may be overlooked or neglected. Given the tenuous, uncertain position of the social welfare service system today, it is worth analyzing the policy experience of victims' services during the last peak time of public attention—the mid- to late 1970s—when victims' services received support from several federal agencies.

NOTES

1. See Stephen Schafer, *The Victim and His Criminal: A Study in Functional Responsibility* (New York: Random House, 1968), pp. 7–38; idem, *Compensation and Restitution to Victims of Crime*, 2nd ed. (Montclair, N.J.: Patterson Smith, 1970), pp. 3–12; Bruce Jacob, "The Concept of Restitution: A Historical Overview," in *Restitution in Criminal Justice: A Critical Assessment of Sanctions*, ed. by Joe Hudson and Burt Galaway (Lexington, Mass.: Lexington Books, 1977), pp. 45–51; Richard E. Laster, "Criminal Restitution: A Survey of Its Past History," in *Considering the Victim: Readings in Restitution and Victim Compensation*, ed. by Joe Hudson and Burt Galaway (Springfield, Ill.: Charles C. Thomas, 1975), pp. 19–28; Donald E. J. MacNamara and John J. Sullivan, "Composition, Restitution, Compensation: Making the Victim Whole," *Victimology*, ed. by Emilio C. Viano (Lexington, Mass.: Lexington Books, 1974), pp. 221–23.

2. Jacob, "The Concept of Restitution," p. 45.

3. Schafer, *The Victim and His Criminal*, p. 15.

4. Ibid., p. 16.

5. Ibid., p. 19.

6. Jacob, "The Concept of Restitution," p. 48. Also see Jeremy Bentham, "Political Remedies for the Evil of Offenses," in Hudson and Galaway, *Considering the Victim*, pp. 29–42.

7. See Schafer, *The Victim and His Criminal*, pp. 23–25; idem, *Compensation and Restitution*, pp. 9–12; Marvin E. Wolfgang, "Victim Compensation in Crimes of Personal Violence" (1965), in Hudson and Galaway, *Considering the Victim*, pp. 118–20.

8. *Report of the Delegates of the United States to the Fifth International Prison Congress*, Paris, July 1895, Senate Document no. 181, 54th Congress, 1st Session (Washington, D.C.: U.S. Government Printing Office, 1896), p. 28.

9. Sheldon Glueck, "The Significance and Promise of Probation," *Probation and Criminal Justice* (New York: Macmillan, 1933), p. 7.

10. See Hans von Hentig, *Crime: Causes and Conditions* (New York: McGraw-Hill Book Co., 1947); idem, *Punishment: Its Origin, Purpose, and Psychology* (London: William Hodge and Co., 1937); idem, *The Criminal and His Victim: Studies in the Sociobiology of Crime* (New Haven, Conn.: Yale University Press, 1948).

11. Von Hentig, *The Criminal and His Victim*, p. 384.

12. Ibid.

13. Ibid., p. 442.

14. Ibid., p. 399.

15. Beniamin Mendelsohn, "The Origin of the Doctrine of Victimology," *Excerpta Criminologica* 3 (1963):239–41.

16. Ibid., p. 241.

17. Henri Ellenberger, as quoted by Nwokocha K. U. Nkpa, in "Armed Robbery in Post-Civil War Nigeria: The Role of the Victim," in *Victims and Society*, ed. by Emilio C. Viano (Washington, D.C.: Visage Press, 1976), p. 161.

18. W. H. Nagel, "The Notion of Victimology in Criminology," *Excerpta Criminologica* 3 (1963):245–47.

19. Marvin E. Wolfgang, "Victim Precipitated Criminal Homicide," *Journal of Criminal Law, Criminology, and Police Science* 48, 1 (May–June 1957):1. For other articles examining the victim from a similar perspective, see Leroy G. Schultz, "Interviewing the Sex Offender's Victim," *Journal of Criminal Law, Criminology, and Police Science* 50, 5 (January–February 1960):448–52; Henry Weihofen, "Compensation for Victims of Criminal Violence," *Journal of Public Law* 8 (1959): 209–18.

20. Wolfgang, "Victim Precipitated Criminal Homicide," p. 3.

21. Margery Fry, *Arms of the Law* (London: Victor Gollancz, 1951), p. 126.
22. Margery Fry, "Justice for Victims," *Journal of Public Law* 8 (1959):191–94. For more information on Margery Fry, see "Victimology and Its Pioneers: Sara Margery Fry," in *Victimology: An International Journal* 1, 2 (Summer 1976):205–9.
23. Fred E. Inbau, "Victims of Criminal Violence," *Journal of Public Law* 8 (1959):202.
24. Weihofen, "Compensation for Victims," pp. 209–18.
25. *Penal Practice in a Changing Society*, as quoted by Jacob, "The Concept of Restitution," p. 51.
26. Harry Elmer Barnes and Negley K. Teeters, *New Horizons in Criminology*, 2nd ed. (Englewood Cliffs, N.J.: Prentice-Hall, 1955), pp. 769–70.
27. Arthur J. Goldberg, "Equality and Governmental Action," *New York University Law Review* 39 (1964):224.
28. Robert Childres, "The Victims," *Harper's Magazine* 228, 1367 (April 1964):160. Also see idem, "Compensation for Criminally Inflicted Personal Injury," *New York University Law Review* 39 (1964):452–62; LeRoy G. Schultz, "The Violated: A Proposal to Compensate Victims of Violent Crime," *St. Louis University Law Journal* (1965), reprinted in Hudson and Galaway, *Considering the Victim*, pp. 130–42.
29. Childres, "The Victims," p. 160. Also see Edward F. L. Bruen, "Controlling Violence v. Compensating Victims," *ABA Journal* 50, 9 (September 1964):855–56.
30. Childres, "Compensation for Criminally Inflicted Personal Injury," p. 455.
31. Ralph W. Yarborough, "S.2155 of the 89th Congress—The Criminal Injuries Compensation Act," *Minnesota Law Review* 50 (1965):258.
32. State Senator J. Eugene McAteer, as quoted by Herbert Edelhertz and Gilbert Geis, *Public Compensation to Victims of Crime* (New York: Praeger Publishers, 1974), p. 76.
33. Michael R. McAdam, "Emerging Issue: An Analysis of Victims Compensation in America," *Urban Lawyer* 8 (1976):353.
34. Edelhertz and Geis, *Public Compensation to Victims of Crime*, p. 93.
35. See Anthony C. Meade, Mary S. Knudten, William G. Doerner, and Richard D. Knudten, "Discovery of a Forgotten Party: Trends in American Victim Compensation Legislation," *Victimology: An International Journal* 1, 3 (Fall 1976):421–33; Burt Galaway and Leonard Rutman, "Victim Compensation: An Analysis of Substantive Issues," *Social Service Review* 48, 1 (March 1974):60–74; Carol Joy Gordon, *Victims' Compensa-

tion, unpublished draft, NIMH Research Project, Kennedy School of Government, Harvard University, 1981.

36. See Galaway and Rutman, "Victim Compensation," pp. 65–67.

37. Cynthia Crossen, "Crime Victims Are Winning Share of Fines, Role in Judicial Process," *The Wall Street Journal,* 18 April 1986, p. 37.

38. Victims of Crime Act of 1984, P. L. 98–473; Office of Victim Assistance, Commonwealth of Massachusetts, *Selected Documents,* 1986; interview with Elizabeth N. Offen, deputy director, Office of Victim Assistance, Commonwealth of Massachusetts, 2 June 1986; Crossen, "Crime Victims Are Winning Share of Fines," p. 37.

39. See James Q. Wilson, *Thinking about Crime* (New York: Basic Books, 1975); Ernest van den Haag, *Punishing Criminals: Concerning a Very Old and Painful Question* (New York: Basic Books, 1975); Robert Martinson, "What Works?—Questions and Answers about Prison Reform," *The Public Interest* 35 (Spring 1974):25; James Q. Wilson, "What Works? Revisited: New Findings on Criminal Rehabilitation," *The Public Interest* 61 (Fall 1980):3–18. Also see "Delinquency Treatment Seen as Failure in 30-Year Study," *Psychiatric News* 13, 3 (3 February 1978):3. As faith in rehabilitation declined, the belief that punishment deterred crime increased significantly. See Gordon Tullock, "Does Punishment Deter Crime?" *The Public Interest* 36 (Summer 1976):103–11.

40. Andrew von Hirsch, *Doing Justice: The Choice of Punishments: Report of the Committee for the Study of Incarceration* (New York: Hill and Wang, 1976), p. 14. Also see Martin R. Gardner, "The Renaissance of Retribution—An Examination of Doing Justice," *Wisconsin Law Review* (1976):781–815; Marc F. Plattner, "The Rehabilitation of Punishment," *The Public Interest* 44 (Summer 1976):104–15.

41. Von Hirsch, *Doing Justice,* p. 51.

42. In the decades prior to 1960, some criminologists tried to develop restitution programs, usually for the rehabilitative effects on the criminal. See Irving E. Cohen, "The Integration of Restitution in the Probation Services" (1944), reprinted in Hudson and Galaway, *Considering the Victim,* pp. 332–39; Albert Eglash, "Beyond Restitution—Creative Restitution" (1958), reprinted in Hudson and Galaway, *Restitution in Criminal Justice,* pp. 91–99.

43. Steven L. Chesney, "Restitution and Social Control," in *Victims, Offenders and Alternative Solutions,* ed. by Joe Hudson and Burt Galaway (Lexington, Mass.: Lexington Books, 1980), p. 55.

44. See Robert Kigin and Steve Novack, "A Rural Restitution Program for Juvenile Offenders and Victims," in Hudson and Galaway, *Victims, Offenders and Alternative Solutions,* pp. 131–36; John Harding, "Community-Service Restitution by Offenders," in Hudson and Gala-

way, *Restitution in Criminal Justice*, pp. 101–30; Mike Patterson, "Oklahoma Department of Corrections Restitution Program," in *Offender Restitution in Theory and Action*, ed. by Burt Galaway and Joe Hudson (Lexington, Mass.: Lexington Books, 1978), pp. 179–83; Alan T. Harland, "Restitution Statutes and Cases: Some Substantive and Procedural Constraints," in Hudson and Galaway, *Victims, Offenders and Alternative Solutions*, pp. 155–69; Paul W. Keve, "The Therapeutic Uses of Restitution," in Hudson and Galaway, *Offender Restitution in Theory and Action*, pp. 59–64.

For a skeptical view of restitution, see John F. Klein, "Revitalizing Restitution: Flogging a Horse That May Have Been Killed for Just Cause," *Criminal Law Quarterly* 20, 3 (June 1978):383–408.

45. For a representative sampling, consult Sidney Hook, "The Rights of Victims: Thoughts on Crime and Compassion," *Encounter* 38, 4 (April 1972):11–15; Morton Bard and Dawn Sangrey, *The Crime Victim's Book* (New York: Basic Books, 1979); Robert Reiff, *The Invisible Victim: The Criminal Justice System's Forgotten Responsibility* (New York: Basic Books, 1979). For a thoughtful review of Reiff's book, see Graham Hughes, "The Plight of the Victim: Review of *The Invisible Victim* by Robert Reiff," *New York Review of Books*, 6 March 1980, p. 3.

46. Scholars of European politics have noted the rise of "antipolitics"—notably, alternative political parties and social movements. See Suzanne Berger, "Politics and Antipolitics in Western Europe in the Seventies," *Daedalus* 108, 1 (Winter 1979):27–50.

47. See Erich Lindemann, "Symptomatology and Management of Acute Grief," *American Journal of Psychiatry* 101, 2 (September 1944):141–48; Donald C. Klein and Erich Lindemann, "Preventive Intervention in Individual and Family Crisis Situations," in *Preventing Mental Disorders in Children: Initial Explorations*, ed. by Gerald Caplan (New York: Basic Books, 1961), pp. 284–305; Reuben Hill, "Generic Features of Families under Stress," in *Crisis Intervention: Selected Readings*, ed. by Howard J. Parad (New York: Family Service Association of America, 1965), pp. 32–52.

48. See Anne Newton, "Aid to the Victims—Part II: Victim Aid Programs," *Crime and Delinquency Literature* 8, 4 (December 1976):508–28; Mary E. Baluss, *Integrated Services for Victims of Crime: A County-Based Approach* (Washington, D.C.: National Association of Counties Research Foundation, 1975); Mary E. Baluss, "Services for Victims of Crime: A Developing Opportunity," *Evaluation and Change*, Special Issue, (1980):94–102; John P. J. Dussich, "Victim Service Models and Their Efficacy," in *Victims and Society*, ed. by Emilio C. Viano, pp. 471–83; "New York Groups Aid Crime Victims," *The New York Times*, 25 December 1983,

p. 39; Molly Ivins, "Victims Say Lives Echo with Grief," *The New York Times*, 21 April 1981, p. B1.

49. See Anthony A. Cain and Marjorie Kravitz, *Victim/Witness Assistance: A Selected Bibliography* (Rockville, Md.: National Criminal Justice Reference Service, June 1978); Nina McCain, "She Aids the Bewildered Victims," *The Boston Globe*, 23 January 1982, p. 2; "The National District Attorney's Association Commission on Victim/Witness Assistance," *Victimology: An International Journal* 1, 2 (Summer 1976):321–26; David C. Bolin, "The Pima County Victim/Witness Program: Analyzing Its Success," *Evaluation and Change*, Special Issue (1980):120–26; *Victim Witness Program of Middlesex County, MA* (Cambridge, Mass.: Middlesex County District Attorney's Office, 1982).

3

CHILD ABUSE

The abuse of children by their parents has been a part of the social condition as long as people have kept records. But it is only relatively recently that a parent's brutality toward his or her child has been an urgent public policy problem. Prior to the 1960s, child abuse was the quiet responsibility of public and private child protection agencies; the issue provoked virtually no public debate. Like domestic violence, rape, and elderly crime, though, child abuse has emerged during the last 25 years from the private world of community and professional discussion into the political arena, where it has become a burning, highly visible public issue. And like these other victims' issues, the discovery of child abuse as a public issue led to federal funding of service programs for abuse victims. This federal funding and the accompanying regulations are a key reason for the continued prominence of the child abuse issue on the social policy agenda in states across the country during the 1980s, a decade when other victims' issues are struggling against waning public interest.

THE DEVELOPMENT OF CHILD ABUSE AS A PUBLIC PROBLEM

Child abuse initially emerged as an important societal concern in the late 1800s, thanks in part to the widely publicized case of Mary Ellen Wilson, who endured grisly beatings with a leather strap at the hands of her stepmother. A "friendly visitor" brought the child's plight to the attention of the Society for the Prevention of Cruelty to Animals, which, in turn, took the case to court and had Mary Ellen removed from the home and her stepmother sentenced to prison. The case helped spur the creation of Societies for the Prevention of Cruelty to Children and helped fuel the growth of a variety of other private, voluntary organizations dedicated to helping victims of abuse and neglect. For the most part, these private child welfare agencies relied upon private donations and fees to support their services.[1]

As in the Mary Ellen case, most such agencies sought punitive measures to correct the abuse: remove the child, jail the abusive parent. However, in the early twentieth century, with the rise of the Progressive movement, another approach took shape. The Progressives favored a rehabilitative view, promoting efforts to keep the child at home and alleviate the social and economic problems that were compromising family life. The successes of the Progressive movement sent the private agencies into a long decline, largely because the rehabilitative approach was at odds with their punitive approach, which relied heavily upon institutional care of abused children. And the creation of many state-administered child protective agencies after 1920 crowded out many established private agencies from the protective service field.[2]

The rehabilitative approach remained in the ascendant through World War II and the early postwar years. However, public discussion of the child abuse problem was virtually nonexistent. Moreover, the victims of abuse who came to public or private attention were usually the most severely injured abuse victims; case finding and aggressive investigation of potential abuse situations were either rare or difficult for social workers to sustain owing to the relatively low level of resources devoted to the child abuse problem.

The transformation of child abuse from a "privatized," nonpolitical issue into a public policy concern began in 1957. That year, the U.S. Children's Bureau released a report recommending that each state's public child welfare department investigate child abuse and neglect, provide the appropriate social services, or report the situation to law enforcement authorities. Then, in 1963, the bureau distributed a model state reporting law, designed to require certain professionals to report suspected cases of abuse and neglect. This model law encouraged state legislators, child welfare advocates, and human service professionals to push for the adoption of reporting laws at the state level—an effort that permanently changed the political environment on the child abuse issue.[3]

The interest of the Children's Bureau staff in child abuse was due primarily to the work of a private advocacy organization, the American Humane Association (which produced reports in the 1950s on the inadequacies of public child protection services)[4] and to research by radiologists and pediatricians. The medical community's early involvement in the child abuse issue had a substantial role in defining the problem for the Children's Bureau and other federal agencies that later funded child abuse programs and research.

Radiologists were the first physicians to call child abuse a serious, neglected medical problem. In 1946, radiologist John Caffey noted a striking series of long bone fractures and bruises among infants but did not speculate on the causes. His work, however, spurred other research, including his own a decade later, which began considering diagnoses that had to do not with medical causes, but with social ones. Tentatively, researchers began to conclude that some children were being brutalized by their parents.[5]

In 1962, the growing body of research culminated in an article in the prestigious *Journal of American Medicine*, "The Battered Child Syndrome," written by Denver pediatrician C. Henry Kempe. The article, which was widely distributed, called attention to abuse as a major cause of death and injury to children. Having surveyed the literature and 302 cases of abuse, Kempe suggested that the causes of abuse could be traced to the personality disorders of certain parents. Abusive parents were not necessarily psychopathic, sociopathic, or poverty-stricken, Kempe suggested. But, he wrote, "In most cases, some defect of character structure is probably present; often parents may be repeating the same type of child care practiced on them."[6]

The impact of Kempe's article was tremendous: the issue suddenly leaped into the pages of newspapers and magazines; it garnered the interest of social workers, psychologists, psychiatrists, and others in the traditional "helping professions." It caught the attention of the Children's Bureau. And most important, it laid down a definition of the issue that has endured to this day.

Kempe's work located abuse in the deviance of abusive parents, rendering "an individually centered psychological construction of the problem that made it seem very self-contained," as political scientist Barbara J. Nelson noted.[7] The definition of the problem as a syndrome, a "clinical condition," suggested there should be a treatment and cure. Such a definition called for programs to identify and adjust the abusive parents' character defects, thus avoiding the stickier point raised by later researchers that abuse was equally a product of socioeconomic factors—such as poverty, lack of education, and unemployment—for which there were no handy programmatic answers.

Though the problem definition was later expanded from physical abuse to include sexual abuse, neglect, and failure-to-thrive cases, it was never redefined out of a deviance model or in a way to encourage efforts to prevent abuse before it occurred. Primary prevention programs—whether they involved plans to screen parents who might be high risk, or blanket high schools with parenting education—won little support from the government agencies that became involved in the issue until very recently.

A GROWING FEDERAL ROLE IN CHILD ABUSE POLICY: 1960–1980

It can be argued that the most influential action initiated by federal policymakers regarding child abuse was the drafting (in 1962) and distribution (in 1963) of the model reporting statute.[8] Within five years, every state had adopted laws encouraging or requiring professionals to report abuse to the designated authorities. The reporting laws were a vital bridge in moving the issue onto policy agendas, for they made awareness of the issue a mandated professional responsibility and thereby forced, at least implicitly, a guarantee that there would be public investment in programs to handle the reports.

The reporting laws also catalyzed a public policy chain reaction that ensured that the child abuse issue would remain a public policy concern. The passage of the laws led to a dramatic rise in the reports of child abuse and neglect. The growing demand for staff and funding resources to address this reporting rise forced an expansion of the role of state protective service agencies; by 1967, only ten states still left responsibility for investigating child abuse reports in the hands of private voluntary agencies.[9] New awareness of the problem led to discoveries of new forms of abuse—sexual exploitation, infants' failure to thrive, child pornography, and incest—which demanded legislative revisions and, in turn, new service programs.

In terms of federal funding, the 1950s and 1960s were a period of mounting federal expenditures for research on child abuse. This research role of the federal government reached a major turning point in 1969 when the federal Department of Health, Education, and Welfare created the Office of Child Development, one of whose main missions was the support of child abuse research and demonstration projects.

Federal policy toward child abuse took a new and important turn in 1974 with the passage of the Child Abuse Prevention and Treatment Act (CAPTA), which established the first categorical funding mechanism for child abuse programs. Federal funds were now available to the states for the development of "new and innovative approaches to child abuse."[10]

CAPTA was introduced by Senator Walter F. Mondale, then chair of the newly created Senate Subcommittee on Children and Youth. Mondale had a long-standing commitment to issues of child welfare, but as Barbara J. Nelson and Ellen Hoffman point out, he was also looking for a new issue on which to establish the subcommittee's reputation.[11] Child abuse was a good bet; it already enjoyed a place on the policy agenda, and, portrayed in the right way, it could be relatively noncontroversial.

Although the definition of abuse in the CAPTA legislation was quite comprehensive—covering physical and mental injury, sexual abuse, negligent treatment, and maltreatment—congressional hearings and debate on the bill focused on a far narrower definition of the problem. Witnesses in hearings on the bill testified to the vast numbers of children who endured horrendously brutal treatment at the hands of their parents or caretakers. The subcommittee's report on CAPTA opened its argument for the bill by stating: "Each year in this country, thousands of innocent children are beaten, burned, poisoned, or otherwise abused by adults."[12]

Nelson maintains that more comprehensive definitions "were actively suppressed in order to enhance the noncontroversial nature of the issue."[13] The narrower definition was consistent with the experience of physicians, who, as Nelson notes, had "early and easy access to officials."[14] And the focus on the most horrific examples of physical abuse headed off challenges from conservative critics who might otherwise have opposed CAPTA as undue interference in the family and parental discipline. Mondale could ill afford a conservative defection. He needed solid support in Congress because the Nixon administration opposed the bill. The legislation would have created a new categorical spending program, and the White House was committed to reducing the federal role in addressing social problems.

Despite the opposition of the Nixon administration, CAPTA was enacted in early 1974. The bill authorized $85 million for four years. The bulk of the annual appropriations was earmarked for research and demonstration projects, although the law also stipulated that 5 to 20 percent of the money must be distributed to the states for child protection service programs. To administer the money, CAPTA established a new entity, the National Center for Child Abuse and Neglect (NCCAN), located in the Office of Child Development of HEW.[15]

When the act came up for reauthorization in 1978, it was passed with little debate, although a section on adoption reform was added to the bill. In recent years, amid budget cuts and newly strong conservative opposition to government intervention in the family, the law has had a tougher time winning reauthorization.

The creation of NCCAN contributed to a widening division between public and private services for victims of child abuse. NCCAN was a boon to private agencies interested in getting involved in the issue; and as private treatment programs proliferated, it was easier for the public agencies, bombarded with reports of suspected abuse, to scale down their treatment efforts and focus on their investigatory role.

Since its establishment, NCCAN has been the center of federal child abuse policy. Aside from the Children's Bureau and the Title

XX program, which funded protective services, HEW (and its successor, Health and Human Services) administered few other programs specifically devoted to child abuse. The National Institute of Mental Health sponsored a few selected research projects but little else. The Law Enforcement Assistance Administration (LEAA), so prominent in other victims' issues, maintained a low profile on child abuse. LEAA provided several grants for training legal, medical, and law enforcement personnel about their responsibilities in cases of child abuse. The agency also offered limited support to law enforcement and social service programs addressing the problem. In 1974 and 1975, LEAA awarded several grants to criminal justice agencies, such as juvenile court programs, to encourage the investigation and prosecution of child abuse and neglect cases; but in many instances, child abuse victims were not the only group served by the programs.[16]

LEAA'S limited role reflected the prevailing professional consensus on child abuse during the 1970s. Prior to the 1960s, law enforcement agencies were key actors in child abuse cases—responsible for investigating reports of abuse and enforcing orders to remove children from their homes. Beginning with Kempe's article in 1962, though, professionals in the field increasingly viewed law enforcement personnel as inappropriate agents for handling the problem of child abuse.

EXPLAINING CHILD ABUSE

The preferred service response to child abuse—treatment and rehabilitation—was largely the product of what some have called "the child abuse industry": the academics, practitioners, and professionals in the mental health, medical, and social service fields who became involved in the issue.[17] The theories and service models generated by these groups had an especially strong influence on the federal programmatic response to child abuse.

The vast literature on child abuse revolved around two basic theoretical and therapeutic schools of thought: the deviance perspective, which emphasized the psychopathology of the abusive parent; and the ecological view, which focused on the socioeconomic stresses that led parents to abuse their children. In academic debate, the two schools represented counterposing "ideal types," the extremes on a continuum of child abuse theory. In practice, the schools were not mutually incompatible. The complicated nature of child abuse defied monothematic explanations or treatment methods; the majority of programs incorporated ideas from both models. Further, as psychiatrist Brandt Steele points out, the selection of treatment modality often was *not* a predetermined process but was instead influenced to a great extent by the wishes and desires of the parent or family.[18] Thus, in practice the models and definitions tended to be much less discrete and precise than the academic literature suggests.

The psychopathology orientation was most prominently put forward by Dr. C. Henry Kempe and his associates. As first developed in "The Battered Child Syndrome," Kempe's model postulated a number of explanations for the abuse, all of which focused on the personality disorders of the parents: emotional immaturity, excessive dependency, poor impulse control, past history of abuse. Kempe stressed that only 10 percent of abusive parents were seriously mentally ill and thus beyond treatment. The remaining 90 percent were influenced by early childhood experiences that set a predisposition for abuse, which could then be triggered by certain stresses and contexts. The suggested treatment involved a variety of techniques designed to meet the dependency needs of the abusive parent. These included professional psychotherapy, either individually or in groups; lay therapy, wherein a lay person befriends the isolated abusive parent; self-help groups; crisis nurseries; special day care preschools; and residential programs for the entire family.[19]

Belief in the identifiable personality traits of abusers and the influences of early childhood spawned several preventive and predictive approaches. Kempe advocated the use of "screening" programs for newborns to identify high-risk families. Kempe's National Center for the Prevention and Treatment of Child Abuse in Denver also operated a Lay Health Visitors Program to evaluate mothers at delivery and shortly thereafter in order to screen for potential abuse and neglect.[20]

The ecological model, developed primarily by social scientists, identified many of the same characteristics of abusive situations as Kempe but offered less individualized explanations. Instead, parental abusiveness was correlated to environmental circumstances such as situational and child-rearing stresses, social isolation, poverty, cultural values in child rearing, and lack of education about child development. Child abuse, then, was seen as a predictable response to particular situations.[21]

Few authors attempted to integrate all of these factors into a comprehensive ecology of child abuse.[22] Rather, most of the literature concentrated on one or more clusters of sociological influences, such as socioeconomic stresses, parenting techniques, or social position. The clusters implied certain intervention strategies to alleviate stresses affecting the family. Thus, one avenue of treatment was through a case-management approach, the traditional response of social service agencies. In a "multiproblem" family (as abusive families are often labeled), case management suggested the coordination of medical, psychological, legal, and social services. Other treatments included parenting education, homemaker/parent aides, and parent support groups, as well as therapy.

Despite their different emphases, the two schools shared several assumptions. Both defined abuse clinically, in terms of injuries—physical or emotional—inflicted on children by their parents. Both posited the abusive family as a special group, deviant from social norms. In different ways, both schools proposed methods of intervention designed to compensate for parental deficiencies. Therefore, although the definitions of parents' needs varied, both schools offered solutions that ultimately reinforced the parent's dependency.

By contrast, sociologist David Gil formulated a third model of child abuse that radically challenged both the psychopathological and the ecological theories.[23] Gil defined child abuse as anything limiting the full and free development of a child's potential and considered it but one of many forms of abuse fostered by the inequities of class structure, poverty, and unemployment. Gil posited an intimate connection between child abuse and cultural norms that sanction violence and physical discipline. Gil deserves mention both because his theories demonstrated an alternative conceptualization of child abuse and because his model was *not* incorporated into child abuse policy or programs. What is left out of policy is frequently as telling as what is contained in policy initiatives: the in/out distinction illuminates the parameters of policy and what policymakers perceived to be an appropriate range of responses to a given problem.

According to Gil, child abuse could be eradicated only through deep structural and cultural changes. This implied a level of intervention beyond the capacity of the helping professions or the inclinations of policymakers (indeed, it can be argued that Gil's prescription for change was so long-range that it precluded the possibility of short-term reforms). Because most theories attributed the problem of child abuse to a deviant group in the population, the suggested treatment approaches were compatible with the conventional scope of policy and/or legislative action. But, according to Gil, acceptance of these "deviance" theories over his own had ideological overtones: "This general conception of the dynamics of deviance seems to derive from a politically 'conservative' premise, according to which the American social structure is basically sound, except, perhaps, for a few minor necessary adjustments."[24] Thus, although Gil was highly respected in the child abuse field and was frequently invited to comment on child abuse policy, his views were not influential in determining a response to child abuse.

THE SERVICE RESPONSE TO CHILD ABUSE: 1960–1980

Although the federal government has never devoted substantial sums of money to the funding of child abuse programs, the impact of federal policy on the development of service programs has been particularly profound. In the 1960s, federal policy encouraged the adoption of reporting laws by states across the country, which in turn forced state governments to upgrade their public protection system. In the 1970s, the federal government provided funds and guidance to states and private agencies to cope with the emergent public policy issue that the federal government had helped "discover" in the 1960s. As a result, the 1970s were a tinkering time: adjusting the reporting laws to cover more professionals and more kinds of abuse; promoting more specialization and professionalization of the state child protection services, and fostering different experiments in treating child abuse through NCCAN's research and demonstration projects.

The effects of federal policy on the child abuse problem are vividly manifest in the service programs devoted to the issue. These programs can be divided into four general categories: public child protection agencies; treatment programs sponsored by private agencies; prevention programs; and projects to promote interagency cooperation.

At the heart of child abuse programming was the child protection service system (CPS)—the state- or county-administered social service agencies mandated to receive and investigate reports of abuse and neglect and to evaluate and refer confirmed cases. Prior to the reporting law legislation, state authorities tended to uncover cases of abuse and neglect through the investigatory casework of welfare department personnel.

The passage of the reporting laws at the state level, and CAPTA at the federal level, precipitated a major shift in public child protection systems at the state level. State welfare agencies began to establish separate child protection units, distinct from other child welfare programs. Many states moved child protection services out of the welfare department and into an agency responsible for social services. Separate child protection units—with distinct administration and staffing—were set up at the local level. Specialized policy and planning departments were also created at the state level. By the end of the 1970s, 45 states had identified a department or individual at the state level responsible for stimulating and promoting services for abused and neglected children.[25]

During the same period, CPS agencies gradually assumed primary responsibility for receiving and investigating reports of abuse. The Children's Bureau model reporting law recommended that reports be sent to law enforcement authorities, and many of the state reporting laws initially followed suit. But by 1974, the laws had changed so that in all but nine states, the CPS agency had exclusive or shared responsibility for receiving reports.[26]

The CPS method of service delivery was traditional case management, described by the American Humane Association in 1967 as "a program which seeks to prevent neglect, abuse, and exploitation of children by reaching out with social services to stabilize family life. It seeks to preserve the family unit by strengthening parental capacity and ability to provide good child care."[27] Case management focused more on changing the life circumstances of abusive parents than on the specific personality of the abuser. CPS caseworkers made a range of services—not all specifically directed at child abuse—available to abusive parents and their children. Depending on the resources of the agency and the community at large, these included psychological counseling, day care, parents' aides, homemakers, parenting education, self-help groups such as Parents Anonymous, peer support groups, employment counseling, drug or alcohol abuse programs, financial assistance, legal aid, and health care.

Ideally, CPS caseworkers marshaled the array of services they believed would alleviate the stresses compromising parents' ability to adequately care for their children. If the parents were uncooperative or the abuse/neglect continued, the CPS agency had the legal authority to remove the child from the home. Indeed, frequently CPS workers depended upon court orders or the threat of removal to gain client cooperation.

That's the way CPS units were supposed to work. In reality, a number of factors, beyond the issue of client cooperation, hindered CPS units in the delivery of child protection services. For one, the interdisciplinary nature of case management meant that intervention was often stymied by a lack of coordination among the services involved. It was frequently difficult for caseworkers to focus the attention of various legal, medical, mental health, and social service programs simultaneously on a single family, as well as on the individual members of that family. Caseworkers' problems were intensified by the fact that they were usually saddled with the most serious and difficult abuse and neglect cases; as the mandated public authorities, CPS units did not have the flexibility that the private agencies often enjoyed in choosing their clients.

Second, child protection workers carried inordinately high case loads, averaging between 40 and 80 families, which meant that caseworkers were able to see each family at best once a month. Most private treatment programs, by contrast, saw clients at least once a week. And, according to a NIMH evaluation, weekly contact seemed to be the minimum necessary to provide intensive, effective intervention.[28]

The lack of specialized skill and training of CPS workers was another impediment. Theoretically, most CPS units were organized along the social work supervision model: caseworkers (ideally with master's degrees in social work) would learn and work under the guidance of more experienced (and often more highly trained) social workers. However, a number of evaluations showed that in practice many agencies suffered from a lack of adequate supervision or formal case review and discussion. According to an evaluation of child abuse and neglect programs sponsored by NIMH:

In all too many cases, staff of the public agency receive no training beyond friendly support. While the emphasis of protective service is said to be the preservation of the family unit, many workers received no training whatsoever in family or couple therapy. . . . most have no training in work with children or adolescents and relatively little specific knowledge of child development which they can usefully transmit to parents.[29]

Thus caseworkers were often ill equipped to deal with the multifaceted problems of abusive families; they were expected to utilize a variety of treatment modalities with "insufficient training in some and no training in others."[30]

The lack of supervision and training was particularly critical given the ambivalent role of caseworkers. CPS workers were in the contradictory position of simultaneously investigating a family and trying to establish a treatment relationship, of being police officers and social workers, investigators and friends. The pressures and frustrations of child protection work tended to produce a high burnout rate, which in turn compounded staffing problems. In some agencies, the turnover rate exceeded 50 percent a year.[31]

Such problems prompted a surge of state efforts to raise the educational and experiential qualifications of CPS caseworkers and supervisors and to institute regular in-service training for all CPS staff. Several states began providing higher salaries, extra benefits, and compensation time for CPS workers.

A number of state social service departments also developed special policies for the local CPS units, further distinguishing them from other child welfare programs. Some 31 states required specialized intake procedures; 16 states formulated standards limiting CPS workers' case loads, holding them to anywhere from 15 to 40 families per worker.[32]

Some counties and states also separated the investigative and therapeutic functions of CPS workers, establishing "protective services" to investigate and provide short-term relief to abusive families and "preventive services" for the delivery of long-term assistance. However, according to an NCCAN evaluation, "the separation of staff functions is often based on a perceived need to investigate cases quickly; [therefore,] staff resources are funneled into protective services, while effective long-term services are limited and overburdened."[33]

Some individual CPS agencies were able to surmount such problems, by structuring—at local initiative—service innovation into the organization of their services. This arrangement was the common thread tying several successful CPS programs noted in an NCCAN publication.

Minnesota's Hennepin County Protective Services, in existence since 1945, was able to maintain manageable caseloads, between 18 and 30 families, and to provide services in fairly intensive treatment relationships. The organization of the Hennepin County service may have contributed to its success. The service consisted of one assessment unit, with a supervisor and six staff, and four field units, each comprised of a supervisor and eight or nine workers. The assessment unit was responsible for taking incoming calls and determining which cases were referred to the field units. The field units were responsible for providing casework, treatment, and co-ordinating services. This separation of responsibilities eased the burden of individual CPS staff members.

Moreover, the unit escaped the problem of high staff turnover, which plagued many CPS agencies. This may have been related to three factors: caseworkers were hired on the basis of experiential, rather than educational, qualifications; the units' supervisors had several years' experience in child protection, which enhanced their supervisory capabilities; and the units strove for service continuity—generally, the same caseworker worked with a family from intake through closure.[34] These factors may have provided Hennepin County caseworkers with an unusually strong sense of support and stability. Nonetheless, this program was still unable to offer family or child therapy. The main emphasis in Hennepin County's program was on "short-term treatment, on goal-setting, and on accomplishment of specific, limited behavioral changes."[35] Thus, although Hennepin County represents an unusually flexible program, administrative and fiscal pressures still constrained the service program.

Another form of organizational innovation was represented by collaboration between protective services and other agencies. The Lehigh-Northampton Counties Coordinated Child Abuse Program in Pennsylvania, founded in 1968, coordinated the services of the counties' Children's Bureau (CB), the local public child welfare agency, and a mental health agency—Mental Health/Mental Retardation (MH/MR). Inspiration for this cooperative arrangement, which was relatively rare, came from a local pediatrician and psychiatrist, who were disturbed by the lack of psychotherapeutic services for abusive parents in the area.

Cases were referred to the program through the Children's Bureau. MH/MR assumed responsibility for operating therapy groups for abusers, and the CB was responsible for providing casework and coordinating support services. Each group had four therapists: two co-leaders (a mental health worker and a caseworker) and two caseworkers (one from each county). The program offered individual and family therapy, but the main emphasis was on group therapy sessions, which approached abuse as symptomatic of both a psychological problem and a lack of parenting education. The NIMH evaluation of the program traced the success of the agencies' cooperation to the personalities of the key actors involved and to historical accident: the director of MH/MR had recently transferred from a supervisory social work position at the Children's Bureau.[36]

Honolulu's Child Protective Services Center exemplified another type of collaboration, in this case, between a hospital and the Hawaii Department of Social Services and Housing (DSSH). The center was established in 1967 in response to accusations that DSSH was not adequately protecting children or providing needed services. Located in Kauikeolani Children's Hospital, the center contained a protective service unit and a medical component. The former was crisis-oriented. Its staff was responsible for assessing reports and handling social service diagnosis and treatment. The social work staff was administratively responsible to DHSS. The medical component was operated by a director, a nurse, two psychiatrists, two psychologists, and a secretary. Their responsibilities included diagnostic medical treatment, psychiatric evaluations, and hospitalizations when necessary. Members of the medical component also served as consultants to caseworkers both from the center and from other CPS units.[37]

One striking trait of the Hennepin County CPS unit, the Lehigh-Northampton program, and the Child Protective Services Center was the small case load carried by the programs' caseworkers: on average, 20 families. Small case loads may have been as important a factor as interagency collaboration and organizational innovations in the programs' ability to offer intensive, highly effective intervention services.

At the heart of the CPS agencies' troubles was a systemic problem: a service demand that was growing far more rapidly than available funding. Rising public and professional awareness of abuse, coupled with revisions in the reporting laws that expanded the definitions of abuse and the professionals required to report it, contributed to a nonstop increase in the reports of suspected cases of abuse and neglect. Yet the agencies were chronically underfunded. Funding, or lack thereof, was a consistent complaint in the American Humane Association's surveys of state and county child protection agencies; indeed, in 1977, more states named funding as a problem than in 1967.[38]

Prior to the 1960s, private child abuse programs had been in a long decline. In the last two decades, though, private child abuse programs have expanded tremendously, owing primarily to two factors. First, to stretch scarce state dollars and enhance program flexibility to deal with the huge increase in abuse reports, many state agencies in the 1970s curtailed their direct service role. In numerous states, the public agencies, either voluntarily or under legislative mandate, started contracting out their evaluation, treatment, and casework functions to smaller private agencies. Frequently, the tasks of investigation and referral were the only remaining public responsibilities. Second, in the wake of CAPTA— and the new availability of federal demonstration and seed grants— a host of specialized child abuse programs emerged, under the aegis of various private agencies and funded primarily with government funds.

Most private programs were oriented toward "treating" the abusive family, and there were as many different types of private treatment programs as there were theories of effective treatment methods. As Anne Harris Cohn, chair of the National Committee for the Prevention of Child Abuse and Neglect, observed:

Although many professionals accept the notion that treatment works, few agree on what kind of treatment works. Theories range from an emphasis on therapeutically oriented intervention (such as psychiatric counseling) to concrete services (such as homemaking and employment and financial assistance) to education (such as parenting classes).[39]

Professional disagreement notwithstanding, few treatment programs exclusively followed one approach. Growing awareness of the complexities of child abuse militated against treatment based on a single strategy. Most programs offered, either directly or indirectly, a mix of therapeutically oriented intervention, concrete services, and education.

Many of the treatment models were first developed by Henry Kempe, Brandt Steele, and Ray Helfer and their associates. Under Kempe and Steele's influence, for example, the first multidisciplinary child protection team was created in 1958; an individual therapy program using specially trained nonprofessionals who would "befriend" the abuser was launched in 1967; and a Families Anonymous self-help organization was started in 1968. In the 1970s, Kempe and his associates continued their innovative efforts via a newly created agency, the National Center for the Prevention and Treatment of Child Abuse, founded in 1972 in Kempe's home city, Denver, Colorado. A crisis nursery was formed at the center in 1973. In 1974, a residential treatment program for families, a therapeutic play school, and a group therapy program for abusive parents were all established. In 1975, the center began to offer group therapy for preschool children. And in 1977, the center's research on abuse prevention through prediction of high-risk families culminated in a Lay Health Visitors program, based on a similar program developed in Scotland. In the late 1970s, the center's efforts increasingly focused on the issues of foster parents, sexual abuse, and failure-to-thrive cases.[40]

As the models developed by Kempe suggest, there was an increasing use of lay people and paraprofessionals in the delivery of child abuse services. Lay people could provide the social support—the simple friendship—that many abusive parents lacked.

They also were a cost-effective way to provide services. Since the early 1970s, more programs have incorporated the services of lay therapists, parents' aides, homemakers, and foster grandparents. In some cases, trained volunteers provide these services; in others, they are delivered by paid staff. Self-help groups—particularly Parents Anonymous, an organization founded by an ex-abuser in the late 1960s—also proliferated, usually under the auspices of professionally staffed, established programs. Yet despite the growing acceptance of lay people and paraprofessionals, most of these staff were supervised by trained professionals with advanced degrees. For example, although staff at the Denver National Center for the Prevention and Treatment of Child Abuse and Neglect approved of the therapeutic benefits of the Parents Anonymous self-help model, they felt that there was a need for professional input. Therefore, until Parents Anonymous began using professional sponsors, the center relied on its own professionally run self-help groups.[41]

Because of the seminal influence of Kempe et al., the evolution of the center's programs is a fair reflection of the development of treatment programs in general during the 1960s and 1970s. Approaches that enjoyed success in Denver were often incorporated into, or made the basis of, programs in other parts of the country. Conversely, the center's most experimental programs were the least frequently replicated. The residential program, discontinued after two and a half years because of its expense, was rarely duplicated elsewhere. The Lay Health Visitors Program suffered a similar fate, primarily because of the controversy surrounding the idea of prevention through prediction. Many professionals and academicians believed that attempts to screen new parents for potential abusers posed an invasion of privacy and a potential intrusion on individual rights.[42]

However influential the experiences of the National Center, they were not the sole determinants of which treatment models were implemented by private agencies. The pattern of implementation, insofar as one can be determined, suggests that other factors were at work as well. The most commonly adopted approaches were those which extended traditional concepts of service delivery, allowed for greater cost-effectiveness, and could be easily incorporated into existing programs or services.

Since few agencies could support as comprehensive an array of services as the National Center, many agencies implemented programs that were based upon a core-treatment strategy. In some cases this involved a particular method of service delivery. For example, the SCAN (Suspected Child Abuse and Neglect Network) volunteer service of Little Rock, Arkansas, was centered on 30 volunteer lay therapists who provided intensive supportive and therapeutic services to abusive families.[43] Other programs developed around the provision of such services as parents' aides/homemakers, special day care centers, psychological counseling, or parenting education.

Another core approach involved building services for a particular population, be it an ethnic group or age group. NCCAN sponsored several programs for specific groups such as native Americans, military personnel, and migrant workers.[44] Kempe's crisis nursery, therapeutic play school, and preschoolers' group therapy were all programs tailored to the developmental capacities of young children and the particular dynamics contributing to abuse at different stages of childhood.

The focus on a particular age group was the basis for Pittsburgh's Parental Stress Center (PSC), billed as "a comprehensive approach to infant care."[45] PSC was formed in 1975 by representatives from the four major agencies addressing children's needs in Allegheny County: the Children's Hospital of Pittsburgh, the Allegheny County Children and Youth Services, the county juvenile court, and the Pittsburgh Child Guidance Center. PSC began as a residential center (subcontracted through the Children's Home) to house abused or neglected infants who had been removed from their families. Derived from Kempe's crisis nursery, the center was intended as a neutral place for parents to visit their children and for staff to assess whether potential rehabilitation was viable. Aside from reinforcing positive parenting, PSC offered its clients individual and group counseling, social activities, and aid in remedying welfare and employment problems. In 1976, PSC established a day center specifically for abused and at-risk toddlers who were living at home.

Private programs were developed most often by the social work and medical communities. Although the professional ethos of each had some impact on the programs that were developed, the setting of programs was less influential than in other types of victims services. Thus, despite the differing treatment outlooks of the social work and medical professions, in the case of child abuse treatment their efforts were relatively compatible. Each employed concepts derived from the other, in many cases building treatment programs that cannot readily be labeled "medical" or "social work" in orientation. The unusual cross-fertilization of therapeutic ideas resulted in a seeming mélange of treatment programs. But beneath the apparent diversity was a fairly uniform effort to integrate psychotherapeutic techniques with the delivery of concrete support services. Moreover, the lack of exploration in preventive directions during this period reinforces the impression that the apparent array of approaches to child abuse rested, in fact, on a fairly narrow set of ideas.

Perhaps the main difference in the services offered by the two professional groups was in scope. The varied and disparate programs based in social service or community agencies generally shared the common goals of strengthening both the psychological and the socioeconomic conditions of abusive parents. Most often that meant a blend of counseling programs; day care services; parents' aide, homemaker, or lay therapy services; and self-help peer support groups. That social service agencies tended to deploy such an array of services may be related to the professional orientation of social work—one that seeks problem resolutions in multiple dimensions. Then, too, social service agencies had a fair degree of flexibility in seeking funding sources. Because they were eligible for both private and public grants, the agencies were often able to implement specialized, innovative service components, such as those developed at Kempe's National Center. The agencies tended to be better funded (in per capita terms) than the public authorities and many other private service organizations; thus, they usually were able to maintain small client/staff ratios and offer long-term intensive services.

Hospital-based programs exhibited less variety. Since states generally required physicians to report suspected cases of abuse and neglect, many hospitals developed a basic protocol for the identification and reporting of abused or neglected children. But few ventured into more extensive service programs. This was not really surprising, given that the medical conception of treatment and cure does not traditionally take account of the types of social, cultural, or economic variables associated with child abuse. Although in recent years, a growing number of medical practitioners have recognized that these factors have a role in health care, medical facilities are not traditionally oriented toward providing social services. Moreover, medical insurance does not reimburse for the type of multidisciplinary treatment required in abuse and neglect cases. Thus, unless hospitals received special grants or had an administrator or staff member committed to addressing the problem, there was little incentive to develop comprehensive treatment resources.[46]

The more common type of hospital program was the in-house multidisciplinary team, a strategy designed to counter the fragmentation of hospital services, improve in-house response to cases of abuse and neglect, and provide medical consultation to other agencies. A model for many hospitals was the Boston Children's Hospital Trauma X team, established in 1970. The Trauma X team was funded by the hospital and included two social workers, a part-time attorney, a nurse-practitioner, several pediatricians, a psychiatrist, a psychologist, and two Department of Social Service workers acting as informal liaisons. The team existed mainly for consultation, to lend its expertise to the primary care group whenever a child was hospitalized and abuse was suspected. The team met weekly to discuss issues arising from various cases, both inpatient and out-patient. When a report was filed, the team did follow-up to ensure that the public authorities provided the needed services.[47]

The success of the treatment programs was debatable. For example, in her evaluation of the National Demonstration Program on Child Abuse and Neglect (jointly funded by the Office of Child Development and the Social and Rehabilitation Service of HEW), Anne Harris Cohn raised a number of questions about the effectiveness of short-term treatment services. Cohn found that 30 percent of the parents studied were reported to have seriously abused or neglected their children while in treatment. Moreover, the highest reincidence rates occurred where inadequately trained workers were conducting intake and case management. In addition, according to Cohn, the project staff reported that only 42 percent of their clients had a reduced potential for future abuse and neglect. Cohn also found that children were as much in need of treatment as their parents, yet only 3 of the 11 projects studied provided such services to children. Cohn concluded that children were not necessarily protected simply because their parents were being treated and that the "success" rate of 42 percent indicated treatment programs were "not nearly as successful as society had been led to expect."[48] Further, Cohn found that although diagnostic skills were necessary for intake and treatment planning, lay services (i.e., parents' aide or Parents Anonymous counseling) were particularly effective in reducing parents' propensity for future abuse. Cohn attributed this success, in part, to the smaller case loads carried by lay counselors (which enabled the counselors to spend more time with the parents) and to the ways peer support and friendship reduced parents' social isolation.

Despite the mixed results of treatment strategies, federal policy consistently favored efforts to treat abuse rather than prevent it from occurring in the first place. This focus was not because of a paucity of preventive strategies: both the psychological and ecological models of child abuse indicated that there were potential ways to prevent child abuse and neglect. For example, Kempe and others argued that abusers and families in which there was a high risk of abuse often exhibited traits that could be identified and treated through special screening programs. Prevention advocates maintained that hospitals and schools could offer educational programs on parenting skills and child development. Health care facilities could enhance their social service programs to provide additional support and assistance to new and expectant parents.[49] In short, the problem could potentially be averted if services that addressed the stresses contributing to abuse were incorporated into the regular operations of the traditional helping agencies.

However, very few agencies offered preventive services, and there were even fewer programs whose central purpose was prevention. One of the few, the Panel for Family Living in Tacoma, Washington, actually was established as a treatment program. An NCCAN grant supported the panel's parents' aide and family counseling programs, but when the grant expired in 1977, the agency was unable to secure adequate local funding to maintain its services. The board of directors then decided to shift the panel's emphasis entirely to primary prevention and to allow local mental health agencies to assume responsibility for treatment services. The prevention program included an extensive library resource; a speakers' bureau of trained volunteers; and a consultation and training component for other agencies and professionals. The panel also sponsored a hospital visitor program through which volunteers were available to help new mothers identify their own support networks. In 1979, the panel received an NCCAN grant for a parent education program that used dramatic skits to deliver information on parenting. Thus, the panel delivered prevention-oriented services and encouraged the implementation of preventive programming in other community agencies.[50] But in general, preventive services—where they existed—were linked with the more immediate programmatic objectives of identification and treatment.

A few speculative reasons may be offered as to why preventive programs were so infrequently implemented. First, the "helping professions" by training are not traditionally oriented toward primary prevention. The professional framework of both medical and social service practitioners is geared to treating a problem *after* it is symptomatically evident. Institutionally, neither health care nor social service facilities are geared toward preventing a problem prior to its manifestation. Moreover, as Peter Coolsen of the National Committee for the Prevention of Child Abuse noted, "it has taken considerable time for professionals in the field to develop a prevention 'mind-set.' Many treatment professionals had viewed prevention as a luxury and were so pre-occupied with after-the-fact cases that they did not pay serious attention to preventive efforts."[51] Coolsen also argued that many professionals considered primary prevention "unworkable" since child abuse was related to such a wide range of societal and individual variables. Strategies to prevent abuse on a secondary level were also problematic in many practitioners' eyes. Many felt ethical qualms about concentrating on high-risk families and high-potential abusers since there was the danger of unfairly stigmatizing nonabusive families. Finally, there was little financial support for prevention on either a primary or a secondary basis. Insurance does not typically reimburse for preventive services. And federal agencies awarded few grants to prevention programs. It was not until 1978 that NCCAN initiated a significant prevention program, which sponsored 32 projects across the country. These included parent education, parents' support groups, information and referral services for family support agencies, and home visitation services.[52]

In the 1970s, federal agencies encouraged efforts to coordinate services addressing child abuse and neglect at all phases of intervention from identification through treatment and long-term prevention. Interagency multidisciplinary teams were the most frequent outcomes of these efforts. The complex problems of abusive families were perceived by many professionals as lending themselves to cross-disciplinary approaches. In addition, laws mandating professional reporting fostered interdisciplinary communication. Team members usually included doctors, nurses, public health nurses, lawyers, social workers (from both public and private agencies), and on occasion staff from schools, the police, and the courts.

The most common multidisciplinary teams were those developed in and operated by hospitals. But as an NCCAN publication pointed out, "because of the coverage given treatment-oriented, hospital-based multi-disciplinary teams, there has been some confusion over what it is and can do. A multi-disciplinary team does not have to be treatment-oriented, nor need it be in a medical center. . . . many community programs have been developed for such specific purposes as better reporting and interagency cooperation."[53]

For example, the Ramsey County (Minnesota) Child Abuse Team, organized in 1969 by the St. Paul–Ramsey County Mental Health Center, combined the functions of interagency cooperation and direct service delivery. Team members represented agencies directly involved in intervention and treatment of abuse and neglect cases—police, the county welfare department, the county juvenile court, the county and city hospitals, the county nursing service, the community mental health services, and the Children's Placement Service. Members routinely used the team in all confirmed cases of abuse to seek recommendations, share information, and coordinate services. However, each member agency retained its traditional role and responsibilities in addressing abuse or neglect. The experience of Ramsey County's team was typical of most team efforts; its smooth functioning depended upon administrative commitments to team involvement from all member agencies and the designation of a coordinator, the team's only funded position.[54]

Most teams did not receive direct federal support through grants. But federal philosophical support is evident in statements and publications such as NCCAN's *Multidisciplinary Teams in Child Abuse and Neglect Programs*, which promoted the multidisciplinary team as an effective intervention strategy and provided guidelines for the establishment of teams.

A coordination effort that received more direct federal support was the Comprehensive Emergency System (CES), which began in 1971 in Nashville with a research/demonstration grant from the Children's Bureau. CES was designed to provide emergency services on a 24-hour basis in cases of abuse and neglect. Initially, the program was aimed at a situation that was specific to Nashville. Tennessee law authorized three agencies to receive reports: the courts, the police, and protective services. The high level of law enforcement involvement, coupled with the lack of 24-hour social services, meant that a large number of abused and neglected children were routinely, and often inappropriately, processed through the courts and placed in foster care. CES was developed to bolster the capacity of Nashville social services and to demonstrate an effective deployment of emergency services. To achieve these goals, CES trained special child protection personnel to handle intake on a 24-hour basis. The intake worker operated as a case manager, coordinating delivery of services, such as caretakers, homemakers, foster family homes, and shelter for families or adolescents on an emergency basis. Some of these components were already in existence; others, like the emergency homemakers, caretakers, and foster homes, were added when CES was implemented. The intake workers were also responsible for outreach and follow-up efforts. The CES program was further enhanced when LEAA contributed discretionary funds to hire additional personnel in the courts, the police department, and the adolescent shelter.

In 1974, the Children's Bureau awarded the program a three-year nationwide information dissemination contract to establish the National Center for Comprehensive Emergency Services to Children in Crisis. The center's five staff members traveled across the country to help communities develop their own comprehensive emergency systems; by 1977, at least 60 communities had instituted all or some part of the CES system.[55]

THE POLICY IMPLICIT IN PRACTICE

For purposes of clarity, child abuse programs have been classified in four categories: public child protection services; private treatment programs; prevention programs; and multidisciplinary, interagency programs. While the categories are useful in distinguishing the service system for child abuse victims and their families, they obscure the overlaps between different programs and service strategies and the similarities they shared.

One common trait of abuse and neglect programs was a common orientation toward the abusing adult. Services focused on adults in the hope that if the abuser's needs (as both program and parent defined them) were met, then the abuse/neglect would be eliminated or deterred. In practice, programs most often worked with mothers, an overrepresentation that was supported by research comparing the likelihood of maternal, as opposed to paternal, abuse.[56] The emphasis on mothers may also have been due to mothers' greater willingness and availability to participate in programs. But very few programs provided therapeutic or other types of services directly to abused children. In 1974, only 3 of 11 demonstration centers funded by NCCAN incorporated a specific children's service component.[57] A conference on children's programs in 1980 had only 10 projects participating, all of which were federally funded.[58] Beyond the options of foster care or permanent placement, there were few intervention strategies specifically for children. This is especially striking in light of the body of literature indicating the intergenerational effects of family violence.

Furthermore, a majority of programs handled abuse cases involving very young children, from infancy to six. This probably was related to early research showing that a high incidence of abuse was directed at children in this age range. Also, hospitals were more likely to come into contact with very young children, since they are more easily and more seriously injured.

One other possible reason for the infant orientation relates to the media's treatment of child abuse. Battered infants made for more dramatic stories; as victims, they evoked greater sympathy and outrage than did school-age children or adolescents. However, the emphasis on toddlers and infants meant a significant portion of abuse cases remained unaddressed, given David Gil's findings in 1973 that about half the reported abuse incidents involved school-age children.[59]

A third trait of programs was the concentration of personnel from the medical and social work fields and a lack of involvement by the mental health community. While psychiatrists and psychologists were frequently members of multidisciplinary child protection teams, their involvement was most often on an individual, rather than on an agency, basis. Mental health agencies and community mental health centers were active in child protection efforts in only a few isolated cases; almost no treatment programs were operated under mental health auspices. This was the result of both professional and structural disincentives. Most mental health professionals are unaccustomed to working with involuntary or unmotivated clients—a common factor in child abuse cases. Further, mental health agencies are not in the habit of providing clients with the kind of concrete services child abuse/neglect programs offer. Mandatory reporting and the issue of confidentiality may have also hindered the involvement of the mental health community. The professional training of mental health workers assumes a confidential counselor/client relationship; yet most child abuse programs consider confidentiality detrimental to rehabilitation, since many abusive parents will not acknowledge their violent behavior or cooperate in treatment programs unless they are legally forced to do so.

During the 1970s, law enforcement agencies, from the federal to the local level, were largely uninvolved in the abuse and neglect programs. This was due primarily to the general shift of responsibility in abuse and neglect cases from law enforcement to social service auspices following the passage of the reporting laws in the mid-1960s. By 1974, only 5 states required that reports be made exclusively to a law enforcement agency (D. A.'s office, police, sheriff, or state police), and only one state directed all reports to the juvenile court. In the 22 states where both law enforcement and social service agencies were authorized to receive reports, the responsibility, in practice, usually fell to the social service agency.[60]

For example, according to NCCAN, "in one state, through a turn of events that neither the police nor child protective workers can explain, the proposed 1973 reporting law was amended just before passage to require reporting solely to the police. No one, including the police, seems to approve of this last minute change, and no one seems to follow it. When they do receive a report, the police immediately refer it to protective services."[61]

Ironically, the proliferation of reporting laws across the country created a set of circumstances that, in the 1980s, has pushed the law enforcement community back into a key role in child abuse cases. As noted, the reporting laws produced a tremendous explosion in abuse and neglect reports. These laws also raised the public's awareness of the child abuse problem and their expectations of the capacity of the public and private treatment system to respond to child abuse. So, when a child abuse incident occurs despite these treatment programs, law enforcement often demands a larger role in intervention decisions regarding child abuse cases. The result has been a trend away from the rehabilitation of abusive parents. In recent years, there has been an increase in criminal prosecution of abusive families and the removal of children from abusive or potentially abusive situations.

Finally, few services began as the result of systematic planning; instead, most programs were developed out of the professional or personal experiences of individuals in a community, or in response to a particularly gruesome and well-publicized incident that highlighted the gaps in the social service systems. For example, the death of a nine-year-old girl at the hands of her parents in Montgomery County, Maryland, sparked an intensive campaign to alert the public to the problem of child abuse and to improve the county's handling of abuse and neglect cases. One outcome was Project Protection, a program to sensitize school personnel to the signs of abuse and neglect and to educate them about their obligation to report it.[62]

This lack of systematic planning was reflected in the superficially related but generally fragmented system of child protection that developed in all states. Despite variations, the child protection "system" of most states and communities included a mandatory reporting process; public and private child protection services; and various other agencies and individuals involved in the identification, disposition, or treatment of cases. But, as pointed out in an NCCAN publication, "this complex of laws, agencies, and people usually resemble[d] more a patchwork of divergent philosophies and procedures than a coordinated and well-functioning system."[63]

On one level, the federal government's involvement in the issue brought about significant changes in the social response to child abuse. The punitive approach that had prevailed until the early 1960s was eclipsed by a determination to preserve the family unit through rehabilitative efforts. Responsibility for the problem was removed from the courts and police and placed squarely in the hands of social workers, doctors, psychologists, and counselors. Subsequently, law enforcement personnel have once again become part of the government's response to child abuse; in many localities and states, they now share responsibility with these other professionals for treatment decisions. An issue that made its way onto policy agendas defined as a problem of physical maltreatment underwent substantial revisions. As defined today, child abuse includes a whole constellation of parental maltreatment ranging from sexual exploitation to mental cruelty.

The early years of child abuse treatment programs were the province of professionals; in the 1970s, a host of service strategies reliant on lay people and paraprofessionals emerged and gained credibility. Self-help groups—particularly Parents Anonymous— have proliferated, often at the urging and under the supervision of established professionally staffed programs. And primary prevention programs, long the poor stepchild of the field, gradually began to secure federal funding.

Yet despite the changes, the substance of child abuse policy remained remarkably static. The theoretical understanding of child abuse never substantively advanced beyond the initial analyses that labeled it deviant. The psychopathological and ecological models developed in the 1960s continued as the keystones of child abuse theory and service practice. As the issue became more prominent, an increased variety of groups and individuals became involved in efforts to address child abuse, and a seemingly diverse array of abuse and neglect programs emerged. Nonetheless, a core set of approaches remained the foundation for the vast majority of these service programs. One set of strategies was oriented toward the particular stage of intervention in abuse and neglect cases: identification, evaluation, prevention, and treatment. A second set of strategies was aimed at one or more causal factors of abuse, such as the psychological and personality traits of the abuser, the environmental context of abuse, individual and social stresses, and the lack of adequate parenting and child development information.

The favored approach was related as much to local circumstances and resources as to changes in the state of the art. Professional researchers and service providers were highly influential in shaping the response to child abuse. Unlike other victims' issues, child abuse programs were dominated by professionals from the medical, legal, and social work fields who brought not only their expertise but also well-developed professional networks to the problem. Thus many innovations, especially in terms of treatment, were disseminated as much through professional channels such as journals, conferences, and collegial associations as through federally initiated technical assistance, research, or demonstration programs.

The domination of child abuse services by professionals in institutional or institutionally affiliated settings was not a byproduct of federal policy, but it was related to the process by which the child abuse issue became the subject of policy. The lack of alternative grass-roots services for child abuse speaks to an advocacy process inherent in children's issues. The children's constituency differs from that of other victims' issues in that children generally do not represent their own interests—they are represented by adults. Thus, the texture of a children's issue is highly dependent upon the adults who become involved in it. In the case of child abuse, the issue was forwarded by adults in the medical and social service professions, whose interest stemmed less from a perspective of social critique than from professional and personal experience and concern.[64]

Unlike other victims' issues, federal grants for child abuse programs did not substantively encourage particular intervention strategies or administrative settings. Instead, federal agencies assumed a broker's role: the establishment of NCCAN provided a vehicle by which the efforts of various professional groups could be subsidized. Indeed, NCCAN was unusually even-handed in its distribution of awards; a wide variety of agencies and treatment methods were supported by NCCAN funds.

Perhaps the only assumption consistently apparent in federal initiatives was the theme of child abuse and neglect as a deviancy, rather than as the tragic but logical product of cultural values or socioeconomic structures, as David Gil maintained. However, this deviancy perspective was as pervasive at the local level in the outlooks of most service providers as it was at the federal level.

The lack of a strong federal funding role and the absence of clear guidelines to state and local authorities regarding the development of child abuse treatment programs fostered fragmentation in state and local responses to the issue. Although the issue carried wide political appeal and inspired unanimous enthusiasm, child abuse was treated in an amazingly unsystematic fashion. On the basis of federally sponsored model laws, states implemented a number of legislative changes that broadened the definitions of abuse, specified the reporting obligations of professionals, and so forth. Yet these legislative reforms were frequently enacted with seeming disregard for the capacities of service agencies involved with abuse or neglect. Moreover, the laws varied from state to state: an offense that constituted abuse in one state may have represented a tragic, but legally permissible, act in another; the legal responsibilities of CPS agencies were broad in some states, while in others they were fairly limited. State administrations had considerable discretion in determining child abuse policy. The choice of an agency to receive reports, the distribution of Title XX block grant money, definitions of abuse and neglect—all were issues largely determined at the state level, thereby fostering divergent child protection systems.

The types of federal grants that were available did, however, exert important influences on direct service programs for abused and neglected children. Funds for child abuse programs were available in two basic forms: demonstration or "seed" grants to initiate or support innovative service projects; and block grants such as Title XX to sponsor the ongoing operation of abuse and neglect programs. The distribution of demonstration monies and block grants contributed to the growing distinction between public CPS agencies with statutory responsibility for abuse and neglect cases and nonauthorized "private programs." The bulk of Title XX monies were allocated to state administrations for distribution; in many states, the public agencies received a large portion, if not all, of the block grant monies. Therefore, smaller "private" agencies were highly dependent on state purchase-of-service contracts, or on demonstration grants offered by federal grantors such as NCCAN, the Public Health Service, the Office of Child Development, the Social Rehabilitation Service, and LEAA. Demonstration grants and contracts produced specialization of services: programs were funded to develop particular service innovations. And, of course, there was never a substantial amount of money available for demonstration projects. As Hoffman notes, CAPTA was deliberately underfunded to avoid a presidential veto, even though it was known that authorizing $85 million for four years was insufficient for "a major and comprehensive attack on the problem."[65]

Additionally, the limited commitment of contracts and demonstration grants led to discontinuities in service. In a number of cases, programs folded or curtailed services when the federal grants expired and no local support was forthcoming. In other cases, projects' functions were assumed by one or several larger institutions, such as hospitals or social service departments. State purchase-of-service contracts enabled several programs to continue after federal funding ended. But this kind of local support, like other types, rarely sustained the level of services that the larger demonstration grants supported.

Moreover, a change in administration could bring significant changes in the nature and flexibility of service delivery. For example, when the Bowen Center in Chicago was able to replace a federal demonstration grant with state funds, state officials required that the center change its referral practice—from a relatively open process allowing the center to receive referrals from the community to a closed process requiring the center to obtain referrals from the state. The state also shifted the focus of the program from long-term treatment to short-term counseling, crisis intervention, and diagnostic evaluations.[66]

THE 1980s

Federal funding of child abuse programs by the National Center for Child Abuse and Neglect (NCCAN) fell to $16.2 million in FY 1982 from $22.9 million in FY 1981. Spending stayed at $16.2 million for FY 1983 and 1984.[67] However, in 1984, the original CAPTA legislation of 1974 (which had been renamed the Child Abuse Prevention and Treatment and Adoption Reform Act during the 1978 reauthorization process) was reauthorized again.[68] Since then, NCCAN spending has risen significantly. Specifically, NCCAN spending in FY 1985 jumped to $26 million.[69]

During the Reagan administration, important changes have occurred in NCCAN priorities. NCCAN grants to the states have received greater emphasis and support: from FY 1981 to FY 1985, NCCAN grants to the states rose from $6.7 million to $12 million,[70] far faster than the rate of increase for NCCAN research and demonstration grants. Also, the 1984 legislation authorized a $5 million annual appropriation for the "identification, treatment and prevention of sexual abuse."[71]

The pattern of NCCAN research and demonstration grants for FY 1985 also indicates a significant shift in program priorities: in contrast to the 1970s, many NCCAN grants were awarded to projects for the exploration and development of innovative preventive and educational strategies to address child abuse. Treatment projects still receive funding, but they no longer receive the lion's share of the research funding. And even the awards for treatment projects show a decided shift: many projects are attempting to demonstrate the feasibility of nonprofessional and volunteer approaches to child abuse. Thus, one consequence of the Reagan administration policy on NCCAN has been to disrupt, at least partially, the nexus of NCCAN professionals and medical and social welfare professionals throughout the country who during the Carter years impressed upon NCCAN a professional treatment focus.[72]

The Reagan administration has also had an effect on other child abuse funding programs of the Carter years. The Omnibus Budget Reconciliation Act (OBRA) of 1981 cut the expenditures for Title XX (renamed the Social Services Block Grant) by approximately 20 percent and devolved responsibility for program administration to the states. Since 1981, expenditures for the block grant have declined from $2.9 billion dollars in 1981 to about $2.6 billion in FY 1986.[73] LEAA and CETA, which played only a minor funding role, were eliminated.

New federal funding for child abuse programs is just beginning to flow to programs from the federal funds authorized under the Victims of Crime Act of 1984 (VOCA). As noted, $68 million was accumulated from fines and penalties on federal criminals for the VOCA fund for FY 1986. The three designated priorities for VOCA funds are child sexual abuse, rape services, and battered women. One of the first states to take advantage of the VOCA funds was Massachusetts; starting in July 1986, seven child abuse programs received funding. However, the future of the VOCA fund is clouded with uncertainty, since the Reagan administration has proposed drastic reductions in funding levels for FY 1987.[74] Further, the existing grants are unlikely to be renewed even if overall funding is stable. Thus, it appears that VOCA funds could fall prey to the same cyclical pattern of growth and decline characteristic of many funding programs for victims in the 1960s and 1970s.

At the state level, state administrators and legislators have stepped up their commitment, developing new regulations and funding to address the child abuse problem. This growing prominence of state governments in the development of child abuse policy is directly attributable to the federal policy of the previous two decades. The dramatic rise in reports of abuse and neglect publicized the issue of child abuse, giving social welfare advocates a potent weapon in lobbying for increases in child abuse funding. In addition, the reporting statutes have facilitated the "discovery" of long-neglected problems such as sexual abuse, incest, and the failure-to-thrive syndrome. These emergent social policy concerns have, in turn, been met with more appropriations at the state level.

Federal funding also spurred the professionalization of state child protection agencies; thus, when federal funding declined in the 1980s, an administrative capacity existed at the state level, capable of responding to and exercising leadership on the child abuse issue. In an era of rising abuse reports, this leadership role has usually meant requests for more money from the legislature.[75]

Federal funding also played a major role in the creation of a "child abuse industry" comprised of academics, service providers, and child welfare advocates. In the face of declines in federal funding, these individuals have continued to carry the flame at the state and local level. Through publicity and direct lobbying, they have pushed state legislators to appropriate more money for child abuse programs.

Public pressure to address child abuse in the face of stagnant overall revenues has led many states to restructure their entire child welfare service system to emphasize the protective mandate of state agencies. Protective services, then, are absorbing a higher percentage of the state child welfare dollar.[76]

Despite this protective emphasis, prevention programs are proliferating. For example, many states have established children's trust funds, which are usually financed through increased marriage license and birth certificate fees or voluntary income tax refund checkoffs. These trust funds generally finance a variety of educational and counseling programs to prevent child abuse, particularly sexual abuse.[77]

In sum, child abuse is firmly entrenched as a social problem needing government attention and support; its place seems so secure that it threatens to crowd out other legitimate social welfare concerns on the public policy agenda. Responsibility for this development lies in part with the reporting laws, which continually call attention to the gravity of the problem. The reporting laws also uncomfortably remind the public that despite the increasing public funds devoted to child abuse, the problem is worsening, as demographic and socioeconomic changes create conditions conducive to child abuse. Unfortunately, David Gil appears to have been right.

NOTES

1. Barbara J. Nelson, *Making an Issue of Child Abuse: Political Agenda Setting for Social Problems* (Chicago: University of Chicago Press, 1984), pp. 7–8. Also see Stephen J. Pfohl, "The Discovery of Child Abuse," *Social Problems* 24, 3 (February 1977):310–21; Samuel X. Radbill, "A History of Child Abuse and Infanticide," in *Violence in the Family*, ed. by Suzanne K. Steinmetz and Murray A. Straus (New York: Dodd, Mead and Co., 1974), pp. 173–79.

2. Nelson, *Making an Issue of Child Abuse*, pp. 9–10.

3. Barbara J. Nelson, "Setting the Policy Agenda: The Case of Child Abuse," in *The Policy Cycle*, ed. by Judith May and Aaron Wildavsky (Beverly Hills, Calif.: Sage Publications, 1978), p. 18.

4. The American Humane Association (AHA) assessment of child protection services, released in 1956, was widely disseminated and helped to focus public attention on the inadequacies of public services for abused and neglected children. See AHA, Children's Division, *Child Protective Services in the United States* (Denver, Colo.: American Humane Association, 1956).

5. Pfohl, "The Discovery of Child Abuse," pp. 316–19.

6. C. Henry Kempe et al., "The Battered-Child Syndrome," *Journal of the American Medical Association* 181, 1 (7 July 1962), as quoted by Nelson, *Making an Issue of Child Abuse*, p. 13.

7. Nelson, *Making an Issue of Child Abuse*, p. 13.

8. U.S. Children's Bureau, *The Abused Child: Principles and Suggested Language for Legislation on Reporting of the Physically Abused Child* (Washington, D.C.: U.S. Department of Health, Education, and Welfare, Welfare Administration, Children's Bureau, 1963). Indeed, a spate of model statutes and legislative guidelines were formulated and distributed between 1963 and 1967. Various model reporting laws were published by the American Humane Association (1963), the Council of State Governments (1965), the American Medical Association (1965), and the American Academy of Pediatrics (1966). See Nelson, "Setting the Policy Agenda," pp. 25–26.

9. American Humane Association, *Child Protective Services: A National Survey, 1967* (Denver, Colo.: American Humane Association, 1967), p. vii.

10. The Child Abuse Prevention and Treatment Act was signed on 31 January 1974; it was Public Law 93-247.

11. See Nelson, *Making an Issue of Child Abuse*, pp. 134–35. Also see Ellen Hoffman, "Policy and Politics: The Child Abuse Prevention and Treatment Act," in *Critical Perspectives on Child Abuse*, ed. by Richard Bourne and Eli Newberger (Lexington, Mass.: Lexington Books, 1979), 157–71.

12. U.S. Senate, Committee on Labor and Public Welfare, *Child Abuse Prevention and Treatment Act, Senate Report no. 308 to Accompany S. 1191*, 93d Congress, 1st Session, 10 July 1973, p. 1.

13. Nelson, *Making an Issue of Child Abuse*, p. 14.

14. Ibid.

15. For a good summation of the provisions of CAPTA, see Hoffman, "Policy and Politics," pp. 157–70.

16. U.S. National Center on Child Abuse and Neglect, *Federally Funded*

Child Abuse and Neglect Projects, 1975 (Washington, D.C.: U.S. Department of Health, Education, and Welfare, Children's Bureau, 1976).

17. David G. Gil, "The United States versus Child Abuse," in *The Social Context of Child Abuse and Neglect*, ed. by Leroy Pelton (New York: Human Sciences Press, 1981), p. 292.

18. Brandt Steele, "A Psychiatrist's View of Working with Abusive Parents," in *Child Abuse: Perspectives on Diagnosis, Treatment and Prevention*, ed. by Roberta Kalmer (Dubuque, Ia.: Kendell/Hune Publishing Co., 1977), p. 141.

19. Kempe's model is represented or discussed in the following: C. Henry Kempe and Ray E. Helfer, eds., *Helping the Battered Child and His Family* (Philadelphia: J. B. Lippincott Co., 1972); Ruth Kempe and C. Henry Kempe, *Child Abuse* (Cambridge, Mass.: Harvard University Press, 1978); C. Henry Kempe et al., "The Battered Child Syndrome," *Journal of the American Medical Association* 181, 1 (7 July 1962):17–24; Brandt Steele, "A Psychiatric Study of Parents Who Abuse Infants and Small Children," in *The Battered Child*, ed. by Ray E. Helfer and C. Henry Kempe (Chicago: University of Chicago Press, 1968), pp. 103–47; Serapio Zalba, "Treatment of Child Abuse," in *Violence in the Family*, ed. by Murray A. Straus and Suzanne K. Steinmetz (New York: Dodd, Mead and Co., 1974); Richard Galdston, "Observations on Children Who Have Been Physically Abused and Their Parents," *American Journal of Psychiatry* 122, 4 (October 1965):440–43; Dante Cicchetti and J. Lawrence Aber, "Abused Children—Abusive Parents: An Overstated Case," *Harvard Educational Review* 50, 2 (May 1980):244–54.

20. Interview with Donald Bross, attorney for National Center for the Prevention and Treatment of Child Abuse and Neglect, 13 June 1981; and National Center for the Prevention and Treatment of Child Abuse and Neglect, *History of Events Leading to and Projects Created by the National Center for the Prevention and Treatment of Child Abuse and Neglect* (Denver, Colo.: 1980).

21. For examples of ecologically oriented models, see Richard J. Gelles, "Child Abuse as Psychopathology: A Sociological Critique and Reformulation," in Straus and Steinmetz, *Violence in the Family*, pp. 190–204. Also see several articles in *Critical Perspectives on Child Abuse*, including Eli Newberger, "The Myth of the Battered Child Syndrome," pp. 15–25; Eli Newberger and James Hyde, "Child Abuse: Principles and Implications of Current Pediatric Practice," pp.27–40; Edward Zigler, "Controlling Child Abuse: An Effort Doomed to Failure?" pp. 171–213. Also see James T. Tracy and Elizabeth H. Clark, "Treatment for Child Abusers," *Social Work* 19, 3 (May 1974):338–42; Elizabeth Elmer, "Child Abuse and Family Stress," *Journal of Social Issues* 35, 2 (Spring 1979):60–72; Murray

A. Straus, Richard J. Gelles, and Suzanne K. Steinmetz, eds., *Behind Closed Doors: Violence in the American Family* (Garden City, N.Y.: Anchor Books, 1981).

22. Richard J. Gelles, however, developed a social-psychological model of child abuse that included factors such as social position of the parents, class and community, situational stresses (e.g., parental relations, structural stresses, child-produced stress), parents' socialization experience, psychopathic states, and immediate precipitating situations. All these factors are interrelated, and through a complex flow chart Gelles illustrates how certain combinations of these variables may contribute to child abuse. Gelles's model assumes that frustration and stress are important factors associated with abuse. See Gelles, "Child Abuse as Psychopathology," pp. 199–200.

23. David G. Gil, "Violence against Children," *Journal of Marriage and the Family* 33, 4 (November 1971):637–48; David G. Gil, *Violence against Children: Physical Child Abuse in the United States* (Cambridge, Mass.: Harvard University Press, 1970); David G. Gil, "Unraveling Child Abuse," in *Critical Perspectives On Child Abuse*, pp. 69–80.

24. Gil, "Violence against Children," p. 638.

25. Data on the shift to separate child protection units from public welfare departments is based on a review of the AHA surveys on child protection services. See AHA, *Child Protective Services: A National Survey, 1967*; and AHA, *Child Protective Services, Entering the 80s* (Englewood, Colo.: American Humane Association, 1979).

26. Vincent DeFrancis and Carroll L. Lucht, *Child Abuse Legislation in the 1970s*, rev. ed. (Denver, Colo.: American Humane Association, Children's Division, 1974), pp. 24–25.

27. American Humane Association, *Child Protective Services, 1967*.

28. Community Research Applications, *Child Abuse and Neglect Programs: Practice and Theory* (Washington, D.C.: U.S. Department of Health, Education, and Welfare, National Institute of Mental Health, 1977), p. 173.

29. Ibid.

30. Ibid.

31. It is worth noting that the American Humane Association's 1977 survey of child protection service agencies found the problem of staff turnover had diminished. According to the AHA, over half the local offices reported no staff turnover in 1977, and only 12 percent reported a turnover rate of 50 percent or more. The AHA offered few reasons for the surprisingly low turnover rate, suggesting only that despite "burnout," child protection service staff may continue their jobs during tight periods in the job market. See American Humane Association, *Child Protective Services, Entering the 80s*, p. 31.

32. Ibid.

33. NCCAN, *Child Abuse and Neglect, Vol. 1: An Overview of the Problem* (Washington, D.C.: U.S. Department of Health, Education, and Welfare, 1976), p. 48.

34. Community Research Applications, *Child Abuse and Neglect Programs*, pp. 15–32.

35. Ibid., p. 68.

36. Ibid., P. 77–92.

37. NCCAN, Child Abuse and Neglect, *The Problem and Its Management, Vol. 3: The Community Team—An Approach to Case Management and Treatment* (Washington, D.C.: U.S. Department of Health, Education, and Welfare, 1976), pp. 172–77.

38. AHA, *Child Protective Services, Entering the 80s*, p. 17.

39. Anne Harris Cohn, "Effective Treatment of Child Abuse and Neglect," *Social Work* 24, 6 (November 1979):514.

40. National Center, "History of Events"; Ruth Kempe and C. Henry Kempe, *Child Abuse*.

41. Interview with Donald Bross.

42. See Cicchetti and Aber, "Abused Children—Abusive Parents: An Overstated Case."

43. Community Research Applications, *Child Abuse and Neglect Programs*, pp. 46–60.

44. NCCAN, *Federally Funded Child Abuse and Neglect Projects, 1975* (Washington, D.C.: U.S. Department of Health, Education, and Welfare, Children's Bureau, 1976), pp. 10–13.

45. Interview with Barbara Schultz, director of PSC, 6 June 1981; informational brochures on the program.

46. Community Research Applications, *Child Abuse and Neglect Programs*, p. 3.

47. Interview with Tim Scheuttge, coordinator of Trauma X Team, 9 July 1981. Information on the Trauma X Team is also found in the following: NCCAN, *Multidisciplinary Teams in Child Abuse and Neglect Programs* (Washington, D.C.: National Center on Child Abuse and Neglect, 1978), pp. 3–4, Newberger et al., "Reducing the Literal and Human Cost of Child Abuse: Impact of a New Hospital Management System," *Pediatrics* 51, 5 (May 1973):840–48.

48. Anne Harris Cohn, "Effective Treatment," p. 516.

49. See Ruth Kempe and C. Henry Kempe, *Child Abuse*; Peter Coolsen, "Community Involvement in the Prevention of Child Abuse and Neglect," *Children Today* 9, 5 (September–October 1980):5–8; National Committee for the Prevention of Child Abuse (NCPCA), *Community Plan for Preventing Child Abuse* (Chicago: NCPCA, 1979).

50. Interview with Helen Metcalf, director of Panel for Family Living, 6 July 1981.

51. Coolsen, "Community Involvement," p. 5.

52. Ibid., p. 8.

53. NCCAN, *Multidisciplinary Teams*, p. 5.

54. Ibid., pp. 5–6.

55. Interview with Patricia Lockett, former director of CES, June 9, 1981. See also National Center for Comprehensive Emergency Services to Children in Crisis, *Comprehensive Emergency Services: A System Designed to Care for Children in Crisis* (Washington, D.C.: U.S. Department of Health, Education, and Welfare, 1974).

56. See Richard J. Gelles, "Child Abuse as Psychopathology"; P. T. Schloesser, "The Abused Child," *Bulletin of the Menninger Clinic* 28 (1964):261–68; Larry B. Silver et al., "Agency Action and Interaction in Cases of Child Abuse," *Social Casework* 52, 3 (1971):164–71. All cited in Marc F. Maden and David F. Wrench, "Significant Findings in Child Abuse Research, *Victimology: An International Journal* 11, 2 (Summer 1977):205–6. Maden and Wrench noted that studies have indicated that if the father is unemployed, the differential incidence diminishes. They also point out that most authors agree both parents share complicity in the abuse, even if only one commits the actual violence.

57. NCCAN, *Federally Funded Child Abuse Projects, 1975*. The three projects were the Family Care Center, Los Angeles; Family Center, Adams County, Colorado; and Family Resource Center, St. Louis, Mo.

58. Interview with Phyllis Rosanski, director, Family Resource Center, 10 July 1981.

59. David G. Gil, in testimony before the U.S. Subcommittee on Children and Youth, 1973, cited in Diane D. Broadhurst, "Project Protection: A School Program to Detect and Prevent Child Abuse and Neglect," *Children Today* 4, 3 (May–June 1975):22–25.

60. NCCAN, *Child Abuse and Neglect, Vol. 1: An Overview*, pp. 30–44.

61. Ibid. p. 44.

62. Broadhurst, "Project Protection," p. 22.

63. NCCAN, *Child Abuse and Neglect, Vol. 1: An Overview*, p. 32.

64. This idea was suggested by the general discussion of children's rights and child advocacy by Hilary Rodman in "Children under the Law," *Harvard Educational Review* 43, 4 (November 1973):487–514.

65. Hoffman, "Policy and Politics," p. 169.

66. Community Research Applications, *Child Abuse and Neglect Programs*, p. 34.

67. NCCAN, "NCCAN Appropriations: 1974–1985," undated memo.

68. The 1984 reauthorization of the original CAPTA legislation was P. L. 98–457.

69. NCCAN, "NCCAN Appropriations: 1974–1985."

70. Commonwealth of Massachusetts, Office of Federal Relations, *Fiscal 1987 Federal Budget Analysis*, February 1986, p. 66.

71. P. L. 98–457, Sec. 5 (D).

72. Clearinghouse on Child Abuse and Neglect, *NCCAN: Discretionary and State Discretionary Grants: Profiles for Fiscal Year 1985* (Washington, D.C.: NCCAN, 1986).

73. Commonwealth of Massachusetts, Office of Federal Relations, *Fiscal 1987 Federal Budget Analysis*, p. 75.

74. Commonwealth of Massachusetts, Office of Victim Assistance, *Selected Documents*, 1986.

75. See John Milne, "Northeast Officials to Discuss Child Abuse," *The Boston Globe*, 12 June 1985, p. 73.

76. See Madeleine H. Kimmich, *America's Children: Who Cares?* (Washington, D.C.: Urban Institute, 1985).

77. Joann S. Lublin, "States Seek Child Abuse Curbs with an Array of Tough Laws," *The Wall Street Journal*, 9 July 1985, p. 31.

4

RAPE

The rise of the women's movement in the early 1970s heightened public awareness of issues relating to women, sexuality, and sex-role differentiation. The issue of rape—as a literal and figurative representation of male power—was thus a fairly natural focus of feminist activity. Feminists drew attention to the frequency of sexual assault, to the myths surrounding rape, and to the devastating effect of rape on its victims.[1] The issue's successful rise to prominence speaks to the growing power, political legitimacy, and clout of the women's movement and to the growing social interest in the victims of crime. In the issue of rape, both women's and victims' advocates found a cause to champion.

Rape victims' advocates framed the issue on two levels, addressing with equal emphasis both the actual crime of rape and the services or gaps in services available to victims of rape. The insensitive treatment accorded rape victims by police, hospitals, prosecutors' offices, and the courts—labeled by Martin Symonds "the second injury"[2]—became a critical focus for those interested in rape. As Morton Bard noted, "Ultimate recovery from the consequences of the stress is largely dependent upon the helping resources available, those that are both skilled and competent. The unavailability of such resources or the incompetent delivery of the help needed can lead to long term effects for both the victim and those closely related to her."[3]

Thus, the first half of the 1970s saw the rapid development of service programs for victims of sexual assault. Initially, rape services were provided by feminist-oriented rape crisis centers staffed by volunteers and geared to alternative forms of service delivery. The centers usually operated independently of any larger institution or service agency; indeed, they often stood as remonstrations to the lack of attention accorded rape victims by the traditional service agencies. In response to the increased awareness of rape, as well as to the pressures of community groups, health care and criminal justice agencies began reorganizing their procedures to better handle victims of sexual assault. Often these efforts were later expanded to establish specialized rape service projects housed in hospitals, district attorneys' offices, and community mental health centers. Services varied from simple referral hot-lines to multifaceted programs offering crisis intervention counseling, advocacy, referrals, information, consultation, and education. By the mid-1970s, the gaps in services for rape victims were beginning to be filled, but often along very different lines from those envisioned by the original antirape activists.

Consequently, today's rape services generally differ markedly from the autonomous crisis centers of the early 1970s.[4] Crisis intervention counseling and the provision of supportive services remain a priority, but present-day centers place more emphasis on improving the response of medical and legal institutions to rape victims and on increasing the prosecutions and convictions of rapists. Fewer services today are staffed entirely by volunteers; most have a core of paid staff, who often are motivated more by professional than by political concern. And significantly more rape services today are associated with larger institutions, such as hospitals and law enforcement, social service, and mental health agencies. The affiliations ensure more stability and funding security; but implicitly they also represent a waning of the political ideals guiding the early rape crisis centers.[5]

FEDERAL FUNDING AND RAPE VICTIMS' SERVICES

The change in rape services is directly linked to the introduction of federal policy on the issue of rape. Policymakers in Washington became involved with the issue in the mid-1970s following the emergence of grass-roots rape crisis centers. In general, two agencies—the National Institute of Mental Health (NIMH) and the Law Enforcement Assistance Administration (LEAA)—assumed the major responsibility for rape-related programs.

Because of NIMH's tendency to sponsor a diverse array of activities to address a social problem, the agency was a fairly natural locus for rape-related research. In 1976, the National Center for the Prevention and Control of Rape (NCPCR) was established under NIMH auspices, largely as a result of pressure from women's groups, especially the National Organization for Women (NOW). Legislation establishing the center authorized it

to develop, implement and evaluate promising models of mental health and related services for rape victims, their families and offenders. Additionally, the legislation authorized the center to encourage and support research into the legal, social, and medical aspects of rape, as well as develop and provide needed public information and training materials related to efforts to prevent and treat problems associated with rape.[6]

The center was also to assist community mental health centers in meeting the costs of providing consultation and education services relating to rape. The center initiated work in five areas: (1) support of research and research-demonstration projects, (2) dissemination of information, (3) development and distribution of training materials, (4) sponsorship of conferences and provision of technical assistance, and (5) establishment of the Rape Prevention and Control Advisory Committee.[7] According to the center's director, Elizabeth Kutzke, "These activities [were] intended to complement many public and private initiatives, preserve local options and control, assist those seeking new and better information, provide tested models for improving policies and services, and improve our understanding of the problem of sexual assault."[8]

According to its legislative mandate, however, the center was restricted in its ability to support direct services. The center could award grants for basic and applied research, research-demonstration models of innovative approaches to rape prevention and treatment, and research-demonstration models providing consultation and education.[9] According to the center's 1979 annual report, of approximately 57 grants awarded, 31 supported basic research, 25 provided for research-demonstration projects (including new programs, consultation and education services, and evaluation of existing services), and 1 grant funded a training program.[10]

The center's limited ability to support direct services meant most grants were awarded to programs that had a strong research component, which limited the number of eligible community-based programs. As the Washington, D.C., Rape Crisis Center explained in its manual, "Many community-based centers do not wish to make research a program priority, or don't have the professional expertise or skills necessary for this work."[11] The distribution of the research-demonstration grants reflects the community programs' difficulty in receiving NCPCR funds: of the 25 funded projects, only 9 made any provision for direct victims' services, and only 3 of those 9 operated in a noninstitutional setting.[12]

According to Mary Ann Largen, a longtime antirape activist and one of the drafters of the bill that established the center, the center's bent toward research was designed to ensure the bill's passage in a political climate hostile to direct federal sponsorship of human services.[13] Proponents of the legislation hoped a service would be added at a latter date. Indeed, a service component was passed when Congress passed the Rape Services Support bill as part of the Mental Health Systems Act of 1980. But the bill was passed without appropriations and was subsequently repealed by the Reagan administration.

LEAA was the other major sponsor of rape-related efforts, with the agency dispensing most of the funds for rape services from its discretionary monies. These grants were most revealing of the agency's policy regarding rape. Although LEAA provided some support to independent rape crisis centers, the majority of the grants were directed toward initiating services connected with or housed in criminal justice agencies. The theme of LEAA's grant awards was to engage the criminal justice system in the issue and to improve rates of rape prosecutions and convictions.[14] But this goal was unpalatable to many service programs, particularly the independent rape crisis centers, which were unwilling to actively encourage victims to cooperate with the criminal justice system.[15]

Other federal agencies, such as the Community Services Administration and the Public Health Service, funded antirape efforts, but on a less-involved and less-sustained basis. The Department of Labor's Comprehensive Employment and Training Act (CETA) program was an important source of inexpensive staffing for centers. In addition, the Community Development Block Grant and General Revenue Sharing programs provided federal funds to state and local governments, which in turn used these dollars for rape crisis centers.[16]

But nonfederal sources, such as municipal, county, or state agencies, private institutions and foundations, and grass-roots fund raising, were the mainstays of many rape services.

The history of rape victims' service programs provides one of the clearest illustrations of the interrelationships between various stages of the policy process. It illuminates the dialectic between federal and local, traditional and nontraditional initiatives. The need for rape services was brought to the attention of policymakers and the public through the efforts of local community groups. Organizations with a grass-roots constituency, such as the National Organization for Women (NOW), vigorously lobbied for legislation and service appropriations at the federal level.[17] These efforts were rewarded with a federal policy toward rape and rape victims that incorporated important aspects of the feminist orientation.

However, as federal policy evolved, the character of rape services at the local level shifted away from these feminist policy objectives. Federal grant programs encouraged the rise of services located in established agencies and institutions and administered by professionals. There is a significant correlation between the evolution of these programs and the demise and instability of the alternative rape crisis centers. To some extent this could have been predicted from the language of the federal Requests for Proposals (RFP) and the guidelines of federal grant programs. But it is only through examining the services themselves, and the effects of federal grants upon them, that the full implications of federal policy becomes apparent.

THE ORGANIZATIONAL EFFECTS OF FEDERAL FUNDING

In 1972, several of the first rape crisis centers were established in cities such as Boston, Detroit, Berkeley, and Washington, D.C. All were towns with large universities and strong feminist communities; and the original centers were most often offshoots of women's centers, consciousness-raising groups, or other women's organizations. Although the founders had no knowledge of one another, the first centers were remarkably similar in their approaches toward organizational structure and service delivery. As Elizabeth O'Sullivan, who surveyed rape crisis centers in 1976, observed, "Reflecting the pervasive attitudes of the women's liberation movement and the methods of alternative community services, [the founders of the centers] formed collectives characterized by a distrust of professionals and a belief in the value of peer support." [18]

Generally the centers opened with an impressive array of services based on a feminist analysis of rape victims' needs: ending the victim's sense of isolation, extending peer support, and heightening public awareness of the rape issue. Thus, the centers offered 24-hour hot-lines; short-term peer counseling on an individual and group basis; accompaniment to hospitals, police stations, and court; and community education and political activism.

The founders of the early centers envisioned them as social change organizations, and this was reflected in all facets of their services. For example, counseling was predicated on a self-help alternative to conventional therapeutic techniques. "In these programs, client participation is seen as the cornerstone of alternative mental health service programs, and indeed of mental health itself," noted James Gordon. [19]

As the Ann Arbor Women's Crisis Center manual stated:

By self-help we mean getting away from traditional therapy. At the heart of traditional therapy is the idea of a person with troubles going to someone more skilled and submitting herself to that person. In place of this approach we have a philosophy of peer counseling. This means that one does not depend upon another to make one's decision. A person has to decide for herself the best way to deal with her problems. The counselor is there to listen to a woman and to reflect her feelings back to her. [20]

Thus, most rape crisis centers stressed that the victim herself must decide whether to seek medical or legal services or to file a report with the police. According to most centers, the counselor's role was to inform the victim about these options and lay out the pros and cons. Rape crisis centers' orientation toward social change also influenced their work beyond direct victims' services. Many centers offered self-defense classes for women and promoted other preventive measures against rape. Bay Area Women against Rape posted flyers describing rapists and their patterns in the community.[21] In a few cases, centers independently published the names of alleged sexual assailants, or those acquitted, or on parole or probation.[22]

The rejection of traditional service delivery methods by rape crisis center staff was accompanied by a challenge to conventional organizational structures. Indeed, many centers argued that alternative services could be delivered only through alternative structures. In a number of the early programs, the two issues were considered equally important. Thus, the earliest guide to organizing a center, "How to Start a Rape Crisis Center," published by the Washington, D.C., center in 1972, was predicated upon the desirability of a collective model in which hierarchy and internal differentiation among staff were minimized by maintaining volunteer and paraprofessional organizations.[23] Early centers depended heavily on volunteers' time, energy, and ideological commitment. Members of the collective were to be equally involved in administration, policymaking, service delivery, community education, and any other work necessary to maintain the center. For example, the present Boston Area Rape Crisis Center was established in 1973 as Women against Rape with an entirely volunteer staff.[24]

In a 1976 survey of 90 rape crisis centers, O'Sullivan found that the size of collectives ranged from 5 to 150 volunteer members, with a median of 24. Members were most often college-educated, white, female students. Usually only the largest centers tried to recruit male volunteers, to act as counselors for male victims of sexual assault or to assist in cases where the victim wanted to work with a man. Many of the early centers believed the presence of male counselors would not be helpful to the victim.[25]

The reliance on volunteers produced a high turnover rate. Of the centers O'Sullivan surveyed, over two-thirds experienced continual turnover in membership, although most had a core of active, long-standing women volunteers. She found that those members who stayed tended to wean themselves from the emotionally draining work of crisis intervention to become active in other areas.[26]

In many cases, however, the all-volunteer collective structure was inadequate to both meet the growing service demand and pursue a variety of other service objectives. The problem was exacerbated by the centers' chronically insufficient funding. Many centers were thus forced to address the conflict between the demand for direct services and other service priorities. According to O'Sullivan, "a few eliminated or severely limited their hot-line hours to concentrate on other activities."[27] Other centers responded to the pressures of demand by substituting less burdensome emergency coverage systems for the hot-lines, such as call-forwarding systems and beepers—which were less than ideal for victims who would have to wait for a counselor to be located. In some cases, centers encouraged women to ask their family or friends to accompany them to the hospital or police station. This solution not only lightened the demands on rape crisis centers but encouraged victims to develop their own support system, thus reinforcing centers' goal of peer support and reassurance.[28]

The difficulties of meeting the demand for services through a collective structure also forced many centers to choose between curtailing services and developing a more formal organizational structure. O'Sullivan found several centers chose to limit their services in order to maintain their collective structure.[29] But more often, centers abandoned the all-volunteer collectivity to build some form of semihierarchical organization. Variations on this theme included the use of standing committees for the division of tasks; steering committees for formulating policy decisions, subject to the review of the membership; and the development of advisory boards with real or symbolic power.

In about half of the centers, the collective was modified by the addition of salaried positions that enabled the centers to upgrade the level and consistency of their services. According to O'Sullivan:

Staffing patterns have reflected an individual center's needs, preferences, and financial condition; consequently, a variety of staff roles, responsibilities and authority are found. In a few centers, staff conducted most activities with limited volunteer participation. In others, volunteers provided most weekday services. Some centers recruited volunteers in staff positions. Others paid volunteers for time spent aiding a victim or carrying out administrative tasks.[30]

Many centers, like the Washington, D.C., Rape Crisis Center, used funding to encourage the involvement of low-income or minority women who could not otherwise afford to participate as volunteers. As the founders of the center explained, "One of the reasons why the women's movement is seen as a white middle class movement is the fact that it is primarily a volunteer movement. . . . We try to be conscious of that and have been able to get one or two salaries which made it possible to hire minority women. This is the way to change the image, and often the reality of the women's movement."[31]

In most cases, the introduction of paid staff did not signify the establishment of a conventional hierarchy. Few centers hired professional counselors or administrators. And usually paid staff served a coordinating rather than a directing role. The commitment to peer counseling generally endured; most centers continued to rely on volunteers to provide counseling and other related services. Many centers also continued to handle policymaking and decision making collectively, with salaried staff and volunteer members wielding equal authority.[32]

However, internal changes in structure were accompanied by changes in the centers' relationships with other community agencies. The earliest rape crisis centers maintained a distance from law enforcement agencies, hospitals, and social service agencies. They offered themselves as alternatives to institutional services, where such existed, and assumed a militant, critical stance toward professionals in the health care, mental health, and law enforcement fields.[33] Over the years, this position was tempered, in part because the development of rape victims' services in established community agencies altered the context in which the alternative service programs operated. Thus, many centers developed formal and informal contacts with relevant public and private agencies— hospitals, police departments, prosecutors' offices, social services agencies, and mental health centers.[34] Centers showed more interest in forming cooperative relationships with the rape victims' programs operating under the aegis of such agencies. For instance, in 1981 the Boston Area Rape Crisis Center, based in a local women's center, began meeting on a bimonthly basis with representatives from other area rape programs, including those housed in the city hospitals, to discuss common problems and share information.[35] In establishing these affiliations, many centers were also responding to the concern of medical and social service professionals that the isolation of autonomous centers from traditional health and welfare agencies was potentially detrimental to the health and emotional recovery of rape victims.

In the course of the 1970s, communication between alternative rape crisis centers also was strengthened. The early centers operated in relative isolation; aside from a national newsletter[36] and intermittent contacts, there were very few attempts to build informational or political networks. In the latter half of the 1970s, however, several statewide rape crisis center coalitions were formed, and shortly thereafter, the National Coalition against Sexual Assault (NCASA) was formed.

Many of the changes adopted by rape crisis centers were related to lack of funding. The alternative service centers rarely won federal funding. In 1976, O'Sullivan found that out of 80 centers, only 32 percent had received LEAA grants—and these were mostly larger centers.[37] Other federal programs supported an even smaller number of centers: 4 percent in O'Sullivan's survey were awarded CETA work slots; 4 percent got money through mental health programs; 4 percent received grants from ACTION; 3 percent received community development funds; 2 percent had Revenue Sharing money; and 1 percent got funding through the Title XX program.[38] (This survey was conducted in 1976, when the NCPCR was just getting started. However, even when NCPCR funding was in full swing in the late 1970s, centers rarely received funding.)

Local public and private grantors also avoided rape crisis centers. According to O'Sullivan's survey, only 8 percent of the centers received funds from city or county government; only 11 percent were awarded local contracts for services. Six percent were awarded United Way money. By contrast, 18 percent received money from local churches or foundations. Foundations usually gave seed money for a limited period of time to get the project started. Church and business donations, while small, were more likely to be continued.[39] Centers also relied upon their own fund-raising efforts to raise revenue—charging fees for services and speaking engagements, holding benefits and bake sales, and selling publications. But this fund raising tended to leave the centers the victims of their own success. The high level of motivation and dedication of center volunteers, and their ability to raise money independently, kept many centers just solvent enough to continue providing basic services. The centers' ability, albeit limited, to exist on shoestring budgets obscured the real need for more enduring, substantial forms of support. A major difficulty arose for the alternative centers when public and private institutions began developing rape victims' services. As a study by the Center for Women's Policy Studies observed in 1975, "hospitals, prosecutors' offices, mental health agencies and crisis intervention centers are all competing with rape crisis centers and with one another for local funds. . . . the rape crisis center is disadvantaged in this competition because most grantors prefer to deal with established institutions and professional credentials."[40] At this time, many centers were neither incorporated nor tax-exempt, making them even less attractive grantees.[41]

The increase in the number of institutionally affiliated programs was paralleled by a drop in the number of independent centers. By 1981, only 200 to 300 independent centers were still in operation, compared to the 600 to 700 in existence five years earlier.[42] Moreover, about one-third of the surviving centers consisted of little more than a hot-line; other services had been dropped.[43] A number of those which closed were centers that had received federal funds but could find no other source of support once the federal funding expired.

The Plymouth County (Massachusetts) Rape Crisis Center (PCRCC) is a good example of the fate of many centers that were established in the 1970s. PCRCC was established in 1977 with approximately five CETA workers as the organizing group of workers. When the CETA program ended in 1981, the center struggled to stay operational with one paid staff person and a small corps of volunteers; expenses were paid with a small United Way grant. Eventually, the financial difficulties of the agency became overwhelming and the agency closed. (Two years later, the center was revived through an allocation of state dollars for rape crisis centers.)[44]

Some centers received federal funds with the stipulation that the service would later be picked up by state or local agencies. However, in a number of cases local agencies carried the service only as long as publicity and visibility lasted; within a year and a half, many services were quietly dropped.[45]

The rape victims' programs developed by hospitals, law enforcement agencies, and mental health agencies represented a response to increased awareness of the problem and community pressure. The programs were also a response to a federal policy that encouraged the creation of rape victims' programs in established community agencies and offered grants as an incentive for traditional agencies to get into the field. As a consequence, by the late 1970s, at least half, if not more, of the service programs for rape victims were operated in affiliation with public or private institutions.

On the surface, these service programs did not appear to be significantly different from those available in the independent centers: hot-lines, crisis intervention, counseling, advocacy, information, referrals, and community education remained the service staples. However, there were differences in the substantive methods of service delivery. The programs housed in larger institutions did not place the same emphasis on peer support and self-help.

Although the independent centers had been successful in bringing out the need for sensitive treatment of rape victims, the interpretations of that treatment varied. Many institutionally based programs incorporated the concept of supporting the victim, without making the surrender of professional control which the self-help model dictated. While many programs, particularly those based in criminal justice agencies, employed paraprofessionals and trained volunteers, the service delivery followed the lines of traditional therapeutic techniques. Consider, for instance, the description of the well-intentioned efforts of the emergency room of Chicago's Billings Hospital. At Billings, the chaplain acted as an advocate to coordinate rape victims' medical and legal treatment. "Very early on after meeting the patient, the chaplain makes the judgement as to what level of feeling she is experiencing—whether it is tremendous shock, denial or whatever. He decides whether to counsel her first or just let her calm down."[46]

The organizational structure of institutionally based rape services contrasted sharply with that of the alternative rape crisis centers. These traditional programs tended to follow the organizational lines of the host institution. Final decisions usually rested in the hands of the institutions' authorities.

Unlike the rape crisis centers, institutionally based programs often employed salaried professional staff who were trained in rape crisis intervention techniques. However, the number and responsibilities of the paid staff varied. In many programs, the regular agency staff's responsibilities were expanded to include rape victims' services, and one or two new people were hired to coordinate the program or to provide clerical and administrative assistance. These people were often hired on the basis of their expertise in rape or victims' counseling. Few programs used volunteers, and those which did cast their volunteers in significantly different roles than the independent centers. Rape crisis centers relied on volunteers precisely because they were nonprofessionals who, for ideological reasons, would be receptive to a self-help approach; while institutionally affiliated programs often sought to instill a professional attitude into their cadre of volunteers. In promotional literature, the district attorney–based Baton Rouge program repeatedly emphasized the "professionalism" of its volunteers to lend credibility to their work.[47]

Moreover, many institutionally affiliated rape services were influenced by the larger objectives of the host agency. The service domain of the host agency could determine which aspects of rape were stressed in the service delivery: for instance, hospitals were geared toward the medical needs of rape victims, prosecutors' offices emphasized the legal ramifications of sexual assault. And the service programs were shaped by the professional ethos of the host institution. Medical and mental health agencies incorporated a "treatment and cure" approach in their rape service programs, based on the idea that the trauma of rape represented a psychological and physical crisis which should be treated to avert more acute disorders. Prosecutors' programs sought ultimate resolution of rape trauma through the prosecution and conviction of the assailant;

counseling and victims' support services were one means to that end.

Hospitals commonly initiated rape victims' programs. The increased acknowledgment of the incidence of rape intensified the demand for quality medical care, both because sexual assault victims frequently needed medical attention and because many states required an evidentiary examination for prosecution. (Several states ultimately enacted laws requiring the free provision of medical services to rape victims.)[48]

Most hospitals, particularly public hospitals, introduced special emergency room protocols for treating sexual assault victims. Often the revision of emergency room procedure was the prelude to more extensive programmatic efforts. A number of hospitals established special units to address both the medical and the psychological aftereffects of rape.[49] Boston's hospitals provide examples of the types of programs. The Beth Israel Hospital formed a multidisciplinary rape crisis team, with specially trained nurses and residents staffing the emergency room and social work, psychology, and psychiatry students providing follow-up counseling. The hospital also integrated rape crisis intervention counseling into the formal training of psychiatry, psychology, medicine, and obstetric/gynecology residents.[50] Boston City Hospital, by contrast, adopted a single-discipline model for service delivery. A trained group of nurses were placed in the emergency room to provide immediate counseling and assist rape victims all the way from the initial medical examination through court proceedings.[51]

In general, however, hospital programs were crisis-oriented. Many hospitals referred victims to independent centers or mental health agencies for longer-term rape-related counseling.

And what services they did offer were delivered by professionals. There is little evidence of any hospital programs using volunteers except where an agreement was reached between the hospital and a local rape crisis center. For instance, Philadelphia Women Organized against Rape was located in Philadelphia General Hospital, and center volunteers were called into the emergency room whenever a rape victim came in.[52]

Criminal justice agencies developed a number of rape-related projects. A number of prosecutors' offices established special sexual assault units to help the victims and witnesses in such cases.

The Philadelphia District Attorney's Office established a Rape Prosecution Unit comprised of 12 assistant D. A.'s, two paralegals, two detectives, and one victims' advocate. The unit handled all sexual assault prosecutions and worked closely with the area rape crisis center. The unit also pioneered a number of innovations in the handling of rape cases, including advance sessions to prepare the victim for the courtroom experience and "vertical prosecution," which allowed the same attorney to handle the case from arraignment through sentencing.[53]

In Minneapolis, the Hennepin County D. A.'s Sexual Assault Services went beyond simply helping sexual assault victims through the judicial process. Backed by the credibility of the D. A.'s office and its central role in the justice system, the service would intervene on behalf of victims who were having difficulty eliciting help from the police, hospitals, or even the prosecutor's office.[54]

In other cases, prosecutors' offices provided the organizational base for a comprehensive rape victims' program. The Baton Rouge, Louisiana, Rape Crisis Center, located in the parish D. A.'s office, offered counseling, advocacy, information, referrals, and related services through a group of trained volunteers.[55]

The prosecutors' services, not surprisingly, remained oriented toward the criminal justice system. To varying degrees, the underlying goal of these programs was to facilitate the criminal justice process for rape victims so more would cooperate with the system and, hence, to raise the rates of prosecution. There was an implicit conflict between this goal and the objectives of rape crisis counseling; at times, the tension surfaced. An extreme example occurred at the Baton Rouge Stop Rape Crisis center. The program's administrator was fired for refusing to comply with a policy change instituted by the program's director—the district attorney—to deny services to nonreporting victims.[56] Although the policy change was never formally implemented, it seems to have been influential: LEAA later designated the center an "exemplary project" for its success in raising the number of rape prosecutions and convictions.[57]

In rare instances, rape victims' programs were affiliated with the court system. In Erie County, New York, for instance, LEAA funds were used to establish the Volunteer Supportive Advocate Court Assistance Program.[58] The court project was part of a countywide initiative to improve county agencies' treatment of rape victims. Trained volunteers were available to meet with victims and their families prior to a trial, to prepare victims for the court proceedings, and to act as a buffer or liaison between the victim and court personnel during the proceedings. They were available on a limited basis after the trial. According to the director of the program, the rationale for the service was that "while changes in the law and improvements in investigative techniques can, and do, increase the likelihood that the perpetrator will be convicted, no real headway can be made until the victims themselves are made more comfortable with the criminal justice process, and, as a result, become more willing to see a prosecution through to a successful conclusion."[59]

During the 1970s, mental health agencies were the least common initiators of rape victims' services, in part because no federal sponsors actively encouraged mental health agencies to deal with the issue through direct service programs. The legislation establishing the National Center for the Prevention and Control of Rape (NCPCR) only authorized community mental health centers to develop consultation and education services for the prevention and control of rape and the proper treatment of rape victims. The National Center designated a specific category of research-demonstration grants to assist community mental health centers in establishing those services. However, the legislation was ambiguous as to the precise meaning of "consultation and education"—the phrase could cover a wide variety of activities.[60]

Most community mental health centers were slow to fill this consultation and education mandate, much less develop direct services for victims. Those rape services which were based in community mental health centers usually represented the incorporation of a previously independent rape crisis center. When the Worcester, Massachusetts, rape crisis center was thrown into a crisis after losing the funding for its hot-line, the community mental health agency gave the center office space, funding, and one and a half paid positions. The center continued to operate as a collective, and a relatively stable relationship evolved. The conflicts that arose were usually due to the mental health center's inability to pinpoint who was accountable in the rape crisis center's collective. The center pressured the rape center's paid staff to assume more power and leadership within the collective. The rape service was also pressed to conform to several of the mental health center's procedures, such as entering their clients into the mental health center's computer file—a policy the rape center resisted because it did not want its clients to be stigmatized as mental health patients.[61]

In some instances, incorporation of a rape crisis center led to the complete appropriation of services and program content by the staff of the community mental health center. The Lynn, Massachusetts, Rape Taskforce joined forces with the community mental health center and the local hospital. However, the coalition was soon beset by countless battles over service structure and publicity. Competition over clients left many of the task force volunteers with nothing to do; eventually the volunteer task force burned out, leaving the responsibility for counseling to a joint crisis team of the mental health center and the hospital.[62]

A number of communities developed joint models, involving two or more of the agencies mentioned above, to coordinate services for rape victims. Such efforts proved one way to spread scarce resources to ensure that rape victims received medical and legal attention, as well as counseling and information. LEAA funded citywide rape reduction projects in Denver and Seattle, which drew together relevant public and private agencies. As in most LEAA-backed programs, these projects were geared toward promoting an increase in prosecution and conviction rates.[63] A number of public and private agencies benefited from these LEAA efforts to coordinate criminal justice, mental health, and medical programs for rape victims. LEAA profited as well: these integrated programs were likely to be more cost-efficient in the long run, and in the short run they brought LEAA publicity and allowed the agency more influence in the funded programs.

Institutionally affiliated programs were better able to secure federal grants than were the independent rape crisis programs. Institutions, particularly hospitals, had more resources to fulfill the research requirements of grantors such as the National Center for the Prevention and Control of Rape. Established public and private agencies had the professional credentials and clearly delineated administrative responsibilities that most grantors preferred. It was also probably more advantageous for grantors to fund demonstration projects proposed by established agencies than to sponsor wholly new programs: a working administrative structure was already in existence, and the likelihood of the project's postgrant continuation was greater.

Yet while institutionally based programs were subject to fewer credibility problems than were the independent centers, it is still difficult to find many agencies operating rape victims' programs on direct federal grants. Most hospital and prosecutors' programs got their main support from city, county, or state funds, via the larger agencies' budget, with federal grants supplying seed money or funding for short-term special projects.[64] The exceptions to this rule were cases where the funds were provided for research or participation in citywide rape reduction schemes. For example, Denver General Hospital received money through a LEAA-supported rape reduction program that was implemented to coordinate the city institutions' responses to rape victims and to generate information about the incidence of rape in Denver.[65]

At bottom, institutionally based programs and alternative rape crisis centers confronted the same basic problem: federal grants were not designed to support the ongoing maintenance of direct services for victims of rape. Grants were instead awarded to projects that indirectly benefited rape victims, such as research projects, sensitivity-training programs for police and health care personnel, and consultation and education services.

Moreover, the federal goal of encouraging the growth of new rape service programs left already-established direct service programs at a disadvantage. For example, the Beth Israel Hospital service applied for a grant from the National Center and was rejected because its program had already been operating for several years without federal assistance.[66] Obviously, however, the bias toward start-up funding encouraged federal dependence. As a result, unless the funding for a rape service program was assumed by local grantors and/or a host institution, the expiration of the federal grant often signaled the demise of the service program.

THE POLITICAL CONSTRAINTS ON FEDERAL POLICY

There are a number of reasons why the federal role in direct services for rape victims remained limited. Rape was, and remains, a sensitive issue, despite the increased public awareness of sexual assault. The women's movement framed the issue in a social-political context, linking rape with the power relationship between men and women. Despite acknowledgment of the seriousness of rape, policymakers accepted this analysis only tentatively at best; at worst, they found it threatening. As the study conducted by the Center for Women's Policy Studies pointed out, "little private or public financial support has been made available to the women's movement, particularly to antiestablishment or 'alternative' organizations, which rape crisis centers are likely to be. This is in sharp contrast to monies made available to other alternative programs, such as those for runaway youths, drug abuse, or free clinics.[67]

Then, too, as antirape activist Freada Klein observed, the delivery of federal support was not a demand of the early rape services movement. Indeed, many centers' staff were philosophically opposed to seeking federal support, believing that it would diminish community ties.[68] Many centers were wary of federal funding for fear of losing their autonomy and control over service policies. This situation was especially the case with LEAA, which as a rule included cooperation with the criminal justice system as a stipulation for funding. The stress on actively encouraging victims to report a rape was considered a violation of the origins of the antirape movement; thus, many centers did not apply to LEAA for funds. There was also concern that federal support would spur the professionalization of services, which would have put many of the early nonprofessional centers out of work, as well as shifting expertise from the alternative services to professional communities.

The fear that federal funding would change the character of a service program was not unfounded. For example, the Baton Rouge rape service was initiated by a volunteer group of women who were concerned by the lack of supportive services for rape victims. The volunteer Rape Task Force began a hot-line. Finding they needed help in bringing rapists to prosecution, the group turned to the D. A.'s office: "[The D. A.] had already expressed an interest in making rape a high priority in his office and agreed to support the establishment of a rape crisis center if the Task Force could secure adequate funding and if the Task Force would permit the program to be run out of the District Attorney's Office."[69]

The resulting LEAA-funded Stop Rape Crisis Center was heavily geared toward increasing the prosecution and conviction of rapists. Counselors escorting the victim to the hospital were charged with the initial responsibility of determining whether a rape had actually been committed. Significantly, the evaluation of the service found that only 74 percent of the respondents regarded the counselor as sympathetic: "Project personnel believe this somewhat negative perception may be due to the counselor's need to get critical information from the victim at a time when she is most upset."[70]

The inexperience of the original rape crisis centers was another reason for the minimal federal commitment to direct services. Many of the alternative service workers lacked skills in political organizing and in administering a service organization. Moreover, the centers in the early 1970s were often preoccupied with overwhelming service demands, which further hindered their ability to pursue other activities. The inability of the early movement to forge a strong national network also undercut its lobbying potential. Mary Ann Largen notes that the absence of a national presence made it even more difficult to press for a service component in the legislation establishing the National Center for the Prevention and Control of Rape (NCPCR).[71]

In addition, the disparate nature of the groups that became involved in the rape issue—mental health, law enforcement, medical and feminist organizations—made for an uneasy coalition. They tended to approach the issue of rape from very different orientations. Women's groups and mental health professionals were often distrustful of each other's efforts. Both were frequently skeptical about the criminal justice system. There was a major distinction between the law enforcement emphasis on rape as a crime against the state and the feminist/mental health stress on rape as an offense against the individual. Issues such as the question of whether to report a rape thus became a major precipitant of conflict. Though increasing communication between the groups smoothed over some of the tensions, the fragility of their alliance may have undercut their ability to act as a coalition to focus federal attention on the problem of rape.

THE REAGAN ERA

The ability of rape crisis centers to find nonfederal means of support has become a critical issue during the 1980s, given the Reagan administration's commitment to scale back or eliminate federal support for many social and health services, including rape services. In 1981, the Mental Health Systems Act was repealed, reducing the capacity of mental health programs and community mental health centers to respond to rape victims. The budget of the National Institute of Mental Health was cut substantially; accordingly, the National Center for the Prevention and Control of Rape (NCPCR) was left with a budget that allowed for little more than the basic fulfillment of outstanding grant obligations. In 1985, the center was abolished altogether; its rape-related funding activities are now part of the Anti-Social and Violent Behavior Branch of NIMH, an obvious diminution of the priority of the rape issue within NIMH.[72] In addition, LEAA was not reauthorized in 1980 (a decision reached under the Carter administration), and in March 1982 the agency ceased operations and the Department of Justice assumed responsibility for any outstanding contracts.

Yet, ironically, the Reagan administration, which opposed categorical grant programs or federal sponsorship of direct services, provided the first specific funding mechanism for rape-related direct service programs. The consolidation of categorical programs into block grants opened an unexpected avenue for rape victims' service programs. In 1981, Congress passed the Preventive Health and Health Services Block Grant, which included a three-year, $3 million appropriation for rape victims' services.[73] In a sense, the inclusion of the Rape Prevention and Treatment Block Grant was a fluke. The National Coalition against Sexual Assault (NCASA) lobbied for the appropriation, arguing that the repeal of the Mental Health Systems Act and the cutbacks in other federal programs would devastate the local service programs for victims of rape. According to Mary Ann Largen, one of the chief lobbyists for the bill, the appropriation passed because it enjoyed strong bipartisan support, represented a comparatively small financial commitment, and was not widely publicized. NCASA made the strategic decision to keep a low profile on the rape service appropriations to avoid drawing fire from conservative groups and legislators.[74]

NCASA was equally strategic when it came to determining how the money would be administered.

When the block grant was passed in 1981, the National Center lobbied to gain authority over the funds; at the same time, NCASA lobbied to have the block grant administered by the Public Health Service. According to Largen, NCASA was concerned that if the block grant was handed over to the National Center, the funds would be diverted from direct services into research and demonstration projects.[75] NCASA won. Thus, the rape appropriations were channeled through the federal public health system, with the Centers for Disease Control based in Atlanta administering the grant at the federal level and departments of public health responsible for the monies at the state level.[76] The decision to place the appropriations within the preventive health block grant rather than in the block grants for mental health or social services was deliberate. The drafters of the bill wanted to support existing rape service programs and feared that if the appropriations were included in either the mental health or social service block grant, only community mental health centers or hospitals would benefit. Advocates of the appropriation believed that the indifference of public health agencies to rape service improved the chances that the money would be awarded to the desired programs.[77]

Regardless of the intentions of its drafters, however, the language of the act was vague as to what constituted "rape prevention and treatment." The act stipulated only that the grants must be used for "providing services to rape victims and for rape prevention" and that not more than 10 percent of the money could be used to administer the block grant.[78] According to individuals familiar with the bill, rape services implied crisis intervention counseling, hot-lines, advocacy, information dissemination, and referrals; and prevention meant community education, professional training, and similar preventive educational measures. Although never explicitly stated, the general consensus held that the block grant was to be used to support existing direct service programs, both the independent rape crisis centers and those programs affiliated with larger institutions.

In some states, public health departments subcontracted the administrative responsibility for the funds to agencies or organizations already dealing with rape victims or rape-related issues. For example, in Texas, the state Association against Sexual Assault administered the block grant beginning in fiscal year 1982. In other states, state coalitions of rape victim advocates worked closely with the public health department to develop the regulations and funding formulas for the block grant.[79]

Evidence suggests that in many states the alternative service rape crisis centers were the predominant recipients of block grant funds. However, the state awards were relatively small. Only eight states received more than $100,000 in FY 82.[80] These state appropriations were in turn divided into relatively small awards with few programs receiving grants exceeding $10,000. But in many cases, this small award meant the difference between a program's survival and its demise.

Further, the federal dollars, despite their relatively low level, often stimulated the expenditure of state dollars for rape crisis centers. Massachusetts is perhaps the most dramatic example of this phenomenon. In 1983, the Massachusetts Department of Public Health (DPH) began a funding program for rape crisis centers that relied on state and federal dollars. By fiscal year 1987, the DPH was funding 16 centers statewide with an average grant of around $40,000. With this modest amount, the rape crisis centers are expected to offer the standard nonresidential services: (1) a 24-hour-a-day telephone hot-line; (2) short-term counseling; (3) information and referral; (4) case management; (5) interagency coordination with medical, law enforcement, and the criminal justice system; and (6) preventive education.[81] Since sufficient funding exists for only two or three paid staff, services are delivered primarily by volunteers in all DPH-funded centers.

Despite this reliance on volunteers, the regulations of the DPH have increased the professionalization of independent centers. DPH regulations require centers to develop ongoing linkages between health and social service agencies in the area. These affiliation agreements are designed to allow rape victims a continuum of care with the independent centers as the focus, rather than leave rape victims reliant on a single center for the evaluation and treatment of their needs.[82]

Massachusetts remains an exception, however, in the level of funding it has devoted to independent rape crisis centers in the 1980s. In many states, independent centers are very scarce. New

Hampshire, for example, currently has no independent center in the entire state. The New Hampshire state allocation from the public health block grant of $18,000 for FY 85 was insufficient to support an independent center, so the money was instead channeled through the New Hampshire Coalition Against Family and Sexual Violence, to be spent by battered women's shelters for rape-related services.[83] Because of this lack of funding, rape victims usually receive treatment through regular hospital and social service agency programs.

The only other source of federal funds for rape victim services is the Victims of Crime Act (VOCA) of 1984. After a two-year planning process, VOCA funds were distributed to the states, which are responsible for distributing the money. In Massachusetts, the first round of contract awards was announced in June 1986: four independent centers and four professional medical and human service agencies received funding. In addition, VOCA funds are being given to several programs that include rape victims within their target populations. But the contract awards are small, for only one year, with prospects for renewal questionable.[84]

The funding uncertainties and problems of rape victims' services are encouraging the continued consolidation of the service network for rape victims within traditional health and welfare agencies, particularly hospitals and community mental health centers.[85] In the opinion of Fern Ferguson of the National Coalition against Sexual Assault (NCASA), this trend has positive aspects for rape victims: rape victims' programs are on a sounder financial footing; and programs are less likely to fail, thus protecting their availability for rape victims.[86]

The comments of Ferguson are representative of an important shift in thinking among advocates of rape services. Gone is the widespread support for autonomous centers, isolated from traditional health and welfare organizations, which was typical of the 1970s. Now, many advocates maintain that rape crisis centers need the legitimacy and support of the traditional, better-financed agencies in order to survive.

NOTES

1. Sandra Sutherland and Donald J. Scherl, "Patterns of Response among Victims of Rape," *American Journal of Orthopsychiatry* 13, 3 (April 1970):403–411; Martin Symonds, "The Rape Victim: Psychological Patterns of Response," paper presented at Seminar on Rape, John Jay College of Criminal Justice and American Academy for Professional Law Enforcement, 10 April 1975.

For a feminist perspective on rape characteristic of the 1970s, consult Susan Brownmiller, *Against Our Will: Men, Women and Rape* (New York: Simon and Schuster, 1975); Susan Griffin, "Rape: The All-American Crime," in *Rape Victimology*, ed. by Leroy G. Schultz, (Springfield, Ill.: Charles C. Thomas, 1975), pp. 19–39; Washington, D.C., Rape Crisis Center, *How to Start a Rape Crisis Center* (Washington, D.C.: Washington, D.C., Rape Crisis Center, 1971); Diana H. Russell, *The Politics of Rape: The Victim's Perspective* (New York: Stein and Day, 1975); Noreen Connell and Cassandra Wilson, eds., *Rape: The First Sourcebook for Women* (New York: New American Library, 1974); *Feminist Alliance against Rape News*, April 1974– .

Academic attention to the issue of rape also increased substantially in the 1970s. See Menachem Amir, *Patterns of Forcible Rape* (Chicago: University of Chicago Press, 1971); Ann W. Burgess and Lynda L. Holmstrom, *Rape: Victims of Crisis* (Bowie, Md.: Robert J. Brady, 1974); Schultz, *Rape Victimology*; M. J. Walker and S. L. Brodsky, eds., *Sexual Assault: The Victim and the Rapist* (Lexington, Mass.: Lexington Books, 1976).

2. Martin Symonds, "The 'Second Injury' to Victims," *Evaluation and Change*, Special Issue (1980):36–38.

3. Morton Bard, "The Rape Victim: Challenge to the Helping Systems," *Victimology: An International Journal* 1, 2 (Summer 1976):264.

4. Interview with Freada Klein, 18 March 1981. Also see Freada Klein, "Developing New Models: Rape Crisis Centers," *Feminist Alliance against Rape* (July–August 1977):9–10. Klein discusses changes in rape victims' services and the implication of the development of institutionally affiliated services for grass-roots rape crisis centers. This change is the product of a complex set of factors. Federal policy contributed to the emergence of institutionally affiliated rape victims' services; however, the generally low level of federal funding precluded the creation of many comprehensive rape victims' service programs. Thus, most medical, legal, and mental health facilities were unable to do more than simply expand their regular specific service operations to better assist rape victims. And most independent rape victims' programs remained reliant on existing medical, legal, psychiatric, and social services. Hence, a premium was placed on

improving those services where and when they were needed. In addition, as the issue gained currency, rape programs attracted an increasingly diverse group of people. In contrast to the original feminist rape victims' advocates, many of the people joining or establishing rape victims' services in the latter half of the seventies were motivated by professional rather than political concerns. These groups and individuals were oriented more often toward reform than radical reconstruction. Thus, there was less interest in alternative models of service delivery than in simply ensuring rape victims could receive assistance from the traditional "helping" agencies.

5. It is worth noting that the policy response to the rape issue not only led to the development of special victims' assistance programs but also resulted in legislative reforms regarding sex offense. Throughout the 1970s, numerous state laws were revised to better protect victims at trial hearings and to enhance the chances of successful prosecution and conviction of rapists. Reforms included the removal of victim-blaming clauses such as the admissibility of rape victims' sexual history, witness corroboration requirements, and the necessity of a show of forceful resistance on the victims' part. In many states, the "single crime" of rape was replaced by a graduated series of offenses accompanied by a reduced, graded penalty structure; this change stemmed from many reformers' belief that juries and judges were reluctant to convict on rape charges when the sentences were as mandatorily severe as those for murder. In addition, a number of states introduced changes or special clauses in the victims' compensation laws to provide for the special needs of rape victims.

For more information on state legislative reforms, see Leigh Bienen, "Rape III: National Developments in Rape Reform Legislation," *Women's Rights Law Reporter* 6, 3 (Spring 1980):171–217. Bienen's article analyzes the trends in rape legislation since 1975 from a legal point of view. For a state-by-state analysis of the sex offense laws, see idem, "Rape IV," *Women's Rights Law Reporter*, Supplement to 6, 3 (Summer 1980):45–57. Also see Wallace D. Loh, "Q: What Has Reform of Rape Legislation Wrought? A: Truth in Criminal Labelling," *Journal of Social Issues* 37, 4 (Fall 1981):28–52. For information on victims' compensation laws, see Rape Action Project, *Com-pen-sa-tion* (Brighton, Mass.: Rape Action Project, 1981).

6. U.S. Congress, House of Representatives, Committee on Science and Technology, Domestic and International Scientific Planning, Analysis and Cooperation Subcommittee, Testimony of Elizabeth Kutzke, *Research into Violent Behavior: Overview and Sexual Assault Hearings*, 95th Congress, 2nd Session, 12 January 1978, p. 519.

7. Ibid., p. 521.

8. Ibid., p. 521.

9. Ibid., p. 522. Testimony included the annual report of the center and the advisory committee's awards for FY 1979.

10. National Center for the Prevention and Control of Rape (NCPCR), *Grants Awarded by the NCPCR: Short Summaries* (Rockville, Md.: NCPCR, 1980).

11. Washington, D.C., Rape Crisis Center, *How to Start a Rape Crisis Center*, p. 35.

12. NCPCR, *Grants: Short Summaries*.

13. Interview with Mary Ann Largen, 25 February 1981.

14. Interviews with Mary Ann Largen, 25 February 1981, and Freada Klein, 18 March 1981. For information on LEAA's involvement in rape services, see Lisa Brodyaga, Margaret Gates et al., *Rape and Its Victims: A Report for Citizens, Health Facilities and Criminal Justice Agencies* (Washington, D.C.: National Institute of Law Enforcement and Criminal Justice, 1975); House Committee on Science and Technology, *Research into Violent Behavior, Hearings*, testimony of Mary Ann Largen, pp. 489–517; *Feminist Alliance against Rape* (newsletter), November–December 1976. Also see House Committee on Science and Technology, *Research into Violent Behavior, Hearings*. The citywide program implemented in Denver, Colorado, is discussed in David Sheppard, Thomas Giancinti, and Claus Tjaden, "Rape Reduction: A City-wide Program," in Walker and Brodsky, *Sexual Assault*, pp. 169–75. A similar scheme was tested in Seattle. See June Burdy Csida and Joseph Csida, *Rape: How to Avoid It and What to Do about It If You Can't* (Chatsworth, Calif.: Books for Better Living, 1974), pp. 157–62, which focuses on Rape Relief, the rape crisis center involved in the rape reduction project; pp. 205–12 discuss LEAA's rape-related initiatives.

15. According to the Washington, D.C., Rape Crisis Center, LEAA offered a national award to the center with the highest percentage increase in the reporting of rape to the police. See Washington, D.C., Rape Crisis Center, *How to Start a Rape Crisis Center*, p. 34.

16. Ibid. For information on funding sources for rape crisis centers, see pp. 32–36. See also House Committee on Science and Technology, *Research into Violent Behavior, Hearings*; Brodyaga et. al., *Rape and Its Victims*; Elizabeth O'Sullivan, "What Has Happened to Rape Crisis Centers? A Look at Their Structure, Members and Funding," *Victimology: An International Journal* 3, 1–2 (1978):45–62. O'Sullivan provides a breakdown of funding sources for 89 rape crisis centers she surveyed.

17. Interview with Mary Ann Largen, 25 February 1981. See Mary Ann Largen, "History of the Women's Movement in Changing Attitudes, Laws and Treatment toward Rape Victims," in Walker and Brod-

sky, *Sexual Assault*, pp. 69–73. See also Csida and Csida, *Rape: How to Avoid It*, pp. 163–66.

18. O'Sullivan, "What Has Happened to Rape Crisis Centers?" p. 45. O'Sullivan's findings were confirmed in interviews and secondary source materials on a number of rape crisis centers including the Boston Area Rape Crisis Center; Worcester, Mass., Rape Crisis Center; Lynn, Mass., Rape Crisis Center; Bay Area Women Against Rape in Berkeley, Calif.; Women Organized Against Rape in Philadelphia; Rape Relief in Seattle; and the Washington, D.C., Rape Crisis Center.

19. James Gordon, "Grassroots Mental Health Services," *Social Policy* 9, 1 (May–June 1978):34. The self-help participatory approach was also central to organizations formed by feminists in the 1970s. However, feminists' efforts to minimize hierarchy were more often derived from concepts generated by feminist thinkers, in relation to sexism, than from critiques offered by mental health practitioners. See Jo Freeman, *The Politics of Women's Liberation* (New York: David McKay, 1975).

20. Quoted in Washington, D.C., Rape Crisis Center, *How to Start a Rape Crisis Center*, pp. 46–47. Also see Brodyaga et al., *Rape and Its Victims*; and Cassandra Wilson, "Rape Groups," in *Rape: The First Sourcebook for Women*.

21. Csida and Csida, *Rape: How to Avoid It*, p. 149.

22. Loret Ulmschneider, "Dallas Rapists See Their Names Printed," *Feminist Alliance against Rape News* (July–August, 1977):2–5.

23. Washington, D.C., Rape Crisis Center, *How to Start a Rape Crisis Center*. Although the center departed from certain aspects of a collective model—e.g., by hiring staff, creating standing committees, establishing an identifiable decision-making body, a steering committee, and a board of trustees—the organization continued to minimize hierarchical work relations. For more information on the D.C. center, see Emilio C. Viano, "Victimology Interview: The Washington, D.C., Rape Crisis Center: A Conversation with Lysandra Brady, Nancy McDonald, Michele Plate, and Ifetayo Nekenge Toure," *Victimology: An International Journal* 1, 3 (Fall 1976):434–45.

24. Interviews with Sohaila Abdulali, executive director, Boston Area Rape Crisis Center (BARRC), 26 March 1985; and Deborah Stolbach, interim executive director, BARRC, 19 July 1985. The Rape Crisis Center of Worcester was completely volunteer from 1973 through 1978. Interview with Donna Steward, assistant director, Rape Crisis Center of Worcester, Mass., 16 August 1985.

25. O'Sullivan, "What Has Happened to Rape Crisis Centers?" p. 52. In addition, O'Sullivan noted that some centers established liaisons with

companion male groups such as the Philadelphia Men Organized against Rape; however male volunteers in general had very limited roles (p. 55).

Many centers also continue to resist the use of male volunteers. For example, the Boston Area Rape Crisis Center still forbids the presence of men on the grounds of the center.

26. Ibid., pp. 52–56.

27. Ibid., p. 47.

28. Ibid. San Francisco's Bay Area Women against Rape (BAWAR) instituted this practice.

29. Ibid., p. 50.

30. Ibid., p. 51.

31. Viano, "Victimology Interview: The Washington, D.C., Rape Crisis Center," p. 138. The Rape Crisis Center of Worcester, Mass., also paid volunteers in order to attract low-income and minority women to the center staff.

32. Brodyaga et al., *Rape and Its Victims*; Washington, D.C., Rape Crisis Center, *How to Start a Rape Crisis Center*; interviews with Mary Ann Largen, 25 February 1981, and Freada Klein, 18 March 1981.

33. Brodyaga et al., *Rape and Its Victims*.

34. In 1977, O'Sullivan found that of 84 centers, 74 percent had liaisons with city police departments, 56 percent with major city hospitals, 54 percent with prosecutors' offices, 43 percent with a mental health center, and 19 percent with the city council. Approximately a third of the centers had made presentations to the police and hospitals, 18 percent had delivered presentations to prosecutors' offices, and only 10 percent had addressed mental health centers. O'Sullivan, "What Has Happened to Rape Crisis Centers?" p. 49.

35. Interviews with staff members of the Boston Area Rape Crisis Center, 19 March 1981; and Sally Bowie, staff member of the Beth Israel Hospital Rape Crisis Center, Boston, Mass., 10 March 1981.

36. The newsletter, *Feminist Alliance against Rape (FAAR)*, was begun in 1974. In 1978, *FAAR* merged with a domestic violence newsletter, *National Communications Network*, to form *Aegis*, a publication addressing the overall issue of violence against women.

37. O'Sullivan, "What Has Happened to Rape Crisis Centers?" p. 56. Significantly, O'Sullivan found that 61 percent (i.e., 20) of the centers with monthly budgets exceeding $1,000 were receiving support from LEAA.

38. Ibid., pp. 56–ro.

39. Ibid.

40. Brodyaga et al., *Rape and Its Victims*, p. 125.

41. Ibid.

42. The precise figures vary. The figure quoted was Mary Ann Largen's estimate. In the process of compiling a directory of services that belong to the National Coalition against Sexual Assault, Largen found almost half the programs had closed, and more than half had eliminated or curtailed many of their service offerings. Elizabeth Kutzke testified in 1978 that there were "close to one thousand independent state and local programs offering services related to sexual assault." House Committee on Science and Technology, *Research into Violent Behavior, Hearings*, p. 518. However, Kutzke's figure probably included both institutionally affiliated and autonomous rape victims' services, and she also may have been referring to programs providing rape-related services as a part of direct victims' assistance.

See also Stuart Taylor, Jr., "Rape Crisis Centers Reduced," *The New York Times*, 31 August 1981, p. B4. Taylor quotes a past president of the National Coalition against Sexual Assault, who estimates that one-fourth of the approximately 600 centers established during the 1970s had folded by 1981.

43. Interview with Mary Ann Largen, 25 February 1981.

44. Interview with Ursula Garfield, executive director, Plymouth County Rape Crisis Center, Brockton, Mass., 18 April 1985.

45. Interview with Mary Ann Largen, 25 February 1981.

46. "How They Help Rape Victims at the University of Chicago," *Resident and Staff Physician* 19, 8 (August 1973):31. In many institutionally affiliated rape victims' programs, there was a greater tendency for staff to take the initiative in working with the victim, advising or making arrangements for her, and, in general, establishing a wider distance between staff and client than existed in alternative rape crisis programs.

47. Debra Whitcomb et al., *An Exemplary Project: Stop Rape Crisis Center, Baton Rouge, Louisiana* (Washington, D.C.: National Institute of Law Enforcement and Criminal Justice, 1979).

48. In most cases, the legislation enacted mandating free medical care for rape victims represented a broader effort to widen victims' compensation coverage for victims of sexual assault. For example, the compensation programs of Alaska, Delaware, Hawaii, Minnesota, and Washington reimburse rape victims for emergency room visits or evidentiary examinations. In Iowa, Ohio, and Texas the state pays only for the evidentiary examination. Reimbursement not only was designed to spare victims the cost of hospital examinations required by the state, but it may also have represented an effort to encourage the reporting and facilitate the criminal prosecution of sexual assaults. See Bienen, "Rape III—National Development," p. 212; and Rape Action Project, *Com-pen-sa-tion,*

pp. 9–10. The Rape Action Project succeeded in winning changes in the Massachusetts compensation law to broaden the coverage to rape victims.

49. Besides information on specific programs listed below, see Brodyaga et al., *Rape and Its Victims*. Charles Hayman et al., "A Public Health Program for Sexually Assaulted Females," *Public Health Reports* 82, 6 (June 1967):497–504. The lead author established a special program for rape victims at the Washington, D.C., General Hospital—one of the first programs of its kind in the country. Also see Charles Hayman et al., "Rape in the District of Columbia," *American Journal of Obstetrics and Gynecology* 113, 1 (May 1, 1972):91–97; Dorothy J. Hicks and Charlotte R. Platt, "Medical Treatment for the Victim: The Development of a Rape Treatment Center," in Walker and Brodsky, *Sexual Assault*, pp. 53–60; Lynda L. Holmstrom and Ann W. Burgess, *The Victim of Rape: Institutional Reactions* (New York: John Wiley and Sons, 1978).

50. Interview with Sally Bowie, coordinator, Beth Israel Rape Crisis Center, 10 March 1981. See also Sharon McCrombie et al., "Development of a Medical Center Rape Crisis Intervention Program," *American Journal of Psychiatry* 133, 4 (April 1976):418–21; and Ellen Bassuk et al., "Organizing a Rape Crisis Program in a General Hospital," *Journal of American Medical Women's Association* 30, 12 (December 1975):486–90.

51. Interview with Sheila Levenseler, Boston City Hospital Victim Counseling Program, 15 March 1981; see also Ann W. Burgess and Lynda L. Holmstrom, "The Rape Victim in the Emergency Ward," *American Journal of Nursing* 73, 10 (October 1973):1741–45.

52. O'Sullivan, "What Has Happened to Rape Crisis Centers?" p. 47. According to O'Sullivan, at least eight other programs had similar arrangements.

53. Lynn Marks, "WOAR and the DA's Rape Prosecution Unit," *WOARPATH: A Semiannual Newsletter to Supporting Members* 6, 4 (Philadelphia: Women Organized against Rape, April 1980):7.

54. Emilio C. Viano, "Victimology Interviewed: Victims' Assistance Program in Minnesota, A Conversation with Deborah Anderson, Susan Gillespie, Mary Maloney and Peggy Specktor," *Victimology: An International Journal* 2, 1 (Spring 1977):88–101.

55. Whitcomb et al., *An Exemplary Project*.

56. *Feminist Alliance against Rape News*, November–December 1976.

57. Whitcomb et al., *An Exemplary Project*. LEAA's National Institute of Law Enforcement and Criminal Justice published a number of informational materials about each exemplary project. The statement prefacing the publication on the Stop Rape Crisis Center briefly explains the criteria used to designate exemplary projects. These include "overall effectiveness in reducing crime or improving criminal justice, adaptability to other ju-

risdictions, objective evidence of achievement, demonstrated cost effectiveness."

58. David Hirschel, "Providing Rape Victims with Assistance at Court: The Erie County Volunteer Supportive Advocate Court Assistance Program," *Victimology: An International Journal* 3, 1–2 (1973):149–53.

59. Ibid., p. 149.

60. Interview with Mary Ann Largen, 25 February 1981. See also House Committee on Science and Technology, *Research into Violent Behavior, Hearings*, testimony of Elizabeth Kutzke, p. 524.

61. Interview with Nancy Farmer, assistant coordinator, Rape Crisis Center of Worcester, Mass., 12 March 1981.

62. Interview with Nancy Farmer.

63. Freada Klein, "Developing New Models: Rape Crisis Centers," *Feminist Alliance against Rape News* (July–August, 1977):9–10; interview with Freada Klein, 18 March 1981; and interview with Irene Russo, executive director, Lynn Rape Crisis Center, 12 March 1981.

64. Brodyaga et al., *Rape and Its Victims*, pp. 55–72, 95–105.

65. Sheppard, Giacinti, and Tjaden, "Rape Reduction: A Citywide Program."

66. Interview with Sally Bowie, 10 March 1981.

67. Brodyaga et al., *Rape and Its Victims*, p. 123.

68. Interview with Freada Klein, 18 March 1981.

69. Whitcomb et al., *An Exemplary Project*, p. 3. The task force was established in 1974 by a committee of the Baton Rouge YWCA and was "comprised of community leaders and other concerned women" (p. 2).

70. Ibid., p. 32.

71. Interview with Mary Ann Largen, 25 February 1981; also see House Committee on Science and Technology, *Research into Violent Behavior, Hearings*, testimony of Mary Ann Largen, pp. 489–516. Freada Klein made the same point when she was interviewed.

72. The Antisocial and Violent Behavior Branch of NIMH continues to fund several research projects on the "etiology, incidence, prevalence, and mental health effects of rape and other sexual assault." The research is usually conducted by academicians in major research institutions. See Antisocial and Violent Behavior Branch, Division of Biometry and Applied Sciences, NIMH, *Research Program Notice*, 30 January 1986.

73. Interview with Mary Ann Largen, 16 December 1981; interview with Tom G. Ortiz, assistant to the director for field activities, Centers for Disease Control, 23 November 1981. See also Omnibus Budget Reconciliation Act (PL 97-35), Section 901, Preventive Health and Health Services, 1981, in *Federal Register* 46:190 (Washington, D.C.: U.S. Government Printing Office, 1 October 1981), pp. 48592–98; and U.S. De-

partment of Health and Human Services, *Health and Human Services Department: Block Grants* (Washington, D.C.: HHS, August 1981), mimeographed fact sheet.

74. Interview with Mary Ann Largen, 16 December 1981.

75. Interview with Mary Ann Largen, 16 December 1981. Largen speculates that the National Center's unsuccessful bid to be awarded administrative authority for the new Rape Prevention and Treatment Block Grant signaled the program's political unpopularity.

76. The National Coalition against Sexual Assault specifically advised its members to offer their expertise and assistance to the state agencies administering the block grants.

77. Interview with Mary Ann Largen, 16 December 1981.

78. Omnibus Budget Reconciliation Act, Section 1904a-d; and Health and Human Services, "Block Grants," pp. 5–7.

79. Interviews with Sylvia Calloway, Austin, Texas, Rape Crisis Center, 20 January 1982; Lisa Cole, Massachusetts Department of Public Health, 10 February 1982; Cindy Dorman, Services to Victims of Sexual Assault (Raleigh, N.C.), 5 December 1981; Peggy Specktor, Minnesota Program for Victims of Sexual Assault, 15 December 1981; Caroline Heusmann, Rape Crisis Center of Worcester, Mass., 5 December 1981; and Marilyn Strachen, California Sexual Assault Victims Services Program, 6 February 1982.

80. The Centers for Disease Control published an allocation table in 1982 for the rape services block grant funds. According to the table, over half the states (and territories) received grants of $50,000 or less. And the states with the largest grant awards were the most populous. Thus, although Texas was allocated $185,541 in the first year, the state had 25 operating rape victims' programs. To ensure that the grants were meaningful, the Texas Association against Sexual Assault decided that the grant's allocation was to be determined by need, and that the better-funded centers were discouraged from applying. These decisions notwithstanding, few centers received grants exceeding $10,000.

81. Interview with Candace Waldron, Director of Rape Victims Services Program, Massachusetts Department of Public Health, Division of Family Health Services, Maternal and Child Health, 25 June 1987; Massachusetts Department of Public Health (DPH), Division of Family Health Services, Maternal and Child Health, *Request for Proposals, Rape Prevention and Victim Services: FY 1985–FY 1986*, p. 4.

82. DPH, *Request for Proposals.* Interviews with Sohaila Abdulali and Debra Stolbach of the Boston Area Rape Crisis Center and Candace Waldron.

83. Interview with Barry MacMichael, executive director, New Hampshire Coalition against Family and Sexual Violence, 13 August 1985.

84. Massachusetts Office of Victim Assistance, *Selected Documents*, 1986. Interview with Elizabeth N. Offen, deputy director, Massachusetts Office of Victim Assistance, 2 June 1986.

85. Data on the availability of rape services in traditional medical and social welfare agencies is scarce. However, a 1980 survey reported that almost one-quarter of the community mental health centers responding to a questionnaire about rape services provided no rape services at all; many of the other responding centers reported that rape services were a low priority within their service mix. Thus, it appears that rape services risk losing their identity within a multipurpose social service agency. See Bruce D. Forman and J. Charles Wadsworth, "Delivery of Rape-Related Services in CMHCs: An Initial Study," *Journal of Community Psychology* 11, 3 (July 1983):236–40.

86. Interview with Fern Ferguson, National Coalition against Sexual Assault, 11 July 1986.

5

CRIMES AGAINST THE ELDERLY

ELDERLY CRIME AS A SOCIAL PROBLEM

One of the strangest and most controversial victims' issues to emerge in the 1970s was that of crime against the elderly. It was an immensely popular political issue that had little basis in reality, as social scientists who studied the problem quickly concluded.

Yet as Fay Lomax Cook, one of the foremost skeptics, noted, the 1970s were "ripe" for the emergence of the issue since it contained three themes already visible: crime, victims, and the elderly.[1] The issue was, at one level, a natural outgrowth of the increased concern with the status of victims in the criminal justice system; and it was a logical splinter in the overall fragmentation of the victims' issue into typologies of victimization, constituencies of victims.

But the age-specific nature of the issue is related to the emergence of the elderly as a policy concern and a powerful political force. Decades of improvements in health care and living conditions have lengthened the life span of Americans, thereby creating a rapidly growing segment of the population who are 65 and older.[2] In the 1960s and 1970s, there was a burst of policy directed at the aged. Congress enacted major pieces of legislation affecting the health, income, employment, and housing of older adults. And an ever-growing number of organizations, agencies, interest groups, practitioners, and professionals became involved in age-related services. Carroll Estes called it the "aging enterprise": "This enterprise grows through developing and creating focused, organized political pressure in favor of age-segregated policies that single out the aged from the rest of society." Thus, with crime an increasing public concern, it was natural that an age-specific twist to the crime problem would emerge: "the aging enterprise may have assumed that if crime was a special problem for Americans in general, then surely it was a *special* problem for elderly Americans. If there was a growing emphasis on the victimization of Americans, then surely victimization of the elderly deserved special treatment."[3] This conviction did not arise in any orchestrated or uniform manner; groups and individuals began articulating the problem more or less independently of one another. As a consequence, the belief that crime held distinctive implications for older Americans gained increasing currency among policymakers and the public in the early 1970s.

Yet just what was special about the problem of elderly crime was redefined several times as policy evolved. As Cook and others have noted, the elderly crime issue provides a striking example of the effects of issue definition on public policy.

The issue originally came to prominence through media reports of burglaries, robberies, and assaults on elderly residents of public housing projects. As the issue became more visible, this focus rapidly expanded; legislators and senior citizens' advocates increasingly referred to the problem as one affecting all older adults, not only those living in housing projects.[4] Many legislators and advocates for the elderly contended that the problem was epidemic and that senior citizens were especially vulnerable to crime and left particularly harmed by it because of their diminished physical, financial, and emotional resources. "Many elderly today are living in environments that resemble prisons," said Senator Harrison Williams at a 1971 Senate hearing on the housing needs of older Americans. "They are afraid to go out; their friends and relatives are afraid to visit them. This environment exists in public housing projects and private apartment buildings as well.[5]

Social science research soon disproved these contentions, showing that with the exception of certain categories of nonviolent crime, the elderly actually had the lowest victimization rate of any population group. (Yet a number of studies did find that the elderly are particularly susceptible to consumer fraud and bunco schemes.) The studies also showed the elderly suffered no worse consequences from crime than any other age group.[6]

Research did suggest, however, that the elderly were more fearful of violent crime than any other group in the population. Many social scientists argued, thus, that fear was the most salient aspect of the elderly crime problem.[7] Carl Cunningham, who conducted one of the most influential studies on elderly crime, contended that in practical terms, the fear of crime and the experience of the crime held the same implications for older adults. According to Cunningham, fear had an equally debilitating effect on the lifestyles of the aged: fear deterred senior citizens from leaving their homes, participating in social events, using public transportation, visiting their doctors, and so forth.[8] Thus, the elderly crime issue was gradually redefined, and the equation of fear of crime with the experience of crime became the foundation of federal policy. Federal initiatives were directed at alleviating the elderly's fear of violent crime and reducing their risks of being victimized. Programs to strengthen security in senior citizens' homes and neighborhoods and to disseminate crime prevention education became the mainstays of federally funded programs. Victims' assistance programs, for elderly who had already experienced crime, were relegated to the back seat of federal policy.

THE FEDERAL RESPONSE

The way in which the issue was defined led federal policymakers to emphasize the criminal justice rather than mental health implications of crime against the elderly. In contrast to other victims' issues, mental health agencies were almost wholly uninvolved. Neither NIMH nor local community mental health centers displayed strong interest in the problem of elderly crime. In part, this lack of commitment was related to the traditional disinterest of mental health professionals in serving the elderly. Senior citizens' age, resistance to psychotherapeutic techniques, and the reduced likelihood of a "cure" often diminished the appeal of elderly clients for mental health professionals.

Conversely, senior citizens have traditionally avoided entanglement with the mental health system. In general, older adults, wary of being stigmatized as mental health clients, are reluctant to seek help from mental health professionals. A Boston psychiatrist, for instance, who tried to provide outreach services to elderly residents in the catchment area of his community mental health center found older members of the community receptive only when the services were oriented toward crime and other social problems.[9]

The federal agencies spearheading elderly crime policy were the Administration on Aging (AoA) and LEAA.[10] As a repository for monies targeting the elderly, AoA was a logical source for elderly victims' programs. When AoA was established, the administration assembled a national network of agencies on aging to coordinate elderly programs on the federal, state, and local levels. With the emergence of the elderly crime issue, AoA mandated that all local agencies make provisions for elderly victims.

LEAA's involvement in the issue began in the mid-1970s, largely because of congressional pressure. The 1975 Safe Streets Act required each LEAA state planning agency to include in its annual plan a component that addressed the problem of crime and the elderly. Many state agencies responded to this directive by subcontracting programmatic responsibility to area agencies on aging.[11] But the state agencies were forced to take a greater role in 1976, when Congress funded the Community Crime Prevention Program. That program required each local grantee to commit itself to addressing crimes against the aged. The general preventive measures instituted under the programs served as a basis for the development and dissemination of more age-specific crime prevention techniques.[12]

Other federal agencies became involved in the issue, but only through their specific policy areas: Housing and Urban Development (HUD) addressed housing issues; the Community Services Administration (CSA) sponsored programs located in community action agencies; and ACTION developed volunteer opportunities for senior citizens.

Thus, the most common recipients of federal funds were established agencies: agencies for the aging, senior citizens' centers, police departments, prosecutors' offices, and community action agencies. Federal funds were available to initiate projects or to demonstrate service innovations that could be incorporated by existing service agencies. Very few grants were awarded to create wholly new service agencies or to sustain the long-term operations of an elderly crime program.

Tackling the problem of crime against the elderly inspired an unusual amount of interagency collaboration, beginning at the federal level and extending down to the local level. AoA and the Department of the Treasury joined forces to create the direct deposit program, which routes benefit checks directly to banks for deposit. Although the program may actually have been implemented to save money, it has been considered a part of federal policy on elderly crime. AoA entered an interagency agreement with LEAA to work together in planning anticrime programs. In 1977, AoA, LEAA, HUD, and CSA joined forces to develop the National Elderly Victimization Prevention and Assistance Program (NEVPAP). The $4.4 million, two-year effort consisted of seven local demonstration projects in six cities and a central coordinating arm—the Criminal Justice and the Elderly Project of the National Council of Senior Citizens.

Three of the NEVPAP projects were sponsored by local community action agencies with $1.6 million from the CSA. Those were New York's Senior Citizens' Crime Awareness and Prevention Program; New Orleans's Elderly Victimization Prevention and Assistance Program; and Milwaukee's Crime Prevention–Victim Assistance Program. AoA supplied $1.8 million for the remaining four projects: Chicago's Senior Citizens' Community Safety program; Los Angeles's Security Assistance for the Elderly; Washington, D.C.'s Elderly Anti-Victimization Project; and New York City's Senior Citizen Anti-Crime Network.[13] The NEVPAP projects constituted one of the few efforts to focus on inner-city, low-income elderly.

The seven demonstration projects were distinctive in that each attempted to alleviate the fear of crime among older adults *and* to help senior citizens who had been victims of crime. As John Hollister Stein of the Criminal Justice and the Elderly Project noted, these services were both relatively new innovations in the criminal justice field, and they had rarely been impelmented in tandem before.[14] But few other federally funded elderly crime programs were as comprehensive. In most cases, crime prevention and victims' assistance services were provided by separate agencies. And the distribution of federal grants tended to favor crime prevention over victims' assistance services.

The preventive thrust of federal policy was unique; no other victims' issue inspired such vigorous efforts to reduce the potential of a specific criminal activity. One of the most commonly implemented preventive strategies was crime prevention education for the elderly—tips on such topics as avoiding purse snatching or making homes more secure. In a survey of 500 police departments, Philip Gross found education programs comprised the most common outreach effort for the elderly.[15] Programs to reduce senior citizens' vulnerability to consumer fraud likewise relied heavily on educational campaigns.[16] In addition to benefiting the older audience, educational programs were seen as a desirable way to improve links between law enforcement agencies and the elderly community and thereby to encourage the reporting of crime.

Education programs followed a routine format: standard lectures delivered to large groups of senior citizens. Most of the sessions were short-term, usually one-time meetings. Police representatives or staff or volunteers from an elderly crime program would conduct the sessions at a center, agency, or housing project for older adults. However, as the evaluation of the seven NEVPAP demonstration projects pointed out, these formats were not necessarily the most effective way to get across the information. Audiences tended to be more receptive to audiovisual formats and participatory approaches such as role-playing.[17]

In addition to the formal educational sessions, elderly crime programs also trained the staffs or senior citizens' agencies so they could impart crime prevention techniques to their clients on an informal basis. And programs worked with police personnel to sensitize them to the special needs of the elderly and to encourage officers to incorporate preventive approaches into their routine work.

The extent to which crime prevention information influenced elderly life-styles is debatable. In a survey of senior citizens who attended the lectures, the NEVPAP evaluation found that almost half said the information prompted them to be more cautious and watchful.[18] However, educational programs were clearly most effective when coupled with the delivery of more substantive services, such as door locks and security hardware.

Efforts to improve home and neighborhood security—so-called target-hardening programs—were among the most popular and effective of the federally funded elderly crime programs. In a few instances, the efforts extended to the slightly bizarre. For example, New York's Division of Criminal Justice Services used LEAA funds to equip several hundred residents of Rochester, New York, with portable two-way CB radios tuned to the frequency of the police dispatcher. The potential for such quick contact with the police, it was hoped, would deter crime against the elderly, alleviate their fears, and improve their mobility.[19]

But in general, target hardening involved checking seniors' homes for security defects; providing locks, when financially possible; and enrolling clients in police departments' Operation Identification property-marking program. Such services, noted the NEVPAP evaluation, "were 'tangible'—the hardware could be seen and touched by the clients—it reduced both fear of crime and chances of victimization and it was free."[20]

Not all programs offered all the services. Indeed, many programs did not initially anticipate how popular something as simple as the provision of locks would be. The NEVPAP demonstration projects originally planned only to provide home security checks. "However it quickly became clear that the so-called home security surveys by themselves were of minimal value to many low-income clients," who constituted a majority of those served.[21] Uncovering defects without being able to correct them tended to magnify the clients' anxiety. Therefore, all the projects began providing locks for no or minimal cost and discovered a "warmer" reception among their clients. The critical factor was the provision of the locks, since clients were generally able to obtain help installing them.

Most programs reported lower burglary rates for participating homeowners. But as the NEVPAP evaluation noted, a shortcoming of the schemes was the difficulty in extending home security aid to apartment dwellers. Legal issues with landlords and building owners deterred most programs from reaching elderly tenants, an unfortunate drawback since the majority of older city residents live in apartments and are likely to be poor, with a good chance of being victimized.

The home security programs were often complemented by efforts to strengthen neighborhoods with a concentration of older residents. Several communities joined LEAA's Neighborhood Watch program (later picked up by the National Sheriffs' Association). In this program, participants acted as block watchers on the lookout for suspicious or criminal activity. Aside from being a way to reduce crime, block watching was considered a way to break down the elderly person's sense of isolation and detachment from his or her neighbors.[22] It was also considered a way to build neighborhood unity in atomized areas.

A particularly extensive citywide block-watching program was developed by the Mansfield, Ohio, police department as part of an overall elderly crime demonstration project funded by AoA. The 1976 campaign to recruit volunteer block watchers signed up 2,000 people, most of them elderly. Signs were posted throughout the town reading: "Warning, this city is protected by Neighborhood Watch, Senior Power."[23]

The NEVPAP demonstration projects also attempted neighborhood organizing, with the different projects pursuing various strategies. The Los Angeles project enrolled clients in a Neighborhood Watch program administered by the police. The Washington, D.C., project bypassed the police and worked directly with elderly tenants of three high-rise complexes to organize a similar building-watch program. New York's project organized task forces comprised of community groups and agencies in its target areas. The task forces, in turn, organized civilian street and car patrols, tenant lobby patrols, and "buddy systems" in which pairs of senior citizens would be responsible for each other's safety. The project also employed CETA youth workers in the summer of 1978 to patrol the streets and senior centers, equipped with police walkie-talkies. Involving neighborhood youth in such efforts was considered a way to bridge the age gap frequently cited as a factor in elderly crime, since juveniles were often the assailants. Milwaukee's program placed a strong emphasis on organizing block clubs. But despite initial success, the project had a difficult time sustaining community interest in forming the clubs; few met after the initial crime prevention educational meeting.

The NEVPAP evaluation suggests two reasons why neighborhood organizing gained only mixed results: projects underestimated the skills and tenacity required for successful community organizing; and programs tried to organize in high-crime neighborhoods, which were often transitional areas without viable community networks. Thus, most successful organizing efforts were in relatively stable, affluent neighborhoods such as Milwaukee's Sherman Park; Mansfield, Ohio; or Sun City, Arizona.[24]

The focus on elderly's fear of crime and their common feelings of isolation led many programs to take a protective bent in their services. For instance, to allay fears about street crime, some programs recruited the services of neighborhood youth or older men who could act as escorts. More commonly, programs operated special buses and vans to drive senior citizens to banks, shopping centers, medical facilities, and religious or community events.[25] To many service providers, the escorts had the added value of getting clients out of their homes.

Efforts to break down the isolation of older adults gave rise to another service strategy. Several programs, particularly those operating victims' assistance services, instituted phone reassurance services. Volunteers, usually elderly, staffed the phones for a daily round of "check-up" calls to immobile or handicapped senior citizens. If the volunteer could not reach a person, he or she would call the police. LEAA funded one such program in the Huntington, West Virginia, police department; under Operation Lifeline, volunteers staffed the phones every morning to receive "check-in" calls from elderly clients.[26]

These varied crime prevention schemes constituted the core of efforts directed at the problem of crime against the elderly. One of the most striking aspects of the programs was their homogeneity. Projects located in a range of settings—from small towns to affluent suburbs to inner-city slums—implemented similar services. And whether projects were housed in law enforcement, social service, or senior citizens' agencies had relatively little influence on the programs.

The essential sameness of the programs may be related to three factors. First, a strong consensus existed among policymakers, senior citizens' advocates, and service providers as to the nature of the elderly crime problem. The issue did not inspire the ideological disputes so frequent among service providers for rape and spouse abuse victims. Most agreed that the problem was one of fear and that education and target hardening represented the most efficacious ways of combating that fear.

Moreover, federal initiative and federal funding were the building blocks for most elderly crime programs; unlike rape crisis centers, only a few of the programs for older adults genuinely emerged from community action.[27] Thus, federal agencies played an unusually large role in determining the programmatic responses to the problem of elderly crime. The high level of interagency cooperation in Washington meant that each federal agency, regardless of its overall policy orientation, took a similar tack to the problem. The elderly crime programs of LEAA and AoA were analogous, although they were implemented through the agencies' respective service systems.

A third factor was the influence of senior citizens' organizations. Two of the most powerful seniors' organizations—the National Retired Teachers Association/American Association of Retired Persons (NRTA/AARP) and the National Council of Senior Citizens (NCSC)—were active in the development of elderly crime programs. For instance, NRTA/AARP was awarded a grant to produce a training program for law enforcement agencies; NCSC received funding to train age-related service providers in the dissemination of crime prevention information. The models developed by the two organizations were widely distributed, and their recommendations were broadly implemented. One manual developed by NRTA/AARP, *Resource Programs: Models and Current Cases*, advised police departments to deploy such crime prevention methods as Operation ID, home security surveys, neighborhood surveillance and patrols, and educational programs, as well as victims' assistance programs. The manual also strongly advocated the employment of senior volunteers, touting benefits such as cost savings, increased crime reporting, arrests and convictions, and improved community relations. It is difficult to document the extent to which such manuals were used by local service programs, but developing recommendations that were consonant with federal policy made for a combination which presumably could not help but be influential.

Despite the emphasis on crime prevention, most federally sponsored programs also offered assistance for those seniors who had already become victims. However, federal agencies rarely funded programs exclusively devoted to aiding elderly crime victims; the few such programs that existed tended to draw support from other public and private sources.

Like other victims' services, programs for elderly victims provided counseling, advocacy, and referrals. However, the programs were striking in a number of ways. The services were usually established outside the domain of the mental health system. Because the thrust of elderly crime services was toward crime reduction, criminal justice agencies assumed a prominent role in aiding elderly victims. For example, the vast majority of programs relied on police referrals and crime reports to find their clients. While this practice eliminated the kinds of dilemmas that confronted other victims' counselors, who debated whether they should encourage their clients to file reports with the police, it provoked new dilemmas for police personnel who were concerned about breaching the confidentiality of crime reports. And police willingness to refer older victims, or give programs open access to the crime reports, had a significant impact on the programs' success.

The NEVPAP demonstration projects found that their ability to reach large numbers of clients "seemed most directly tied to the efficiency of the victim referral process. And this efficiency varied greatly."[28] Milwaukee's police chief initially refused to release names to the Crime Prevention Victim Assistance Program, thereby forcing the project to rely on extensive, less effective outreach efforts. On the other hand, the Los Angeles project enjoyed the full cooperation of the Los Angeles Police Department, receiving the names of elderly victims on a daily basis.

The dependence on police referrals also inevitably skewed programs' clientele to those who reported crime; programs had difficulty reaching nonreporting victims.[29]

Another characteristic of elderly victims' services was that they rarely handled more than the immediate crime-related trauma. Most relied on referrals to get their clients longer-term counseling or to help them obtain money, housing, or medical care; replace valuable items; or fill other postcrime needs. Therefore, most programs worked hard to establish strong referral networks with the appropriate social service agencies.

Elderly victims' programs also depended extensively on older volunteers to act as counselors. The issue of volunteerism had been controversial among rape crisis centers, but the use of senior volunteers was roundly endorsed by the professional staff of elderly victims' programs. Many professionals in the field waxed enthusiastic about the benefits of elderly peer counseling, as did federal grantors. The success of a Tampa program, which used seniors to counsel older victims in their neighborhoods, inspired the Florida LEAA state planning agency to offer a demonstration grant for programs following the Tampa model: the Request for Proposals promised "extra 'points' for programs using non-professional staffing."[30]

The acceptance of senior volunteers by government grantors—who had looked askance at rape crisis center volunteers—reflects the different conceptualization of the role of volunteers in the elderly victims' service delivery system. Elderly victims' programs did not approach the question of volunteers ideologically. Instead, the use of volunteers was considered a way to stretch services when budgets were tight and signified professional acknowledgment of the efficacy of peer support. While a number of projects used senior volunteers to provide counseling and reassurance, the volunteers remained accountable to the paid, professional staff. Senior volunteers worked under close supervision in a limited capacity. The traditional hierarchies remained essentially intact.

Although the types of services offered by elderly victims' programs were similar, the breadth of service offerings varied. In general, programs located in law enforcement agencies were limited and tended to be subordinated to crime prevention efforts. Some police-based programs offered crisis intervention counseling, usually by trained volunteers. One of the few wide-ranging programs, the Yonkers Senior Security Unit, was actually begun outside the police department, as a crime prevention service funded by AoA. The program's volunteers found many of the clients had been previously victimized and needed to talk about their experience. Soon the staff was doing ad hoc counseling and sending a growing number of clients to the area agency on aging. In 1977, the city asked the head of the program to develop a victims' service for the elderly, which would be based in the Yonkers police department.[31]

Generally, programs designed to comprehensively meet the mental health needs of older victims were operated by social service agencies, aging agencies, or senior centers. The Victims' Assistance Project (VAP) in Jamaica, New York, was exemplary. VAP was housed in a neighborhood senior center, an outgrowth of a larger seniors' program, the Jamaica Service Program for Older Adults.[32] That affiliation enabled VAP to draw on established resources and contacts, one reason, perhaps, for the comprehensiveness of its services. VAP offered clients individual counseling, transportation to court, emergency housing and financial assistance, help in filing for the state's victims' compensation program, and advocacy through the criminal justice process. One of VAP's most innovative services was the provision of long-term counseling through peer support groups, some of which were led by seniors who had themselves been victims of crime. The groups were not only designed to ease the trauma of victimization; they were also considered a way to reduce the isolation and loneliness of many of the elderly participants.

VAP was not alone in branching out its services beyond its clients' immediate crime-related needs. The seven NEVPAP demonstration projects found that while counseling represented a much-needed service, it did not address the concrete needs of clients' lives. Thus, several of the projects began providing services they had not originally planned to give. One of the offices of the Los Angeles project established its own emergency food closet. Staff of the New York project began helping clients caught in legal disputes with their landlords, testifying on the clients' behalf in court. The New York and New Orleans projects hired carpenters to do repairs for victims.[33]

The special needs of elderly victims gave rise to a second variant of victims' assistance programs: criminal justice programs designed to improve the system's treatment of elderly victims and witnesses. Such projects hoped to gain better cooperation from senior victims and witnesses by making the criminal justice system more compatible with their needs. The widely publicized Bronx Senior Citizens' Robbery Unit represented one law enforcement approach. The unit was begun in 1975 by five Bronx detectives who were frustrated by a rash of burglaries of elderly residents' homes. After struggling to gain departmental approval, the unit was authorized to provide specialized services for burglary victims aged 60 and over. The unit developed special interviewing techniques: meeting with the victims in their homes, using a portable mug shot, and incorporating crisis intervention skills in the investigation process. The unit provided escorts to and from court, helped victims relocate and replace stolen ID cards, and generally ensured sensitive police treatment.[34]

Courts were another focus of law enforcement efforts. Several court-based programs were established to assist older victims, prepare elderly witnesses, and monitor the court treatment of cases involving senior citizens. Milwaukee's Court-Watch program was initiated by the county executive, who asked the county office on aging to develop a program for elderly persons appearing in court. The program received LEAA funding and was located in the district attorney's office to ensure speedy access to all relevant cases. Court-Watch volunteers, mostly senior citizens, appeared in court for all cases involving older adults and provided assurance, information, and occasional escorts to all victims or witnesses aged 60 and over. One paid staff person coordinated the volunteers.[35]

There was a retributive edge to the court-watch concept, as exemplified in a description by the senior citizens' organization NRTA/AARP:

Court watch is an advocacy program designed to bring pressure to bear on the judge at a criminal trial. It is based on the premise that much of the efforts of law enforcement agencies and prosecutors have been frustrated in the past by lenient sentencing in the courts. The essence of the court watching program is the use of volunteer observers in the courtroom to systematically record information about the behavior of lawyers and judges, specifically including the severity of sentences given convicted criminals. With the passage of time, a record is constructed that will identify judges who tend to deliver inordinately light sentences. This record may then be used to seek dismissal of the apparently biased judge or to affect changes in his behavior.[36]

Court-watch programs added a new dimension to the process of victims' assistance. The programs were not really developed to aid the older victim or witness; usually this responsibility was assumed by elderly victims' assistance services or by generic victim/witness programs. Instead, the fundamental objective of court watching was to maximize the possibilities of successful prosecution and minimize the likelihood of the victim's abandoning the case or failing to testify. In this respect, as NRTA/AARP acknowledged, the programs were "directed less at the victim than at the criminal."[37]

THE POLICY IMPLICATIONS OF FEDERAL FUNDING

The issue of crime against the elderly was prominent on public policy agendas during much of the 1970s. Yet unlike the issues of rape, spouse abuse, or child abuse, the issue inspired no major pieces of legislation, no categorical grants programs, special agency bureaus, or other formal incarnations of policy. Thus, elderly crime policy can only be apprehended in the process of implementation, in the programs and service approaches encouraged through federal grants.

Despite the high visibility of the issue, the actual financial investment in addressing elderly crime was small. For example, according to the National Council of Senior Citizens, LEAA spent less than 0.2 percent of its grants funds on elderly-focused projects in its first ten years.[38] The low level of funding is not surprising given the emphasis on crime prevention: such efforts involved relatively inexpensive, short-term expenditures. Still, the minimal fiscal commitment was exacerbated by the fact that the majority of federal grants were intended as seed money, or to initiate demonstration projects. As the NCSC noted, "while it is true that in areas where comprehensive anti-crime programs are operating these services have proven to be of great benefit to seniors, these experimental programs are still too few in number to be available to most seniors, especially those most [in] need: the minorities, the poor, and those living in center cities."[39]

Moreover, the implicit expectation in awarding demonstration grants was that the service model would be disseminated and that state or local governments would assume responsibility for the project when the federal grant expired. The extent to which the demonstration models were employed by other agencies varied a great deal. And not all demonstration projects were equally successful in achieving local sponsorship. In some instances, when a LEAA grant expired, a program was able to obtain money through the Aging network; less frequently an AoA-sponsored project later got money from LEAA. But in general, the services which enjoyed the greatest longevity were those which either were absorbed by a larger institution, such as court advocacy programs, or had established multiple sources of funding in both the public and private sectors.

The reliance on demonstration grants and seed monies held the federal government's role to that of an initiator rather than an ongoing sponsor of projects—a typical role in victims' policies. But it may be that in the case of elderly crime, where the programmatic response to the problem was largely initiated at the federal level, it was particularly difficult for programs to rally local support once the federal funding ended. Across the country, elderly crime programs were short-lived. Activists in the field complained that as soon as a directory of services was published, it was out of date.

Perhaps more than any other victims' issue, elderly crime illustrates the impact of issue definition on policy formation and implementation. Elderly crime policy was predicated on the assumption that the elderly represented a special class of victims. As Fay Lomax Cook noted, there were four ways in which the special treatment of elderly victims was justified.[40]

The first, the "numbers rationale," asserted that the problem of elderly crime was one of crisis proportions; that vast numbers of senior citizens were targets for robberies, burglaries, and assaults. Policy efforts were later justified by the "physical rationale," the argument that the elderly suffered more severe physical consequences because of their frailty and diminished physical capabilities. A third claim for federal action, the "economic rationale," was that crime bit deeper into the pocketbooks of older adults because they frequently lived on fixed incomes and had relatively fewer economic resources than other age groups. Finally, many people argued the "fear rationale," that fear of crime was devastating to senior citizens' life-styles. "Isn't the elderly widow who cowers in her home, imprisoned by fear, equally a victim of crime as the one who ventures out and meets it firsthand?" asked two vocal advocates for elderly crime policy, Sharon and Jack Gold-smith.[41]

As Cook and others noted, these rationales were based on un-documented assumptions and conventional wisdoms.[42] Initially, there were few attempts to substantiate whether the elderly faced a distinctive crime problem, or to define what the problem ac-tually entailed. Over time, however, several statistical studies on the problem were conducted which concluded that the major jus-tifications for treating elderly crime as a special problem were er-roneous. The National Crime Surveys (NCS), conducted by the Census Bureau for LEAA, found that the elderly were less fre-quently victimized than were other age groups; that the physical consequences of crime were no more severe for the elderly than for younger age groups, and that the economic impact of crime was no worse than that faced by other age groups. However, the NCS data confirmed that the elderly were more fearful of crime than were younger people and that fear did have a detrimental impact on the quality of senior citizens' lives.[43] The NCS data was confirmed by the findings of other studies.[44]

The release of the NCS data in 1976 sparked a debate on the efficacy of elderly crime policy. Several social scientists, led by Cook and Wesley Skogan, argued that fear was the most salient aspect of the problem. In part as a result of the research findings, the focus of federal policy gradually shifted: first to the differential impact of crime and the threat of crime on the aged, and then to the elderly's fear of crime. Still, assumptions die hard. Many pol-icymakers and service providers continued to refer to the special vulnerabilities of older adults as a justification for elderly crime programs.

And when state policymakers "discovered" the issue, the issue definition process nearly went back to square one. State policy-makers, backed by state studies, resurrected the old arguments about the differential impact of crime on seniors. These rationales became the basis for a new generation of state-administered el-derly crime programs.

The respecification of the issue from a problem of rates to one of consequences to one of fear explains how the issue definition process occurred and how the elderly were classed as a special category of victim. It is worthwhile to speculate briefly on why the issue assumed this direction. For implicit in discussion of the issue definition process is the assumption that the problem could have been construed in different ways.

A number of commentators, most notably Cook, maintained that the vulnerability of the elderly to crime is related more to the problems of poverty than to the process of aging. Cook's research showed that "the most fearful elders are the poor, blacks, renters, those who lived alone, big-city residents, and women. . . . The list is similar to the characteristics of those under 65 who are most fearful. These people are most likely to be found in the inner areas of big cities."[45] This conclusion suggested that to adequately address the problems and consequences of criminal victimization of the elderly would require a public undertaking of mammoth proportions. Federal policymakers (as well as state and local administrations) were unwilling to make a commitment to this type of effort. Thus, the problems attendant to the theft of Social Security checks were circumvented by encouraging senior citizens to enroll in direct deposit programs. Yet the programs failed to touch the fundamental problem exposed by the theft of benefit checks—that income maintenance programs barely cover their clients' cost of living, much less provide a margin for emergencies. Likewise, the unreliability and dangers of public transportation were resolved through special elderly escort services. The financial and emotional difficulties provoked by forced retirement were met by governmental sponsorship of numerous volunteer programs, such as ACTION's Retired Senior Volunteer Programs. While such programs certainly provide meaningful opportunities for many older persons, volunteerism has little relevance for the very poor. For that reason, perhaps, many of the programs using older volunteers were based in middle-income and leisure communities. Thus, one explanation of the orientation of elderly crime policy was the need to limit the policy implications of the issue. Defining crime problems—of any type—in the context of systemic social and economic inequities would call for a policy response involving a wholesale redistribution of resources.

Challenges to the direction of policy were also minimized, because the senior citizens' lobby, particularly NRTA/AARP, supported the crime-oriented policy response. NRTA/AARP is essentially a middle-class organization whose members are mostly retired professionals. Their policy positions are conservative—a general stance that influenced their policy recommendations regarding criminal victimization of the elderly. Although NRTA/AARP was active in focusing public and legislative attention on the issue of elderly crime, the organization assumed a retributive "law and order" approach to the problem and pushed for cooperation with the criminal justice system. The organization's retributive outlook, coupled with surveys showing that older persons consistently rank crime as a major concern (along with health and income issues), made the "gray lobby" congenial to definitions portraying the issue as solely a crime problem. A deepened understanding of elderly victimization was hindered because the "most needy" aged—those who are poor, minorities, and non-English-speaking—are a difficult group to mobilize and lack the access to the policymaking circles which NRTA/AARP enjoys.

The content of elderly crime policy was also affected by social attitudes regarding the aged. The status of older adults is fastened in a complex, contradictory net of social values and mores. On the one hand, tradition holds the older person in esteem, revering him or her as a wise and experienced member of the community. The deputy commissioner of the Philadelphia Police Department, Harry Fox, hearkened to this view in his defense of crime prevention programs for the elderly: "To find a 97-year-old widow raped by a teenager or an 89-year-old woman to have her purse snatched and knocked to the ground is directly opposite to the American tradition of respect for the elderly."[46] Elderly crime policy was justified on the grounds that society has a special obligation to protect its older citizens and that for reasons of age, senior citizens were especially deserving of attention.

But beneath the tradition of reverence for our elders are a set of daily practices that marginalize the aged—mandatory retirement, age discrimination, the removal of the elderly to age-segregated housing and nursing homes. Thus, the symbolic weight of Fox's scenario is counterposed by the point made by Jeffrey Reiman: "Victimization of the aged cannot be fully understood unless it is seen in a larger social context in which aging itself has been rendered a process of victimization. We have created and we sustain (in a variety of ways) a society in which becoming old is not merely becoming different . . . becoming old is becoming less human and more dead."[47]

This dichotomized view of the aged was reflected in the debate concerning elderly crime. Age-specific policy was advocated on the grounds that the elderly represented a distinct population with special needs and circumstances. But while senior citizens may have special age-related needs, frequently specialness is equated with lesser capabilities. Arguments that the elderly were more vulnerable, frail, and dependent reinforced many of the negative perceptions of older adults which are used to justify depriving senior citizens of meaningful social roles. As Bernice Neugarten notes, age-based policies may inadvertently foster age discrimination: "Policies and programs aimed at 'the old,' while they may have been intended to compensate for inequity and disadvantage, may have the unintended effect of adding to age-segregation, of reinforcing the perception of 'the old' as a problem group, and of stigmatizing rather than liberating older people from the negative effects of the label 'old.' "[48]

Conflicting perspectives regarding the elderly created competing pressures on the development of policy for aged victims. The dominant advocacy efforts treated the elderly as a group with common interests and concerns based upon age; other advocates argued on behalf of particular, often intersecting subgroups of the aged, such as minorities, women, and the poor. In general, policy was a product of the tension between these two poles. The result was that what *appeared* to be a plethora of services for senior citizens *in fact* had little impact on the life situations of most elderly persons. For example, home security checks benefited many homeowners, but the majority of city-dwelling senior citizens live in apartments. Ironically, the age-specific orientation of policy left many older adults untouched by its implementation.

Many commentators have suggested that age-based policy—policy using age as an eligibility criterion—may not be the most efficient or equitable way to address social problems.[49] Indeed, as Cook notes, policy for elderly crime victims was not originally age-based. At one of the earliest forums introducing the issue, the 1971 White House Conference on Aging, the problem was specified to elderly tenants of public housing projects. "According to Lewis Atwell, . . . the coordinator of the White House Conference, interest in criminal victimization of the elderly emerged because of victimization incidents in housing projects for the elderly in Boston that had been described in newspaper reports. These were incidents in which juveniles were harassing and victimizing older people who lived in the projects."[50] Congressional hearings in 1971 and 1972 on the housing needs of the elderly included as a focus the problem of criminal victimization of elderly tenants in federally funded housing projects.[51] However, this initial focus soon broadened to a conceptualization of a problem afflicting old people in general.

The shift to an age-based policy may be related to several factors. Age-specific policies are more easily implemented: they do not require the kind of complicated means tests and needs criteria demanded by the administration of age-irrelevant policies. Moreover, age-based policies were less likely to engender conflict because there were precedents for considering the elderly as a group especially deserving of aid. And senior citizens' powerful role in politics creates additional pressure for age-based policy. As Henry J. Pratt noted:

The elderly constitute an "unrivalled minority," a politicized group which has no institutionalized and self-proclaimed political adversaries. It confronts no interest groups which continuously lobby against a wide range of its policy objectives in the ways that road builders' groups, for example, are opposed by conservation groups, farm workers' groups by organized farm owners, pro-abortion by anti-abortion lobbies, and so forth.[52]

As in the case of child abuse, crime against the elderly represented a convenient political issue; no one could be reasonably pro–elderly victimization. Politicians' support of elderly crime programs gained them favor with the powerful senior citizens' organizations. Yet the record of elderly crime policy suggests that the clout of the senior citizens' lobby does not necessarily give rise to substantive age-based policies. Indeed, it may be that the "gray lobby" is often susceptible to symbolic politics.

Thus, a host of influences combined to fix the policy response to the problem of elderly crime to an age-specific, crime-oriented course of action. Yet even the evaluation of the federally sponsored NEVPAP demonstration projects pointed to the need for service flexibility to address problems beyond the immediate criminal victimization, suggesting that the issue of crime is linked to deeper problems facing the elderly:

Many of the problems which victims mentioned were things which most victim assistance programs are not equipped to deal with. For example, financial assistance, direct medical care, relocation and property replacement are not services generally supplied by the projects. Victim dissatisfaction expressed (to the evaluators) may thus be a reflection of the lack of social services available to victims, rather than dissatisfaction with the projects' services.[53]

These identified programmatic needs failed to substantially alter the anticrime orientation of policy for elderly crime victims. While such anticrime efforts have undoubtedly aided many older Americans, one must conclude that the commitment by policymakers to genuinely improve the lives of the elderly was largely symbolic. The intentions of policymakers or service providers were neither cynical nor insincere; rather, there were structurally embedded constraints on policy options. Problem resolutions that imply extensive restructuring of social, political, or economic institutions are beyond the conventional scope of the political and policymaking process. The short life of elderly crime efforts, and of the issue of elderly victimization as a whole, reinforces this impression. Far fewer services exist today than in the mid-1970s when the issue was at its peak. As attention shifted to other victims' issues, the salience of the problem of crime and the elderly declined on policy agendas.

NOTES

1. Fay Lomax Cook et al., *Setting and Reformulating Policy Agendas: The Case of Criminal Victimization of the Elderly* (New York: Oxford University Press, 1981), p. 5.

2. "In 1900, one of every 25 persons (3 million) was 65 or over; in 1975, one of every ten persons (22.4 million) was elderly; and by 2000, it is projected that one of every eight persons (30.6 million) will be 65 or over" (Cook et al., *Setting and Reformulating Policy Agendas*, p. 6; the analysis on the introduction of age-related policy is largely drawn from pp. 6–8).

3. Carroll Estes, *The Aging Enterprise* (San Francisco: Jossey-Bass, 1979), cited in Cook et al., *Setting and Reformulating Policy Agendas*, p. 8.

4. As Cook notes, even at the 1971 conference, Seymour Glanzer (of the U.S. District Attorney's Office of the District of Columbia) spoke on elderly victimization, and his talk focused on more than just crimes against elderly tenants of public housing. Glanzer claimed the aged were particularly vulnerable to thefts and assaults committed by teenagers, fraud schemes, and con games. See Cook et al., *Setting and Reformulating Policy Agendas*, pp. 10–12.

5. Ibid.

6. See Cook et al., *Setting and Reformulating Policy Agendas*. (Cook provides a full analysis of the data on crime against the elderly and elderly crime policy.) Also see Michael J. Hinderlang, *Criminal Victimization in Eight American Cities: A Descriptive Analysis of Common Theft and Assault* (Cambridge, Mass.: Ballinger Publishing Co., 1976). Hinderlang testified before the House Select Committee on Aging that the elderly were victimized less frequently than younger people. See U.S. Congress, House of Representatives, Select Committee on Aging/Committee on Science and Technology, Subcommittee on Domestic and International Scientific Planning, Analysis and Cooperation (joint hearings) *Research into Crimes against the Elderly, Hearings*, 95th Congress, 2 Session, 1978, pp. 35–40. Also see Warren Weaver, "Fear of Elderly about Crime Found Exaggerated," *The New York Times*, 11 November 1981, p. A17.

For a discussion of the problem of elderly crime as a crisis, see Jack Goldsmith and Sharon Goldsmith, "Crime, the Aging and Public Policy," *Perspective on Aging* 4, 3 (May–June 1975):16–19; Paul Hahn, *Crimes against the Elderly: A Study in Victimology* (Santa Cruz, Calif.: Davis Publishing Co., 1976).

7. Interview with Fay Lomax Cook (Northwestern University School of Education, Evanston, Ill.), 31 March 1981. Also see Cook et al., *Setting and Reformulating Policy Agendas*; Fay Lomax Cook, "Criminal Victimization of the Elderly: A New National Problem?" in *Victims and Society*, ed. by Emilio C. Viano, (Washington, D.C.: Visage Press, 1976), pp. 130–43; Fay Lomax Cook, "Criminal Victimization of the Elderly: The Role of Social Science Data in Moving the Issue onto and off of the Policy Agenda," paper presented at A Conference on Knowledge Use, Pittsburgh, Pa., 18–20 March 1981; and Fay Lomax Cook, Wesley Skogan, et al., "Criminal Victimization of the Elderly: The Physical and Economic Consequences," *The Gerontologist* 18, 4 (1978):338–49.

8. Carl Cunningham, "The Scenario of Crimes against the Aging," paper presented at the Mid-Atlantic Federal Regional Council Workshop on Reducing Crime against Aged Persons, 23 and 26 October 1973, Wil-

mington, Delaware, p. 10. Also cited in New York State Office for the Aging, *Internal Working Paper: Criminal Victimization of the Elderly: Unique Causes—Distinctive Effects* (Albany: New York State Office of the Aging, 1976), p. 13. Cunningham had formerly been principal social scientist at the Midwest Research Institute and conducted one of the most influential studies on crime against the elderly. See Midwest Research Institute, *Crimes against the Elderly* (Kansas City, Mo.: Midwest Research Institute, 1974).

9. Bennett Gurian, "An Overview of Geropsychiatry," *National Association of Private Psychiatric Hospitals Journal* 10, 1 (Fall 1978):52–55.

10. For information on activities of LEAA, AoA, and other federal agencies, see U.S. Congress, House of Representatives, Select Committee on Aging, Subcommittee on Federal, State, and Community Services, *Crime against the Elderly, Hearings*, 94th Congress, 2nd Session, 1977; U.S. Congress, House of Representatives, Select Committee on Aging, Subcommittee on Housing and Consumer Interests, *Crime and Its Effect upon the Elderly in Indianapolis, Indiana, Hearings*, 95th Congress, 1st Session, 1978, pp. 5–14; U.S. Congress, House of Representatives, Select Committee on Aging, Subcommittee on Housing and Consumer Interests, *Elderly Crime Victimization (Federal Law Enforcement Agencies—LEAA and FBI), Hearings*, 94th Congress, 2nd Session, 1976; U.S. Congress, House of Representatives, Select Committee on Aging, *Elderly Crime Victims' Compensation, Hearings*, 95th Congress, 1st Session, 1977; U.S. Congress, House of Representatives, Select Committee on Aging, *Federal Responsibility to the Elderly (Executive Programs and Legislative Jurisdiction), Hearings*, 94th Congress, 1st Session, 1975; U.S. Congress, Senate, Committee on Labor and Public Welfare, Subcommittee on Aging, *Crime and the Elderly, Hearings*, 94th Congress, 1st Session, 1975.

11. According to Victoria Jaycox, director of the Crime and the Elderly Project of the National Council of Senior Citizens, many LEAA state planning agencies simply responded by writing a disclaimer of the problem into their annual plans. Interview, 26 March 1981.

12. For example, Pennsylvania initiated a statewide elderly crime program that relied heavily on local officers trained under LEAA's community crime prevention program. The officers were trained in the particular needs of the elderly and in methods for disseminating age-specific crime prevention information. Interviews with Herbert Yost, Pennsylvania Commission on Crime and Delinquency, 28 December 1981; and James Bubb, Pennsylvania Department of Aging, 16 December 1981.

13. Information on the NEVPAP project is drawn from interviews with Marlene Melcher, Chicago Senior Citizens' Safety Program, 13 April 1981; Marilyn Lurie, Los Angeles Senior SAFE, 14 April 1981; Anna Townes,

Milwaukee Crime Prevention–Victim Assistance Program, 12 April 1981; Andrew Bradley, Washington, D.C., Elderly Anti-Victimization Project, 6 April 1981. See also Lawrence J. Center, *Summary Report: Evaluation of the National Elderly Victimization Prevention and Assistance Program* (Washington, D.C.: National Council of Senior Citizens, 1979), an evaluation funded jointly by HUD, CSA, and AoA; Criminal Justice and the Elderly, *CJE Newsletter*, Summer 1978–Summer 1980. (The newsletter was published quarterly by the Criminal Justice and the Elderly Project of the National Council on Senior Citizens. It contained profiles of the NEVPAP demonstration projects and other programs, as well as information on new legislation and research.)

14. John Hollister Stein, *Anti-Crime Programs for the Elderly: Combining Community Crime Prevention and Victim Services* (Washington, D.C.: National Council of Senior Citizens, 1979), pp. 1–3.

15. Philip Gross, "Summary Report: Crime, Safety and the Senior Citizen," *The Police Chief* 44, 2 (February 1977):18–26.

16. For example, California carried out a major public awareness campaign directed at reducing the elderly's vulnerability to consumer fraud. See Evelle J. Younger, "The California Experience: Prevention of Criminal Victimization of the Elderly," *The Police Chief* 43, 2 (February 1976):28–32.

17. Lawrence J. Center, *Summary Report*, p. 14.

18. Ibid., p. 14.

19. Gregory Byrne, "Rochester Seniors Report Crime by Two-Way Radio," *CJE Newsletter* (Winter 1979–80), p. 3.

20. Lawrence J. Center, *Summary Report*, p. 16.

21. Ibid.

22. George Sunderland et al., *Resource Programs: Models and Current Cases* (Washington, D.C.: National Retired Teachers Association/American Association of Retired Persons, 1980), pp. V33–V38.

23. Wayne L. Cairns, "Senior Citizens Turn Cop Spotters," *The Police Chief* 44, 2 (February 1977):34–37. The other IACP demonstration project sites were the Miami Beach (Fla.) Police Department; Syracuse (N.Y.) Police Department; Omaha, (Neb.) Police Division; Jersey City (N.J.) Police Department.

In Akron, Ohio, 9,000 residents enrolled in the two-year-old Senior Citizen Crime Prevention Unit's "Senior Power" program. "According to the Unit's director, since it began the number of burglaries against those over 55 years old has halved, and the rates of robberies and aggravated assaults have also decreased." Quoted by Gregory Byrne, "Serious Crime Decreases against Akron's Elderly," *CJE Newsletter*, Fall 1979, p. 3.

24. Arizona law contains the unusual provision allowing county sher-

iffs to call and form posses. In Maricopa County, where Sun City is located, over 2,000 elderly volunteers provide their time, money, vehicles, and equipment to aid the sheriff's department. The Sun City posse, by definition, is made up entirely of senior volunteers. The posse is responsible for patrolling the city and reporting any suspicious activity to the sheriff; members have citizen's arrest powers only, however. Posse members also provide traffic direction, crowd control, escort services, and crime prevention.

25. George Sunderland et al., *Resource Programs: Models and Current Cases*, pp. V41–V45. The guide describes "protective senior escort services" as "designed to respond directly to the fears of older citizens concerning various forms of street crime" (p. V41). The guide identified two kinds of services: (1) those which use community youth as companions for older residents and (2) those which organize older men into a volunteer escort service. A third type actually provides transportation along special routes or to frequent destinations. This last type was the one most commonly employed in the demonstration projects.

26. George Sunderland et al., *Resource Programs: Models and Current Cases*, pp. V47–V51. This guide provides specific information on Operation Lifeline, as well as general information on programs for elderly people who live alone. Operation Lifeline is a general label for the type of phone reassurance program instituted in Huntington, West Virginia.

27. Many programs had community advisory boards or representatives for the community on their boards of directors. However, it is difficult to determine how much, if any, influence they exerted.

28. Center, *Summary Report*, p. 8.

29. There is some question as to how willing senior citizens are to report crime. According to Wesley Skogan, analysis of the National Crime Survey indicated that the elderly were the most likely age group to report crimes to the police. See U.S. Congress, House of Representatives, Select Committee on Aging, *Research into Crime against the Elderly, Hearings*, statement of Wesley Skogan, appendix, p. 79. However, other commentators claim that the elderly tend to underreport crime. See, for example, Marcia Greenstein, "An Invitation to Law Enforcement," *The Police Chief* 44, 2 (February 1977):46–47.

30. Gregory Byrne, "Tampa Seniors Help Peers Recover from Crime," *CJE Newsletter* (Fall 1979), pp. 6–10. The program was begun in 1978.

31. Interview with Deborah Matystik, director of Yonkers Senior Security Unit, 15 March 1981.

32. Interview with Fran Seward, director, Victims' Assistance Project of the Jamaica Service Organization for Older Adults, 31 March 1981.

33. Center, *Summary Report*, p. 12.

34. John Hollister Stein, "Detectives Take on Crime against the Elderly," *CJE Newsletter* (Spring 1979), pp. 1, 9–11; and "Cleveland Elderly Seek the Improbable: Their Own Cops," *CJE Newsletter* (Summer 1979), pp. 5–11. Interestingly, although some 100 police agencies contacted the unit for information, as of 1981 only seven similar squads had been established, six of them in New York City.

35. Interview with Judith Wick, coordinator of Court-Watch, 6 April 1981.

36. George Sunderland et al., *Resource Programs: Models and Current Cases*, p. V59. An example of the retributive aspect of Court-Watch is seen in the efforts of the Wilmington, Delaware, Monitors Aiding Justice in Court (MAJIC). According to *Resource Programs*, MAJIC volunteers claim credit for the introduction of a new Delaware law that set mandatory sentences for repeat juvenile offenders (p. V61).

37. Ibid., p. V58.

38. National Council of Senior Citizens, "Educating Service Providers on How to Respond Effectively to Older Americans Adversely Affected by Crime" (a grant proposal for the Administration on Aging, 1980), p. 22.

39. Ibid., p. 36. The proposal also notes that despite these experimental projects, there are still inadequate connections between social service and criminal justice agencies: "it is just this feeling of separation between the social service and criminal justice worlds that keeps the number of elderly clients for existing criminal justice services—like victim assistance, compensation, security surveys, and block watch—to a minimum. Lack of connections, then, leads to a lack of access by seniors to existing criminal justice services" (p. 36).

40. Fay Lomax Cook, "The Application of a Model of Decision Making about Age-Based versus Age-Irrelevant Policies," paper presented at Gerontological Society Annual Meeting, San Diego, Calif., 22 October 1980, pp. 2–4.

41. Goldsmith and Goldsmith, "Crime, the Aging and Public Policy," p. 18.

42. Fay Lomax Cook, *Criminal Victimization of the Elderly: The Role of Social Science Data*, p. 16.

43. Ibid.

44. See Cook et al., *Setting and Reformulating Policy Agendas*; Hinderlang, *Criminal Victimization in Eight American Cities*.

45. Cook, "Application of a Model," pp. 28–29.

46. Harry G. Fox, "Senior Citizen's Castle: The New Crime Scene," *The Police Chief* 44, 2 (February 1977):62.

47. Jeffrey H. Reiman, "Aging as Victimization: Reflections on the American Way of (Ending) Life," in Goldsmith and Goldsmith, *Crime and the Elderly: Challenge and Response*, p 77.

48. Bernice L. Neugarten, "Policy for the 1980s: Age or Need Entitlement?" *Aging: Agenda for the Eighties* (Washington, D.C.: National Journal Issue Book, 1980), cited in Cook, "Application of a Model," p. 5.

49. Critical opinions of age-based policy are presented in Cook, "Application of a Model"; Bernice Neugarten, *Aging*; and Elizabeth A. Kutza, "Toward an Aging Policy," *Social Policy* 12, 1 (May–June 1981):39–43. Kutza argues that age as an eligibility criterion may be inefficient because "benefits become available both to those who need them and to those who do not. Additionally, some critical needs within the group—the needs of the most vulnerable person—may not be well served" (p. 42).

50. Cook, *The Role of Social Science Knowledge*, p. 6.

51. Ibid. See also U.S. Congress, Senate, Special Committee on Aging, Subcommittee on Housing for the Elderly, *Adequacy of Federal Response to Housing Needs of Older Americans, Hearings*, 92nd Congress, 1st Session, October 1971, and 92nd Congress, 2nd Session, August and October 1972.

52. Henry J. Pratt, *The Gray Lobby* (Chicago: University of Chicago Press, 1976), p. 83, cited in Cook, *The Role of Social Science Knowledge*, p. 5.

53. Center, *Summary Report*, p. 10.

6

SPOUSE ABUSE

INTRODUCTION

Ancient law stated that a man might beat his wife provided he used a stick no thicker than his thumb.[1] Over the centuries, the practice lost that explicit social approval; yet wife beating continued with society's tacit sanction. Even when the North Carolina Supreme Court in 1874 nullified a husband's right to beat his wife, the Court still contended, "If no permanent injury has been inflicted nor malice, cruelty, nor dangerous violence shown by the husband, it is better to draw the curtain, shut out the public gaze and leave the parties to forgive and forget."[2] It was not until the 1970s that public officials began to view spouse abuse as anything more than a "private self-generated misfortune."[3]

The change began in 1971, when a group of British women set up the first refuge for women fleeing the violence of their mates. The creation of Chiswick Women's Aid in London stood as a remonstration to society's neglect of battered women; its creation served notice that women were no longer going to quietly accept violence as a part of their lot.[4]

Within a few years, the issue had captured the attention of American policymakers. Victims' policy had already begun turning toward the family, with public awareness moving beyond child abuse to a whole matrix of violent behavior among family members. In the late 1970s, spouse abuse took center stage.

At the time, no one knew the exact dimensions of the problem; statistics documenting the incidence of spouse abuse varied. In 1978, the National Crime Survey concluded that in 1973, 1974, and 1975, 150,000 people had been assaulted by their spouses or ex-spouses annually.[5] Sociologists Murray Straus, Suzanne Steinmetz, and Richard Gelles surveyed a random sample of families in 1975 and found that 28 percent of the couples interviewed had been involved in physical violence.[6] Straus argued that further extrapolations of the data indicated that physical violence afflicted half of all American marriages.[7] Although the tallies differed, all indicated that spouse abuse represented a widespread, if largely invisible, problem.

The transformation of spouse abuse into an *issue*, a policymaker's concern, was related to several temporal factors. The growth of the women's movement helped to awaken recognition of sensitive issues involving sex roles and the family. Women's organizations were instrumental in bringing the issue of spouse abuse to public attention: at the local level, women's groups organized hotlines and shelter facilities for battered women; at the state and federal levels, feminist organizations lobbied to attain legislative changes and funding to support services for victims of domestic violence.[8] In addition, the precedent set by the issue of rape and rape-related policy facilitated the development of other policies and service programs for women. Indeed, many women's advocates first became attuned to the problem of spouse abuse when rape crisis centers and other women's services began receiving calls from battered women.[9] Recognition of the problem was also sparked by researchers and service providers in the child abuse field. In an effort to further understand the causes of child abuse, many researchers and practitioners had begun exploring other facets of family violence.[10]

The proliferation of service programs for battered women also helped raise public and public officials' awareness of spouse abuse. In general, two types of service programs emerged from local initiatives in the mid-1970s: residential programs—shelters designed to provide refuge to battered women and their children; and nonresidential programs aiding battered women who remained in their homes, either unable or unwilling to enter a shelter. Both types of programs offered women a range of counseling services, advocacy, information, referrals, and other related services.

In the early years, the provision of shelter was not the only difference between the two types of programs; they were also distinguished by their methods of service delivery. Usually, shelters were independent, paraprofessional organizations with their philosophical roots in the women's and alternative service movements.[11] Nonresidential programs tended to be organized by the traditional helping agencies—social service, mental health, and law enforcement—and followed conventional, professional methods of human service delivery.

The variation in service delivery methods was buttressed by differing ideas concerning the causes and dynamics of domestic violence. In her manual for battered women's lobbyists, Julie Hamos identified two schools of thought regarding domestic violence. The first viewed the family as a system and considered family violence "an intergenerational cycle of behavior and learned response."[12] Children who grew up in violent homes were likely to become violent adults. Thus, spouse abuse was linked to other forms of family violence, such as abuse inflicted on children by their parents, on parents by their children, or between siblings. This perspective was most frequently represented in sociological and clinically oriented social work literature. Its proponents emphasized the structural factors, in families and society, which contribute to domestic violence, such as society's high tolerance for violence, or its sanction of physical discipline. Sexual inequality was seen as an important factor in spouse abuse, though sociologist Murray Straus cautioned, "as important as sexism is in understanding wife-beating, it is only one part of a complex causal matrix."[13]

At times, the emphasis on *family* violence obscured the fact that the victims of spouse abuse were overwhelmingly women. For example, in 1977, sociologist Suzanne Steinmetz published "The Battered Husband Syndrome," which purported to uncover yet another facet of domestic violence—husband abuse. Steinmetz claimed that husband abuse represented a fairly sizable, wholly invisible problem, though admittedly of smaller proportions than wife abuse. She viewed her discussion of husband abuse as an opportunity to further awareness "of the pervasiveness of all forms of family violence."[14] The article made headlines in newspapers across the country. But many other academics were critical of her argument. One group of critics, piqued by inaccurate media reports that her study showed husbands were more often abused than wives, expressed concern that her study would jeopardize public attention to and funding for battered women.[15]

By contrast, sexism was considered the central cause of spouse abuse by advocates of the second school of thought, derived from feminist theory. The feminist approach viewed spouse abuse as a direct and logical product of social values and conditions that relegate women to a subordinate status. Other forms of family violence were considered related but substantively different from spouse abuse.[16] As Hamos put it, feminist analyses "perceive the need to overhaul some of the values which make men feel the need to abuse women, as well as systems which make women feel the need to remain in abusive relationships. The focus is not on the individual family, except as that as family experiences and expresses the conditions and pressures of larger society."[17] Frequently articulated outside academic circles and in conjunction with political activism on behalf of battered women, the feminist theory was closely intertwined with feminist advocacy.

The sociological and feminist models of domestic violence were not necessarily incompatible—indeed, over time each drew on the other. Advocates of both outlooks believed the elimination of spouse abuse required long-term fundamental social and cultural changes. In the short term, each encouraged the development of services to support battered women, and if possible, to rehabilitate abusive men, and to counsel children so the violent behavior would not be carried into the next generation.

In practice, however, the feminist analysis was most often articulated by alternative service shelter programs, while traditional service organizations tended to subscribe to the sociological model. Service providers in the two camps often viewed one another with skepticism; and at times, the scramble to win what little public money was available widened the breach.

THE FEDERAL RESPONSE

Although feminists had been responsible for bringing the problem of spouse abuse into public light, the resulting public policy was more closely aligned with sociologists' take on the problem. In the policy formation process, the problem feminists defined as "wife abuse" was gradually translated into one of "domestic violence." The semantic shift served to submerge the potentially threatening issue of male violence against women into the more manageable issue of the "violent family." Defined in these terms, the problem lent itself to conventional methods of intervention and service delivery.

Until the late 1970s, federal involvement in the issue was restrained. The National Institute of Mental Health funded scattered demonstration projects. And between 1969 and 1978, LEAA spent some $15 million on battered women's and domestic violence projects, including $4 million on projects to improve police response to domestic violence situations—considered among the most hazardous calls for officers.[18] In the late 1970s, though, federal interest suddenly and dramatically increased.

A striking array of federal agencies became involved in the battered women's issue. LEAA launched its Family Violence Program (FVP) in 1977. During its three-year existence, the FVP funded a diverse set of projects, most of which were located in law enforcement or social service agencies. The thrust of the FVP grants was twofold: to involve and coordinate the efforts of relevant public and private agencies for a comprehensive approach to family violence, and to establish special procedures within the criminal justice system for handling domestic violence cases.[19] "By concentrating its resources on the role of the justice system, LEAA does not imply that the part which criminal justice agencies play in the resolution of family violence should be enlarged. Instead, it seeks to define the relevant responsibilities of the justice system and to improve its response to violence in the home," LEAA program manager Jeannie Niedermeyer told the Commission on Civil Rights in a hearing on battered women's policy in 1978.[20] Since these objectives lay beyond the scope of most shelter programs, few received money through the FVP.[21]

Two years later, the Department of Health and Human Services

(HHS) established a special division, the Office on Domestic Violence (ODV). Lacking legislative authority, ODV could not fund services directly. It did, however, support public information projects, technical assistance and training, and research and demonstration projects. ODV also collaborated with ACTION on a $300,000 grant to establish ten Regional Technical Assistance centers. The centers were funded "to develop state and local networks of consultants who can provide information and educational resource materials to traditional and non-traditional providers . . . by which existing resources can be more effectively used to meet the range of needs of victims of domestic violence."[22] Unfortunately, ODV's lack of legislative mandate meant that it was also short-lived. When legislation to set up a funding mechanism for battered women's services failed in Congress in 1980, ODV's functions were absorbed by the National Center on Child Abuse and Neglect, whose budget was subsequently reduced in the early years of the Reagan administration.[23]

In addition, HHS supported domestic violence programs through Title XX of the Social Security Act.[24] Title XX block grants were awarded to the states for the delivery of social services, including adult protective services. Counseling services for battered women who remained in their homes were thus available under some Title XX funded programs. However, the regulations governing Title XX limited its utility for shelter programs. According to the regulations, the funds could be used for emergency shelter only when it was part of or subordinate to other social services; the funds could not be applied to the operating costs of a program; and because the monies were channeled through state administrations, their distribution depended upon state priorities. Shelter staff had a difficult time obtaining Title XX money in states where domestic violence programs were not a priority. As of early 1980, only two states specifically referred to domestic violence in their annual Title XX service plans.[25]

The federal Department of Housing and Urban Development (HUD) was another source of funding for battered women's programs. HUD's Community Development Block Grant Program, which awarded grants for the acquisition and renovation of emergency housing facilities, helped get about 35 shelters off the ground between 1978 and 1980.[26] But, like Title XX, the funds could not be used to cover operating and maintenance expenses.

The staffing needs of many shelter programs were occasionally met through ACTION, the program that recruited and placed professional and paraprofessional volunteers who wanted to do a stint of community service. But by far the most common source of staff salaries, indeed the most common source of federal support for shelters, was the Department of Labor's CETA program.[27] Winning a CETA work slot was what finally enabled many communities to open shelter facilities. "Without CETA funding, and extensive volunteerism, many programs would not exist or would be unable to offer the surprisingly wide range of services currently available," concluded the Colorado Association for Aid to Battered Women after surveying 163 programs in 1977.[28]

Also, in 1979, President Carter created an Interdepartmental Committee on Domestic Violence. Comprised of representatives of the major cabinet departments, the committee's mission was to share information and to coordinate federal funding efforts in the area of domestic violence.

Despite the number of agencies involved in the issue, the federal commitment to domestic violence remained thin, rarely penetrating deep into the field of battered women's services. In its survey, the Colorado Association for Aid to Battered Women (CAABW) found that of 138 programs, 50.9 percent received CETA funds. But the number receiving other federal grants dropped off dramatically: slightly more than 10 percent of the programs were awarded LEAA grants, 8.6 percent were the recipients of Community Development Block Grants, 6.7 percent had Community Services Administration monies, 6.1 percent received ACTION support, and 5.5 percent were awarded HUD rent subsidies. Title XX funds were granted to only 3.3 percent of the programs. Grants from the Economic Development Administration and the Department of Labor's programs for displaced homemakers were awarded to slightly less than 2 percent of the surveyed programs.[29] This pattern did not change significantly after 1977, despite the creation of the Office on Domestic Violence and the Family Violence program.

As the late Manuel Carballo, acting assistant secretary of HEW, noted in 1980, although a number of federal programs responded to the issue of domestic violence, "no agency [was] able to support emergency intervention, in terms of shelter for battered women and their children, on an ongoing basis."[30]

Ironically, most people in the field agreed shelter was the most pressing need of battered women. As June Zeitlin, former director of ODV, observed, the safety and support offered by shelters were unique and unavailable elsewhere, whereas the long-term, less acute needs of battered women could be met by any number of other agencies and service models.[31]

Shelters were the first service remedy offered battered women, and to this day they remain central to the panoply of services available to domestic violence victims. Like rape crisis centers, the first shelters were organized by women who had come to the issue through their involvement in the women's movement. The early shelters were often consciously political and organized along a collective, nonhierarchical decision-making basis.

Increased awareness of the issue, along with the advent of federal policy, broadened the field; in later days, shelter founders were as likely to be social workers, psychologists, or members of YWCA boards as feminist activists. These groups were inclined to use fairly traditional organizational structures and service delivery methods. The later shelters were often affiliated with private community groups or established women's organizations. Public agencies operated or created shelters only in rare circumstances.

Yet unlike the rape crisis centers, alternative grass-roots organizations continued to dominate the shelter field, even after more traditional agencies moved into the turf. Having created the shelter concept, feminist advocates for battered women fought hard to protect their service prerogative. They based their strategy, in part, on lessons drawn from the experience of rape crisis centers. The feminist advocates determined that the health of their movement depended on ensuring that any forthcoming public support would target direct services and that the delivery of services, especially shelters, would remain in the hands of grass-roots providers. As a statement by the shelter movement's national organization recounted:

As a body we were concerned with avoiding the experience of the anti-rape movement, whereby federal monies appropriated for services to rape victims were channeled into non-feminist professional service agencies rather than the grass-roots groups whose years of unpaid work had provided initial service models and brought the issue to public attention in the first place.[32]

To this end, the establishment of shelters was almost immediately accompanied by political organizing. Networks and coalitions were created to link shelters at the state, regional, and national levels. As of 1981, there were coalitions of independent shelters in almost 30 states, and the national group, the National Coalition against Domestic Violence (NCADV) boasted 249 member organizations, representing 45 states, Puerto Rico, and the Virgin Islands.[33] Established in 1978, the NCADV was active in lobbying, disseminating information, and helping to build state and regional coalitions in different parts of the country.

These coalitions, backed by the women's movement, exerted a powerful political force on behalf of battered women in general, and independent shelters in particular. As a statement by the NCADV noted, "We are hoping that by forming a regionally-based national coalition of *feminist* service providers that we can lobby *as a group* for monies that are needed, and against programs, guidelines, legislation, etc., that we feel will ultimately be harmful to the women we're trying to serve."[34]

At the federal level, the NCADV was effective in persuading the Department of Agriculture to extend food stamp benefits to women in shelters and in pressuring HUD to allow shelters to compete for Community Development Block Grants.[35]

The state coalitions also helped keep the movement unified and funded. Many of the state coalitions encouraged cooperation, rather than competition, between member groups struggling for funding. Some state coalitions even applied for grants on behalf of their members as a way to maintain control over the distribution of money. For example, in 1980 the Pennsylvania Coalition against Domestic Violence won the contract to be the state conduit of Title XX funds, receiving $1.5 million to distribute in 1980 and $2.2 million the following year.[36]

Further, the technical assistance efforts of coalitions facilitated the development and growth of independent shelters. Most of the state coalitions devoted time to this activity, and several won federal support for their outreach efforts. Three of the ten ACTION technical assistance grants to encourage contact between domestic violence services were awarded to state coalitions.[37] The Community Services Administration awarded $100,000 grants to the Pennsylvania coalition and to the Massachusetts Coalition of Battered Women's Service Groups for education and training of shelter staff, volunteers, and residents.[38]

The growth of independent shelters was in some measure correlative with the strength of various state coalitions. For example, when the southern California coalition started in 1976, there were only two shelters in the area. Five years later, there were 32 shelters, the vast majority of which were grass-roots, feminist organizations. Not a single program was operated by county or state agencies.[39] Conversely, where the coalitions were weak or nonexistent, there was a greater proportion of shelters operating under the auspices of public authorities. In New York State, a coalition was not organized until 1978, and then it was slow to gain power. As a result, in part, shelter settings varied tremendously, from the grass-roots to the institutionally based. In New York City, the Human Resources Administration took responsibility for operating several of the city's shelters.[40]

The substitution of independent shelters for public service delivery was not due solely to the efforts of the shelter movement. Private shelters offered government an opportunity to provide a service without taking direct responsibility. Moreover, public officials were sensitive, at times to the point of reluctance, about intervening in the family. Shelters allowed "private" solutions to the public social problem of battered women. The secrecy surrounding shelter operations, designed for residents' protection, reinforced this private character.

SHELTER CHARACTERISTICS

Regardless of affiliation or method of service delivery, the types of services offered by shelters were similar. Refuge, of course, comprised their primary service offering, usually in a central facility. However, in many places, especially rural areas, programs met the need for emergency housing through safe-house networks, whereby volunteers opened their homes to battered women and children for a limited period of time.[41]

According to the CAABW survey, the next most common direct service was job counseling, which was offered by 95.1 percent of the shelters surveyed. The provision of this service reflected the conviction of shelter staff that a strong relationship existed between economic independence and the ability to leave an abusive relationship.

The next most frequently provided services, according to the CAABW survey, included peer support groups, education, transportation, welfare referral, and counseling. Between 60 and 70 percent of the programs offered referrals to other shelters, help with new housing, couples counseling, education of abusers, hotlines, and job training. To a lesser extent, shelters got involved in legislative reform, community education, self-defense training, parenting skill development, assertiveness training, financial assistance, advocacy, and legal assistance. Fewer than half the programs provided counseling for abusers, reinforcing the impression that shelter programs were primarily victim-oriented.[42]

A number of shelters later expanded their service programs to encompass the children of battered women. As Women's Advocates of St. Paul, Minnesota, explained in a publication chronicling the history of the house, "In our shelter, as in most shelters, the children are afterthoughts. They come with their mothers, and it took a year for us to realize that the children need separate staff focus, advocacy, and support. . . . Gradually we discovered the problems children have coming from a violent home, and with that discovery, began to develop a children's program."[43] The expansion of Women's Advocates' children's program included a policy of no physical punishment, or threat of physical punishment; the creation of separate children's play space; special child care workers; and designated children's advocates who could help meet the medical, educational, physical and emotional needs of the children. In 1979, in response to the increasing recognition of the needs of children, ODV, the National Center for Child Abuse and Neglect, and HEW jointly sponsored three demonstration projects (two based in shelters), to develop services for children of abusive parents.[44]

The differences between shelters were most apparent in the programs' methods of service delivery. For example, in surveying shelter programs, the CAABW found that three counseling methods were used. There was the mainstay of alternative services, peer support counseling, which was predicated on the benefits of interaction between battered women and, often, ex–battered women. Many shelters required participation in these peer support sessions. In addition, lay counseling, an extension of peer counseling, was often done on a one-to-one basis to give "the women an opportunity to confide in and develop a close relationship with one other person."[45] Many shelters used volunteers or noncredentialed counselors. Psychotherapy was the third, least frequently used counseling method. Most shelters considered psychotherapy unnecessary, except in cases in which a battered woman had severe psychological problems.

The type of counseling used depended largely on the philosophy and staff resources of the shelters, though most respondents to the CAABW survey felt that all the counselors should be women. In general, many independent shelters relied on peer and lay counseling in accordance with the principle of self-help. Encouraging women to make decisions about their lives and act upon them was considered the best way to bolster battered women's self-esteem and reduce their emotional dependence upon their mates.

Shelters also varied according to the degree of structure built into their programs. Like any residential program, most shelters had rules restricting residents' behavior. Most shelters prohibited violence and limited or forbade the use of alcohol and drugs. In addition, many shelters had policies regarding housekeeping, meal planning, visits by spouses or other men, and the discipline and supervision of children.[46] Shelters also generally set policies about who was admissible and how long they could stay, or how many times they could return. Usually shelters allowed residents to stay between two and six weeks. Faced with an enormous demand and long waiting lists, shelters often chose the women they accepted on the basis of the urgency of the call and the resources of the caller. Thus, a large proportion of shelter residents were lower-income and minority women.[47] Shelter fees varied but were usually on a sliding scale. Because of the expense of housing a woman, most shelters encouraged, and in some cases required, their residents to apply for public assistance to cover the cost of their stay.

During the 1970s, the types of regimens imposed by shelter staff on their clients ranged from highly structured to almost nonexistent. Casa WOMA in San Jose, California, required residents to undergo an extensive intake procedure and to make at least a two-week commitment to the program. Residents were required "to submit a weekly evaluation of their progress which addresses long-term goals, previous weeks' efforts at meeting those goals . . . and areas in which the resident may require assistance from the counselor."[48]

The House of Ruth in Washington, D.C., established a counseling schedule for each resident that included rap groups, individual sessions, and weekly group meetings. The House of Ruth also required its residents to file assault charges against their abusers and to request a restraining order from the police.[49] By contrast, the main requests Women's Advocates made of its residents was that they assume household responsibilities and attend evening house meetings to help organize house chores, appointments, and child care. The residents were encouraged but not required to attend weekly support sessions for both residents and nonresidents.[50] Transition House, in Boston, followed an even looser structure: there was no one-to-one counseling; while staff were available to provide counseling and advocacy, the program basically rested on the spontaneous mutual support of the house residents.[51]

The correlations between methods of service delivery and organizational structure were not as direct among shelters as they were among rape crisis services. Many independent shelters used nontraditional methods of service delivery but conformed to more conventional modes of organizing staff and administrative responsibilities. While a number of independent shelters called themselves collectives, their organization in fact contained modifications of the type of antihierarchical structures used by many rape crisis centers—rotating job responsibilities, all-volunteer paraprofessional staffing, and consensual decision making.

It is difficult to determine how many programs began as collectives and changed, and how many simply started with a semihierarchy. For example, in contrast to rape crisis centers, most shelters immediately sought to establish their organizational credentials and credibility. Even in the early stages, most shelters incorporated, filed for tax-exempt status, and assembled boards of directors so as to be eligible for private and public grants. The CAABW survey found that of 163 battered women's programs, only 12.3 percent had neither a board of directors nor an advisory board.[52] Many shelters responded to or anticipated grantors' preferences for hierarchical structures by creating staff delineations or designated lines of authority.

The pressures and expense of operating a shelter militated against the kinds of collective structure embraced by rape crisis centers. And as one observer noted, the difficulties of running a collective were multiplied when people of different ethnic and cultural backgrounds were living side by side.[53] One of the few "pure" collectives in New York State was Buffalo's Simple Gifts, which was operated solely by women, supported wholly by the community, and dependent on weekly day-long meetings to maintain the collectivity. This intense, demanding commitment was beyond the capability of most shelters.[54]

In many instances, the founders and staff of independent shelters searched for midpoints between conventional and alternative organizational models, compromises that would satisfy both grantors and alternative service advocates. This was most apparent in the issue of staffing, with shelters debating the merits of using volunteers or paid staff, grass-roots paraprofessionals, or counselors and social workers with credentials.

Few programs, aside from safe-house networks, were entirely volunteer. Once a full-fledged shelter facility was established, most programs tried to maintain paid staff. In practical terms, paid staff were less transitory and could provide credibility and accountability to outside funding entities. Paid positions were also a way for some shelters to encourage the participation of minority and lower-income women in what were often white, middle-class enterprises.[55] In the majority of cases, shelters relied on CETA and occasional Volunteers in Service to America (VISTA) grants to subsidize paid staff positions.

But the emphasis on developing staff salaries did not rule out the use of volunteers; shelters depended very heavily on volunteer workers for economic and philosophical reasons. The CAABW study in 1977 found that volunteers outnumbered paid staff by three to one and that "volunteers provided all levels of expertise— lay, paraprofessional and professional."[56] Most often volunteers handled the hot-lines, staffed the shelter at night or on weekends, offered peer counseling (especially true of ex–battered women), provided advocacy, and contributed to community education and outreach. Where shelters stressed a peer counseling philosophy, there were probably few distinctions between the direct service responsibilities of paid staff and volunteers. However, administrative and clerical tasks, and in some cases housekeeping work, were usually reserved for paid staff people.

Most shelters opted for a tenor of paraprofessionalism in their staff.[57] Few independent shelters employed staff solely on the basis of professional credentials. Indeed, some shelters hired staff primarily on the basis of life experience, sensitivity, and commitment to battered women. In other cases, shelters hired staff who had the academic degree to satisfy grantors' preferences but who were nonetheless committed to alternative methods of service delivery. Not surprisingly, programs affiliated with public agencies or established service organizations tended to stress educational qualifications, most often hiring social workers and counselors with degrees. Interestingly, the CAABW survey indicated that even in independent shelters, professionals with degrees frequently held primary responsibility for administration and fund raising.[58] This suggests that although shelters were relatively successful in gaining grantors' acceptance of the self-help service philosophy, grantors' confidence in traditional credentials was still unshaken. It also implies that "professionalism" was a point on which shelters were more willing to compromise than were rape crisis centers.

The pressures to conform to conventional organizational models came from both within and without. Grants and grantors' preferences contributed to the dissolution of collectivities. For instance, New York's Department of Social Services, which funded a number of shelters, allocated salaries according to job descriptions. This practice tended to reinforce traditional staff hierarchies by making administrative positions more highly paid than either direct service or clerical work.[59]

The New England Learning Center for Women in Transition

(NELCWIT), which started as a collective in a conservative part of rural western Massachusetts, was threatened with the loss of its county funding if it failed to hire a director. After substantial discussion, the staff decided to accommodate the County Commissioners, because they could ill afford to lose a major source of their budget, and because they recognized that some of the shelter functions could be facilitated by a director. The staff then hired a woman with professional credentials who had experience in battered women's services and shared the alternative service philosophy of NELCWIT.[60]

Many other shelter collectives were modified because the staff found the program ran more smoothly when job responsibilities were delineated. Women's Advocates of St. Paul, Minnesota, for instance, operated for four years as a pure collective: all staff members had the same salaries and the same job title—advocate— and assumed equal responsibility for day, night, and weekend shifts. Administrative, organizational, and maintenance work was done in their spare time. But after four years, the threat of staff burnout forced them to abandon an "everyone-does-everything" collectivity. First, the shelter hired a part-time maintenance worker; next, the staff created the position of "children's advocate." Specialization continued in 1977, when the shelter employed a part-time chemical dependency specialist, and in 1978, when it was awarded CETA grants to hire a lawyer, develop a follow-up and outreach staff, and designate two more children's advocates. That same year the shelter hired a bookkeeper. In a further reorganization, the staff divided the shelter's work load into three parts—the women's program, the children's program, and a business section.[61]

As alternative service organizations, the independent shelters were also atypical in their emphasis on maintaining contacts with a variety of other community agencies. Alternative service programs usually tried to distinguish and distance themselves from other public and private agencies; yet most shelters sought to establish formal, if not strong, relationships with law enforcement, mental health, and social service agencies. The contacts facilitated the advocacy efforts of shelter workers; they were seen as a good way to build local support, a priority of many shelters. The community agencies, in turn, were relieved that they finally had a place to send battered women.[62]

Some shelters invited representatives from community agencies to sit on their boards. A number conducted educational programs and in-service training to sensitize service providers to the problem of domestic violence. Many shelter staff considered in-service training to be a particularly valuable way to influence law enforcement personnel. For example, Bradley-Angel House in Portland, Oregon, worked with legal aid and the police to train officers in the enforcement of a new law regarding domestic violence.[63]

As the above discussion has implied, the service delivery and organizational structures of shelters were often determined in reference to the need to obtain funding. Shelters could not ignore grantors or be self-supporting in the fashion of rape crisis centers; the costs of operating a shelter facility precluded that approach. But shelters were unable to rely entirely upon federal support either, for little aid was available to cover the operating and maintenance costs of sheltering, and what grants were available posed other types of problems. For instance, while CETA supported many staff positions, the short-term nature of CETA contracts, which were usually nonrenewable after 12 to 18 months, meant a fair amount of staff turnover.

LEAA funds were viewed with ambivalence. Many shelter workers were skeptical about LEAA funds because of the experience of rape crisis centers, the agency's emphasis on a criminal justice approach, and the family orientation of LEAA's Family Violence Program (FVP).[64] These doubts often deterred independent shelters from applying for, or receiving, many LEAA awards. And because the agency's FVP required demonstrated experience in the field, newly developing programs were ineligible to apply. However, in practice the "strings" attached to LEAA's domestic violence grants were less binding than in the case of rape. The few shelters that received LEAA monies were relatively unrestricted in planning their service programs. The one complaint voiced by a few shelters related to the statistics and records LEAA required them to keep. Other funding sources, such as HUD, HHS, and CSA, had less problematic grant-giving histories, but they also awarded grants less frequently.

As with other service programs, shelters' success in obtaining funds was partly related to the effort programs could afford to put into raising funds. Few shelters could afford a full-time fund raiser, yet that advantage contributed greatly to a shelter's vitality. The survival of shelters depended equally on *creative* fund raising and the ability to establish multiple layers of support. For example, one of the oldest shelters, Women's Advocates, received support through community donations, mental health grants, county general assistance funds, Title XX, Minnesota's Child Care Facilities Act, the Community Development Block Grant program, and a $3 million fund allocated by the state legislature for battered women's programs. During the first few years of their funding search, the shelter staff did not discuss feminism or collectivism as important principles, and instead concentrated on demonstrating the need for emergency housing. As their credibility grew in the community, these issues posed less of a problem.[65] Notwithstanding their success in maintaining their organizational integrity and gaining community support, staff of Women's Advocates continued to complain that "funding still took too much staff time."[66]

NONRESIDENTIAL PROGRAMS

The concentration of grass-roots organizations in shelter services left the nonresidential field open to traditional service providers. Most people in the field recognized the need for nonresidential support services as a complement to shelters. Statistics compiled by a San Francisco nonresidential program, WOMAN (Women Organized to Make Abuse Nonexistent), Inc., indicated that given the limited capacity of the Bay Area shelters and the numbers of women seeking help but not emergency housing, the shelters were aiding only about 15 or 20 percent of all the battered women who called for assistance.[67]

While there were crisis lines and counseling centers operated by independent, feminist organizations, the nonresidential field was basically colored by the experiences and perspectives of traditional service providers. Nonresidential programs generally treated wife abuse as a facet of the family violence problem. This perspective spawned three main types of service strategies: (1) developing legal options for cases of domestic violence; (2) providing counseling, advocacy, and support services to members of violent families; and (3) coordinating and expanding existing services to handle the needs of violent families.

The first strategy was an outgrowth of the expansion of legal options for battered women in the 1960s and 1970s. During this period, nearly every state passed legislation, at the urging of battered women's advocates, to provide civil and criminal remedies for spouse abuse victims.[68] A number of states, for instance, criminalized spouse abuse, allowing battered women for the first time to file charges against their abusers. However, many battered women tended to file charges and later drop them. As a result, LEAA sponsored several programs that encouraged prosecutors to relieve victims of the responsibility of deciding whether to press assault charges against their mates.[69] LEAA funding helped a number of prosecutors' offices establish special domestic violence units that "treat[ed] spouse abuse as a crime against the state, and assert[ed] that the prosecutor, not the victim is responsible for enforcing the law."[70] Since the programs' objective was essentially rehabilitative, most were designed to use the leverage of prosecution to force the abuser to seek treatment.[71]

One of the most comprehensive prosecutor programs was the Domestic Intervention Program (DIP) of Miami, begun in 1978 through an LEAA discretionary grant. The program developed a two-pronged approach: prearrest diversion to provide crisis intervention and advocacy to victims of family violence; and postarrest diversion offering defendants in domestic violence cases an alternative to prosecution. Prearrest intervention represented an alternative to the usual police "nonaction" response to domestic disturbance calls. Counselors rode with police, provided on-the-spot intervention, and accepted referrals from other police and victims' agencies. The prearrest unit was victim-oriented, providing counseling for the woman and, if possible, family therapy and/or treatment for the abuser.

The postarrest unit was geared toward the defendants in domestic violence cases. Within 24 hours of the arrest, both the victim and the defendant were contacted by the unit. If the victim consented, a unit staff member would interview the defendant and recommend that the court release him to take part in DIP. The postarrest unit offered therapy and/or counseling to help the abuser acknowledge and curb his violent behavior. Both units were staffed by a supervisor, a family therapist, and three counselors, and the units shared two paralegals who acted as advocates and liaisons for jailed clients.[72]

In 1980, the program was awarded an ODV grant for a model demonstration advocacy project to help battered women outside of shelters obtain services and support. With the ODV grant, the program supported a third unit, the Community Advocacy Unit (CAU), which was designed, in the wake of the Miami's Liberty City riots, to reach victims of family violence in the public housing projects of the riot area.[73]

Few other communities developed prosecutor programs as wide-ranging as Miami's. In some cases, prosecutors' offices merely responded with more sensitivity to the victim of domestic violence. Many others increased their efforts to help battered women get protection orders; one prosecutor began sending letters to abusers threatening legal action if the violence continued. In a few places, the adjudicatory process itself was altered to allow the victim a role in determining the conditions of the defendant's release.[74]

Social service agencies generally dominated the second type of nonresidential strategy: providing counseling and support services to battered women and their families. These programs were usually staffed by professionals with counseling or social work degrees and were often affiliated with or developed by established agencies—family service agencies, community action agencies, and counseling or crisis intervention centers. Some agencies established programs specifically for battered women. Others simply expanded their existing services to assist victims of domestic violence. Very few community mental health centers developed programs for battered women, although psychologists, psychiatrists, and counselors became involved on an individual basis. Nor did many hospitals develop programs for battered women, though, like victims of child abuse, battered women were bound to be seen by the staff of emergency rooms.[75]

Whatever the professional orientation, nonresidential services usually offered some arrangement of the following service elements: long-term and short-term counseling for individuals, couples, and families; victims' or abusers' support groups; advocacy; community education and outreach; information and referrals; and crisis hot-lines.

One of the most publicized counseling programs was the Victim's Information Bureau of Suffolk County, New York (VIBS), a program established with an LEAA grant in 1974. The VIBS counseling plan was structured according to the specific goals of its clients. For those wanting to separate from their mates—the smallest group of clients—VIBS counselors provided help in locating the necessary legal aid, public assistance, housing, and job training. For women who felt they had no choice but to remain in the abusive relationship, VIBS offered individual counseling as well as peer groups with women in similar situations, where they could "share experiences with one another and explore ways to survive."[76]

The largest group of VIBS clients were women who were unwilling to leave their mates but wanted to eliminate the violence and had succeeded in getting their mates to make the same commitment. In those cases, VIBS used individual and couple counseling aimed at teaching the men how to curb their tendency toward violence and helping the women learn how to defuse it.[77]

San Francisco's WOMAN, Inc. was one of the few grass-roots programs responding to the nonresidential needs of battered women. Originally developed to provide shelter, WOMAN, Inc. soon became aware of the large numbers of women who were looking for help other than refuge. Over the years, its volunteer staff marshaled an impressive array of services: counseling, intervention with the police, court accompaniment, peer counseling for abusers, referrals, and community outreach. The program recruited attorneys and legal interns who donated time to help battered women file for restraining orders. And each day, WOMAN, Inc. took inventory of the shelters and emergency housing facilities in the Bay Area to keep track of where shelter space was available.[78]

In 1980, WOMAN, Inc. won a demonstration grant from the ODV. The grant could not be used to support any preexisting services. With the funds, the organization hired several paraprofessionals from among its corps of volunteers and developed three new projects to help battered women identify the services they need, improve the response of the agencies used by victims, and help minority women gain access to existing community resources.

This type of effort—identifying and coordinating services that could help victims of domestic violence—was the third nonresidential strategy funded by federal officials. The appeal of this strategy for federal grantors was not surprising: it represented a way to address the issue without establishing any new programs. Indeed, efforts to coordinate existing general service programs increased in popularity as funds became scarcer. Most of the programs funded by LEAA's Family Violence Program referred to this goal of a "comprehensive" approach to domestic violence.[79] This often implied the creation of links between criminal justice, social service, mental health, and battered women's agencies. LEAA placed special emphasis on the coordination of social service and law enforcement intervention in cases of domestic violence. For example, the agency supported two projects operated by branch agencies of the Family Service Association. One agency in Rhode Island paired police officers and social workers, who would work out of police stations at night to respond to domestic disturbance calls. The other agency, in North Carolina, placed trained staff, primarily social workers, in the local police department to counsel victims of domestic violence.[80]

In certain respects, nonresidential programs were more attractive to federal grantors than were shelter programs. Nonresidential programs were less expensive to operate than residential facilities. Furthermore, most nonresidential programs were affiliated with a larger organization, such as a family service agency or police department, which could cover operating and maintenance expenses and eventually pick up the service once the grant expired.

The traditional service organizations that developed nonresidential programs tended to view the problem and the methods of intervention in ways consonant with federal policy. Moreover, because traditional service providers tended to share the same philosophy regarding these issues, federally sponsored efforts to achieve interagency communication and coordination were more easily implemented. Finally, several of the nonresidential strategies promoted by federal agencies complemented state and local initiatives. For example, the development of domestic violence units in prosecutors' offices dovetailed with a movement among state legislatures to upgrade the civil and criminal options available to battered women; in turn, the new legislation enhanced prosecutors' ability to aid victims of domestic violence.

Yet despite the appeal of nonresidential services and the efforts of federal grantors to involve traditional service agencies in the problem of spouse abuse, financial support for the programs remained on a small scale. Nonresidential programs faced many of the same funding constraints as shelters. Money was unavailable for the ongoing maintenance of services. Nonresidential programs were perhaps better equipped to obtain certain research grants, by virtue of their institutional affiliations and the involvement of professionally trained practitioners. Yet research awards could not sustain direct services.

True, most federal funding made available was for direct services. But most often these funds were distributed through demonstration grants, which represented a short-term, indefinite source of support.

THE 1980s

Ultimately, traditional and nontraditional, residential and nonresidential services faced the same problem: by the end of the 1970s, federal policymakers in the legislative and executive branches had begun to lose interest in the issue of domestic violence. The disengagement of federal agencies from the issue was in part a product of the demise of LEAA and the ODV, the two sources of categorical funding for domestic violence services. But the process was hastened by the budgetary policies of the Reagan administration. The administration's commitment to fiscal retrenchment and a reduced federal role in direct service programs sharply reduced the federal funding available to domestic violence programs. After assuming office in 1981, the administration eliminated or substantially cut every major Carter administration funding initiative for battered women's services.

This steep decline in federal funding for battered women's services has been partially reversed by two recent pieces of legislation: the Victims of Crime Act (VOCA) of 1984 (P. L. 98-493) and the Family Violence and Prevention Act of 1984 (P. L.98-457). Spouse abuse was one of the three priority areas designated by the administration for receipt of VOCA money. One of the earliest states to take advantage of VOCA funding has been Massachusetts, which awarded 7 out of 27 grants to battered women's programs for FY 1987. However, the grants are only for one year; thus, programs will face stiff competition from other victim service programs when the grants come up for grant renewal.[81]

The second new funding source, Title III of the Family Violence and Prevention Act, authorizes federal funding for services to battered women. Like the federal initiatives for battered women in the 1970s, Title III authorizes demonstration grants to state and private nonprofit agencies (administered by the Department of Health and Human Services) and technical assistance grants for the training of law enforcement personnel in domestic violence issues (administered by the attorney general's office).[82]

The initial optimism of battered women's advocates over this legislative victory is turning to frustration. Congress recommended a total of $63 million over three years: $11 million for FY 1985, $26 million for FY 1986, and $26 million for FY 1987. Instead, the actual appropriation levels were $6 million for FY 1985, $2.5 million for FY 1986, and an as yet to be decided figure for FY 1987. The ballooning budget deficit and the Gramm-Rudman budget-cutting act leave scant hope that FY 1987 appropriations will even match FY 1986 levels.[83]

Despite the rather bleak funding picture at the federal level during the course of the Reagan administration, the number of battered women's programs nationwide has been increasing—from approximately 700 in 1980 to over 900 in 1986. The funding for these new programs has come from a mixture of private, municipal, and state dollars.[84]

However, the rise in the number of programs has been uneven: in some states, domestic violence programs have had to struggle to stay operational because of a lack of commitment from state governments for these programs. For example, some states have simply passed along federal cutbacks, thus forcing shelter programs to reduce service.

In the intensifying competition for money, shelters' move away from a political collective orientation has accelerated. More shelters are requiring an M.S.W. or Ph.D. of their staff; and many shelters are merging with traditional social service agencies or, less frequently, other women's programs.

Even the once-unquestioned issue of secrecy is being debated as a possible liability. Many professional and lay battered women's advocates are suggesting that the secrecy of shelter locations may be counterproductive for the treatment of battered women and may diminish the ability of shelter staff to build political and financial support within the local community.[85]

The continued net growth of domestic violence programs despite cutbacks in federal funding is the result of several factors. The statewide coalitions of battered women's advocates have continued to be very aggressive in their political organizing on behalf of services. Also, the publicity generated by the media about the plight of battered women has produced widespread awareness of the issue. Federal funding of services in the 1970s appears also to have helped, in an indirect fashion. As noted, funding was never very substantial, and it was almost always on a short-term demonstration basis. But federal funding did contribute to a proliferation of nonresidential alternatives to shelters and the limited expansion of shelter programs. This federal support, albeit short-term, and the resultant visibility of battered women's programs has helped boost total public and private support for shelters and other battered women's services.

Finally, the history of battered women's programs during the last ten years demonstrates the benefits of a diversified funding base. Programs for elderly crime victims and rape victims were highly dependent on federal funding; thus, they were extremely vulnerable to shifting political currents. Funding for these programs was declining even before Ronald Reagan took office. Battered women's programs, on the other hand, were often started after a period of grass-roots organizing to obtain public and private support. Federal funding, when it was available, allowed an expansion of services, at least temporarily. When federal funding declined, these shelters were often able to build upon their state and local funding to compensate for federal cutbacks. The success of their efforts has varied, though, reflecting the different political and economic circumstances across the country. The challenge for battered women's advocates in the coming years will be to try to generate solid support across the states in an era of shrinking federal support.

NOTES

1. Del Martin, "Overview—Scope of the Problem," consultation report, in U.S. Civil Rights Commission, *Battered Women: Issues of Public Policy: A Consultation Sponsored by the United States Commission on Civil Rights* (Washington, D.C.: U.S. Commission on Civil Rights, 1978), p. 209.

2. Robert Calvert, "Civil and Criminal Liability in Husband-Wife Assaults," in *Violence in the Family*, ed. by Suzanne K. Steinmetz and Murray A. Straus (New York: Dodd, Mead and Co., 1974), p. 89.

3. Jane H. Pfouts and Connie Renz, "The Future of Wife Abuse Programs," *Social Work* 26, 6 (November 1981):451.

4. The shelter actually was begun as a neighborhood advice center intended to provide information on legal rights, welfare rights, and other general social issues. When the organizers found battering—and the need to escape it—was a recurring problem for which women sought the center's help, they turned it into a shelter. See Jo Sutton, "The Growth of the British Movement for Battered Women," *Victimology: An International Journal* 2, 3–4 (1977–78):576–84; Erin Pizzey, *Scream Quietly or the Neighbors Will Hear* (Short Hill, N.J.: Ridley Enslow, 1977).

5. Dierdre A. Gaquin, "Spouse Abuse: Data from the National Crime Survey," *Victimology: An International Journal* 2, 3–4 (1977–78):633. Assaults ranged from verbal attacks to assaults with a weapon.

6. Murray A. Straus, "Wife Beating: How Common and Why?" *Victimology: An International Journal* 2, 3–4 (1977–78):446. The study was based on a probability sample of 2,143 families surveyed in 1975. The 28 percent figure referred to violence experienced in the duration of the marriage or relationship. For the 12 months immediately preceding the study, 3.8 percent of the survey respondents reported one or more physical attacks. Straus notes that "applying this incidence rate to the approximately 47 million couples in the U.S. means that, in only one year, approximately 1.8 million wives are beaten by their husbands" (p. 445).

7. Ibid., p. 447. And Straus's extrapolations did not include abusive incidents involving couples who were not cohabitants.

8. See Susan Schechter, *Women and Male Violence: The Visions and Struggles of the Battered Women's Movement* (Boston: South End Press, 1982); Jean Bethke Elshtain, "Politics and the Battered Woman," *Dissent* (Winter 1985):55–61.

9. In interviews with advocates and service providers for battered women, many said they had previously been involved with rape crisis programs.

10. For example, two of the most prominent researchers on spousal

violence—Murray A. Straus and Richard J. Gelles—have also done significant work regarding child abuse; indeed, Gelles and Straus see strong theoretical connections between the two. Both Straus and Gelles developed social-psychological models to explain the causes of spouse and child abuse. See Murray A. Straus, "Wife Beating," p. 450; Richard J. Gelles, "Child Abuse as Psychopathology: A Sociological Critique and Reformulation," in Steinmetz and Straus, *Violence in the Family*, pp. 200–201.

11. Lois Ahrens, "Battered Women's Refuges: Feminist Cooperatives vs. Social Service Institutions," *Radical America* 14, 3 (May–June 1980):41–47; Schechter, *Women and Male Violence*.

12. Julie E. Hamos (NCADV), *State Domestic Violence Laws and How to Pass Them: A Manual for Lobbyists*, Domestic Violence Monograph Series no. 2 (Rockville, Md.: National Clearinghouse on Domestic Violence, 1980), p. 79.

13. Straus, "Wife Beating," p. 456. Also see Richard J. Gelles, *The Violent Home: A Study of Physical Aggression between Husbands and Wives* (Beverly Hills, Calif.: Sage Publications, 1974); Suzanne K. Steinmetz, *The Cycle of Violence: Assertive, Aggressive and Abusive Family Interaction* (New York: Praeger Publishers, 1977). Also see Murray A. Straus, Richard J. Gelles, and Suzanne K. Steinmetz, *Behind Closed Doors: Violence in the American Family* (Garden City, N.Y.: Anchor Books, 1980).

14. See Suzanne K. Steinmetz, "The Battered Husband Syndrome," *Victimology: An International Journal* 2, 4 (1977–78):499–508.

15. See Elizabeth Pleck et al., "The Battered Data Syndrome: A Comment on Steinmetz's Article," *Victimology: An International Journal* 2, 3–4 (1977–78):680–82. Pleck noted that one immediate consequence of Steinmetz's article was the withdrawal of funds from a proposed shelter facility in Chicago.

16. For a representative sampling of feminist opinion regarding spouse abuse, consult Terry Davidson, *Conjugal Crime: Understanding and Changing the Wife Beating Pattern* (New York: Hawthorn Books, 1978); Ann Jones, *Women Who Kill* (New York: Holt, Rinehart and Winston, 1980); Del Martin, "Society's Vindication of the Wife-Batterer," *Bulletin of the American Academy of Psychiatry and the Law* 5, 4 (1977):391–401; Jocelynne Scutt, *Even in the Best Homes: Violence in the Family* (Ringwood, Victoria, Australia: Penguin Books Australia, 1983), pp. 96–140; Betsy Warrior, *Wifebeating*, 2nd ed. (Somerville, Mass.: New England Free Press, 1976); Schechter, *Women and Male Violence*; Elshtain, "Politics and the Battered Woman"; Ahrens, "Battered Women's Refuges."

17. Hamos, *State Domestic Violence Laws*, p. 79.

18. Commission on Civil Rights, *Battered Women: Issues of Public Policy*, testimony of Jeannie Niedermeyer, p. 177.

19. See Center for Women Policy Studies, Resource Center on Domestic Violence, *Federally Funded Projects on Domestic Violence* (Rockville, Md.: National Clearinghouse for Domestic Violence, 1980); Susan Cohen, Resource Center on Family Violence, *Funding Family Violence Programs: Sources and Potential Sources for Federal Monies* (Rockville, Md.: National Clearinghouse on Domestic Violence, 1979).

20. Neidermeyer, in *Battered Women: Issues of Public Policy*, p. 178.

21. For a discussion of the issues raised by LEAA funding for feminist shelter staff, see Schechter, *Women and Male Violence*, pp. 185–89.

22. Center for Women Policy Studies, *Federally Funded Projects*. For information on the ten specific projects, see Center for Women Policy Studies, *Response to Violence in the Family* 2, 2 (February 1979):6–7.

23. Center for Women Policy Studies, *Response to Violence in the Family* 4, 4 (March/April 1981):3.

24. Connie Downey, "Presentation," in U.S. Commission on Civil Rights, *Battered Women: Issues of Public Policy*, pp. 171–74. Downey was director of the Women's Action Program for the Department of Health, Education, and Welfare. According to Downey, HEW policy aided battered women through the Aid to Families with Dependent Children (AFDC) program, Title XX, and the funding of research and demonstration projects under different authorities such as the NIMH.

25. National Coalition against Domestic Violence, "Response to Representative Ken Kramer," from "Proceedings of the First NCADV Conference," February 1980 (unpublished). Kramer was a major opponent of the Domestic Violence Service Bill (HR 2977), which would have allocated funds for domestic violence service programs.

26. Center for Women Policy Studies, *Response to Violence in the Family* 3, 3 (March 1980):1. The figure was cited by Richard Fleming, then general assistant secretary for neighborhoods, voluntary associations, and consumer protection, HUD. According to the NCADV conference, as of February 1980, only $1.5 million had been made available to shelters under HUD's Community Development Block Grant Program. See "Using HUD to Establish Shelters," *Response to Violence in the Family* 2, 9 (August 1979):1–2.

27. Susan Cohen, *Funding Family Violence Programs*, pp. 13–14. See also U.S. Department of Labor, Women's Bureau, *Use of CETA Funds for Battered Women's Projects* (Washington, D.C.: U.S. Department of Labor, Office of the Secretary, Women's Bureau, 1978).

28. Colorado Association for Aid to Battered Women (CAABW), *A Monograph on Services to Battered Women* (Washington, D.C.: U.S. Department of Health and Human Services, 1979), p. 25. Also see Ahrens, "Battered Women's Refuges."

29. CAABW, *Monograph*, p. 25. Also see Camille Ascuaga, *Political Agenda Setting and the Battered Women's Issue: The Effects of Government Funding on Battered Women's Programs*, unpublished master's thesis, Massachusetts Institute of Technology, Department of Urban Studies and Planning, June 1985, pp. 24–26.

30. Manuel Carballo, quoted in "HEW Official Cites Need for Shelter Funding," *Response to Violence in the Family* 3, 3 (March 1980):4. Carballo's statement was made before a Senate committee in testimony supporting the Domestic Violence Services and Prevention Act (S. 1843) on 6 February 1980.

31. Interview with June Zeitlin, former director of the Office on Domestic Violence, 19 May 1981.

32. Mary O'Hara, "National Coalition Underway," *National Communications Network Newsletter*, (December 1977):3.

33. Interview with Ann Brickston, staff member, National Coalition against Domestic Violence (NCADV), 6 May 1981.

34. O'Hara, "National Coalition Underway," p. 3.

35. Interview with Ann Brickston. The coalition was also active in lobbying Congress for federal funds for battered women's services, albeit unsuccessfully, most notably in 1981.

36. Interview with Susan Dreiss, Pennsylvania Coalition against Domestic Violence, 20 May 1981. The Illinois Coalition against Domestic Violence (based at Sojourn Women's Center, Springfield, Ill.) also received a $1.8 million Title XX contract to deliver services on a statewide basis. The New Hampshire Coalition against Family and Sexual Violence has played a key role in encouraging cooperation among its members, lobbying the state legislature for support, and monitoring the service quality of its member agencies. Interview with Barry MacMichael, executive director, New Hampshire Coalition against Family and Sexual Violence, 13 August 1985.

37. The three were Nebraska Taskforce on Domestic Violence (Region VII), Colorado Association to Aid Battered Women and Safe House (Region VIII), and Southern California Coalition on Battered Women (Region IX). See Center for Women Policy Studies, *Response to Violence in the Family* 3, 2 (February 1979):7.

38. For Pennsylvania, see Center for Women Policy Studies, *Response to Violence in the Family* 2, 2 (November–December 1978):1–2; and for Massachusetts, see *Response to Violence in the Family* 3, 3 (February 1979):3.

39. Interview with Kerry Lobel, staff member, Southern California Coalition on Battered Women, 20 May 1981.

40. Frances Cline, "Haven for Battered Wives," *The New York Times*, 15 November 1977, p. A44.

41. The CAABW found 28 percent of programs surveyed provided shelter through safe homes, rather than a central facility. See *Monograph*, p. 19.

42. CAABW, *Monograph*, p. 20.

43. Women's Advocates, *The Story of a Shelter* (St. Paul, Minn.: Women's Advocates, 1980), p. 35.

44. Center for Women Policy Studies, *Response to Violence in the Family* 3, 1 (October 1979):3; and 3, 10 (July 1980):4.

45. CAABW, *Monograph*, p. 85.

46. Gretchen Vapner, *The Shelter Experience: A Guide to Shelter Organization and Management for Groups Working against Domestic Violence*, Domestic Violence Monograph series no. 4 (Rockville, Md.: National Clearinghouse on Domestic Violence, August 1980).

47. Most studies emphasize that the incidence of spouse abuse *is not* linked to income levels or any particular class or ethnic or racial background. However, battered women frequently are economically dependent upon their mates. For example, the CAABW survey found that 78.7 percent of battered women clients of programs had an income level under $9,999, while 60.3 percent of abusers earned less than $9,999. The CAABW *Monograph* suggests that, at least in New York City, lower-income women more frequently use shelters: "The publicly supported programs are now used primarily by poor women since welfare eligibility is a requirement. Middle-class women who do not want to consider applying for public assistance do not enter shelters. This suggests that segregation of services by class and race may occur as it does in the health system and other public programs" (p. 97).

48. CAABW, *Monograph*, p. 57. Established in 1977, Casa WOMA was operated by the San Jose Women's Alliance; originally the shelter was a program for low-income and minority women.

49. Ibid., pp. 72–77. The program was funded in 1975 and primarily serves minority women.

50. Interview with Lisbeth Levy, advocate, Women's Advocates, 12 May 1981.

51. Emilio C. Viano, "Victimology Interview: Working with Battered Women, A Conversation with Lisa Leghorn," *Victimology: An International Journal* 3, 1–2 (1978):91–107. Leghorn was a founder of the shelter.

52. CAABW, *Monograph*, pp. 24, 91. As the study noted, "Decision making generally followed traditional hierarchical lines of authority between board and staff."

53. Interview with Yolando Bako, former director of New York Volunteers against Violence Project, 5 May 1981.

54. Interview with Ellen Gavin, New York Coalition against Domestic Violence, 14 May 1981.

55. Interview with Paulea Mooney McCoy, Casa Myrna Vasquez, Boston, 19 May 1981. Casa Myrna, a pioneer in the development of multiracial shelters in Massachusetts, maintained its commitment to the participation of minority women by continually making paid staff positions a priority.

56. CAABW, *Monograph*, pp. 23, 83. The term *volunteer* does not always imply unpaid labor. A number of shelters pay volunteers a small wage for services rendered at an hourly rate comparable to the salary of full-time members.

57. Ibid.

58. Ibid.

59. Interview with Ellen Gavin.

60. Interview with Tish Sinclair, staff member, New England Learning Center for Women in Transition (NELCWIT), 11 May 1981.

61. Interview with Lisbeth Levy. See also Women's Advocates, *Story of a Shelter*, pp. 45–58.

62. Emilio C. Viano, "A Conversation with Lisa Leghorn," pp. 98–99.

63. CAABW, *Monograph*, p. 34.

64. Betsy Karl, "LEAA Funds and Battered Women: The Patriarchal Lure," *National Communication Network Newsletter* (December 1977):4–5. Also see Schechter, *Women and Male Violence*, pp. 185–202.

65. Women's Advocates, *Story of a Shelter*, pp. 90–91.

66. Ibid.

67. Interview with Linda Pershing Foley, staff member, WOMAN, Inc., 14 May 1981. Information also derived from WOMAN, Inc., *History and Summary of WOMAN, Inc. Program* (undated promotional material).

68. See Elizabeth Truninger, "Marital Violence: The Legal Solutions," *Hastings Law Journal* 23, 1 (November 1971):259–76; *Battered Women: Issues of Public Policy* (Washington, D.C.: U.S. Commission on Civil Rights, 30–31 January 1978), pp. 20–96; Julie E. Hamos, *State Domestic Violence Laws and How to Pass Them: A Manual for Lobbyists* (Washington, D.C.: National Clearinghouse on Domestic Violence, January 1980).

69. See Lisa Lerman, "Criminal Prosecution of Wife Beaters," *Response to Violence in the Family* 4, 3 (January–February 1981):1–19. The entire issue is devoted to explaining prosecutorial strategy and examines the philosophical basis, empirical basis, and programmatic experience of

prosecuting abusers. The articles were excerpted from a monograph by Lisa Lerman (staff attorney for the Family Violence Project of the Center), entitled *Prosecution of Spouse Abuse: Innovations in Criminal Justice Response* (Washington, D.C.: Center for Women Policy Studies, 1981). The articles are based on the experience of programs funded through LEAA's Family Violence Program.

70. Ibid., p. 5.

71. In recent years, many studies have concluded that women who call the police to intervene in an abusive situation greatly reduce the chances they will be abused again. See "Calling Police Protects Abused Wives, Report Says," *The New York Times*, 18 August 1986, p. A9.

72. Information on the Domestic Intervention Program (DIP) is based on interview with staff member of DIP, 19 May 1981; Miami State Attorney, *Annual Report: Initial Grant Period, July 1, 1978–December 31, 1979* (Miami, Fla.: Domestic Intervention Program, 1980); Lerman, "Criminal Prosecution," pp. 12–15.

73. Center for Women Policy Studies, "ODV Advocacy Projects to Increase Use of Community Service," *Response to Violence in the Family* 4, 2 (November–December 1980):1–2.

74. Lisa G. Lerman, "FVP Project Develops New Criminal Remedies," *Response to Violence in the Family* 3, 2 (January 1980):3.

75. New York City took the unusual step of setting up four Borough Crisis Centers in the emergency rooms of city hospitals. See David Bird, "Abuse Victims Get Help at Crisis Centers," *The New York Times*, 7 February 1978, p. 25.

76. Janet Geller and James Walsh, "A Treatment Model for the Abused Spouse," *Victimology: An International Journal* 2, 3–4 (1977–78):627–32.

77. Interview with Linda Pershing Foley. The Victim Services Agency of New York City initiated a nonresidential program for battered women in 1985. The program specializes in long-term treatment for battered women. See "New Center Offers Workshops to Battered Women," *The New York Times*, 10 February 1985, p. 53.

78. Center for Women Policy Studies, *Federally Funded Projects*, pp. 6–11.

79. Center for Women Policy Studies, "Family Service Association Responds to Domestic Violence," *Response to Violence in the Family*, 3, 2 (March 1980):5.

80. The difficulties of developing a multidisciplinary approach between lawyers and social workers to address the plight of battered women are the focus of an article by Cathy Costantino, "Intervention with Battered Women: The Lawyer-Social Worker Team," *Social Work* 26, 6 (November 1981):456–60.

81. Commonwealth of Massachusetts, Office of Victim Assistance, *Selected Documents*, 1986. Interview with Elizabeth N. Offen, deputy director, Massachusetts Office of Victim Assistance, 2 June 1986.

82. *Family Violence Prevention and Treatment Act*, P. L.98-457.

83. Interview with Janice Moore, Information and Referral Coordinator, National Coalition against Domestic Violence, 11 July 1986.

84. Ibid.

85. Interview with Jean Weiss, New Hampshire Coalition against Family and Sexual Violence, 10 July 1986.

7

CONCLUSION

In the last 25 years, issues of criminal victimization have achieved unprecedented public visibility. The problems of rape, spouse abuse, child abuse, and crime against the elderly were not insignificant in 1960, nor were they invisible. But in the 1960s and 1970s, these problems were "discovered" by practitioners, interest groups, the media, and elected and appointed government officials. Through the discovery process, long-standing social problems were transformed into "issues": matters warranting, indeed demanding, public and policy attention. Victims' issues became the subject of legislative debate and action and the focus of numerous grant programs. Concerted efforts were undertaken at the federal, state, and local levels to assist those victimized by crime and to redress what many perceived to be an excessive preoccupation with the offender rather than the victim of the crime.[1]

The ensuing policy response to victims of crime has been the subject of this book. In many types of policy analysis, the policymaking process is treated as a series of distinct or causally related stages. Policy, as defined in this study, is an ongoing process in which issue definition, agenda building, legislative and agency action, and implementation comprise equally relevant and integral parts.[2] Where many policy analyses examine implementation as the outcome or effect of policy, this analysis treats implementation as a continuation of the policy process, as another facet of policymaking. Consequently, an analysis of the programs and services developed for victims at the local level was considered critical to a full and accurate understanding of victimization policy.

The major focus of our analysis was the services and organizational structure of programs. The service structure was not evaluated for its therapeutic benefits; rather, it was examined in terms of the types of services available in each victims' category, the service models that seemed most politically viable, the methods of service delivery, and the ways in which services shrank or expanded with the policy cycle of an issue. In looking at the organizational structure of victims' programs, we focused on particular organizational characteristics that were typically reflective of policy objectives. These included staffing patterns, decision-making processes, institutional affiliations, community contacts, and budget distribution. Further, our study investigated which structures were accepted as effective vehicles for service delivery, the types of organizational conflicts that arose, the types of institutions that were involved in the various victims' issues, and how they adapted to new fields of interest. A recurrent theme throughout the study was the effect of federal funding, as the most concrete representation of federal involvement. What programs were funded? For how much and how long? How did federal funding affect the service and organizational life of victims' programs?

The salience of these factors varied in the analysis of policy regarding each victims' issue. In some cases, the emergence of particular service or organizational models was clearly related to federal policy; in others, they were less relevant to the policy process. For instance, in the cases of rape and, to a lesser extent, spouse abuse, federal funding clearly played a role in the shift from grassroots alternative service programs to more traditional institutionally affiliated programs. Federal funding spurred the professionalization and institutionalization of rape and battered women's services. In the cases of child abuse and elderly crimes, federal involvement had little effect on the character of existing services.

Despite the discrete evolution of each issue, there were important similarities in the way each was treated in the policy process. These similarities suggest themes that are relevant not only to victimization policy but to public policy in general.

The history of all four issues underscores a major point: the various phases of the policy process—agenda building, issue definition, statement of policy objectives, implementation, and redefinition—are vitally linked in a dynamic and complex relationship. The milieu in which an issue is raised sets the context for developing government programs and projects. The experiences of implementation influence the further life of a policy and, indeed, may affect the very axes of future discussion. The shaping of an issue at the federal level has an impact on how policy is implemented at the local level; local contexts and concerns have an influence on federal initiatives.[3]

The joining point, and perhaps the chief determinant, of these phases is the process of issue definition: that is, the definitions that become associated with a specific problem as it evolves into an object of policy. As political scientist Charles Lindblom noted, "Policymakers are not faced with a *given* problem."[4] Through the activities of the media, interest groups, universities, private and public organizations, and individuals, as well as efforts within formal government circles, the definitions of a problem assume shape. The "naming" or defining of an issue is critical to the overall evolution of policy. For definitions not only set the boundaries of the problem; they also imply explanations and solutions that are built into subsequent policy implementation.[5]

The labels that "stick" to an issue depend upon a number of factors. Issue definition is in part a highly political process, whose outcome often reflects the definition forwarded by a particular interest group. Thus, the prevailing definitions bespeak the relative status and power of various interest groups at a given time.

The role of interest groups was particularly critical to the definition of victims' issues because victims themselves do not tend to be politically mobilized. Instead, they rely on political advocacy supplied by groups representing a larger constituency and broader interests than simply victims or ex-victims. Thus, the expression of victims' issues depended greatly on how these interest groups articulated the issues. Inevitably, these groups lent their own political cast to the victims' issues. The issue of child abuse was forwarded by adults in the medical and social service professions, whose outlooks and professional perspectives had a formative influence on child abuse policy. Policy on elderly crime reflected the relative consensus among elderly advocates regarding the nature of the problem. And the politically conservative, middle-class character of the most powerful senior citizens' lobbying group, the National Retired Teachers Association/American Association of Retired Persons (NRTA/AARP), helped keep the issue from being defined as anything but a crime problem. Since the aged poor and minorities are neither as well organized nor as politically powerful, their potential for redefining elderly victimization policy was less significant. The women's movement articulated the issues of rape and spouse abuse, which meant that, at least initially, both issues were defined in terms of social conditions that give rise to male violence against women. That this type of definition was more readily accepted on the battered women's issue than on rape may have been partly related to the greater clout and legitimacy enjoyed by the women's movement in the late 1970s than earlier in the decade.

Issue definitions are also often the result of political tactics designed to rally as much support as possible. Barbara Nelson calls the products of this strategy "valence issues . . . those which elicit a strong, fairly uniform affective response and thus do not have an adversarial quality."[6] In her study of child abuse, she notes that although child neglect posed a more pervasive and difficult problem than child abuse, neglect was deliberately downplayed in the effort to garner support for federal legislation addressing child abuse.[7]

The ability of particular labels to evoke a uniform, strong response is contingent on the times; the power of a label depends upon a preexisting network of attitudes, assumptions, and ideational currents. These, in turn, influence policymakers and issue advocates as to what represents an acceptable, manageable range of issue definitions and policy options. This contextual factor represents the most profound and perhaps least tangible influence on the issue definition process.

For example, the parameters of policy discussion on all four victims' issues were set by certain ideational barriers regarding the appropriate level of public intervention in personal affairs. As criminal issues, rape, spouse abuse, child abuse, and elderly crime represented salient problems for public authorities. Yet the intimate, personal dimension of victimization issues cast the role of public authorities into uncertainty. The problem of intrafamily violence raised questions concerning the sanctity of the family. The scope of policy options for victims of child and spouse abuse was narrowed by fears of government intrusion in family relations. Policymakers (as well as service providers) were wary of strategies that potentially intruded on individual rights or privacy.[8]

Similar concerns arose in discussions of rape and sexual assault. As a violent act expressed through sex, rape implicitly raised questions concerning sexual norms. Although there was general agreement that the most clear-cut and brutal rapes were a violation of these norms, that consensus disintegrated in discussion of marital rape, acquaintance rape, or sexual assaults not involving penetration. These forms of sexual assault, in which the relationship between victim and perpetrator was more ambiguous or the violence less apparent and hence more easily dismissed, generated considerable controversy. Many questioned whether rape could occur between two intimates, or whether unwanted sexual attentions could constitute assault. The tentativeness with which policymakers approached these situations reflected a profound anxiety about legislating on issues involving sexual behavior that is not unambiguously deviant. And the issues of marital and acquaintance rapes again raised the specter of government intrusion on individual privacy; there was a certain resistance to the notion of public intervention in the relationship between husband and wife or boyfriend and girlfriend.

Policy discussion on the issue of crime against the elderly was bounded by different ideas. As defined by policymakers and senior citizens' advocates, the elderly's vulnerability to and fear of crime was strongly related to the isolation of older adults. But redressing this isolation provoked two concerns. On the one hand, there was continued uneasiness with public intervention into the life-styles of senior citizens. But perhaps a more important influence on policy involved generalized attitudes concerning the elderly. The tendencies to paternalize the elderly, to treat them as dependent, as incapable of fulfilling meaningful social roles, as physically and mentally weak[9]—all these deeply embedded attitudes militated against policy which would significantly reduce the marginal status of the elderly. Indeed, the policy reinforced these assumptions.

One consequence of the issue definition process was that the qualities ultimately associated with the four victims' issues were very similar, despite the differences in the initial articulation of these issues. In the course of policy development, the definition of the issues assumed three (not unrelated) traits. First, in each case policy started from a conception of the victims as helpless, frail, vulnerable, and trauma-stricken. Although the incidence of victimization was acknowledged to be widespread, the concept of victimization was isolated and individualized to a particular woman, a specific kind of family, a hapless old person. The prevailing definition suggested that the circumstances of victimization were anomalies in the social norm, derived from the deviance of the offender. This view reinforced the impression that victims were somehow weaker, more vulnerable, more dependent than—in short, different from—nonvictims.

Second, policy for each issue was formulated on the basis of definitions that often represented the extremes in a given victims' problem. Ambiguities were excluded or submerged. Focusing on the extremes skewed policy away from the "gray" situations, in which, in fact, a large portion of victimization occurs. Thus, the policy response was narrowed, excluding cases where questions of culpability entered and where the victim failed to fit stereotypes. For example, discussion of spouse abuse portrayed battered women as the quintessential victims: physically and financially vulnerable and hooked into absolute dependency on their brutal mates. This understanding of spouse abuse precluded recognition of more ambiguous situations where battered women either contributed to the situation through their own violent behavior or responded to the violence in kind. Indeed, there was considerable resistance to self-defense pleas by battered women who killed their assailants, which suggests the extent to which the category "victim" is reserved for those who fulfill standards of dependency and helplessness.[10] In the same way, determining who is eligible for assistance has been a persistent problem for victims' compensation programs. As an article in *The Boston Globe* noted, "The basic questions of who is a victim and which victims qualify for compensation have led to long and costly legal battles, several of which have run all the way to the Supreme Judicial Court."[11]

Finally, the definitions associated with the issues tended to eliminate the issues' potential value as reflections or manifestations of deep-seated social attitudes or socioeconomic arrangements. It is crucial to recognize that each of the issues potentially represented powerful points of social critique. On the one hand, each type of criminal victimization could be related to more systemic issues of social victimization. In that sense, it is not coincidental that the four victims' issues involved women, children, and the aged. Rape, spouse abuse, child abuse, and elderly crime each could be considered a product of the relative powerlessness and subordinate status that women, children, and old people endure. Alternatively, each of the issues could be construed as a reflection of inequities based on class, as cultural values sanctioning violence, or as symptoms of the malaise afflicting the nuclear family.[12]

Yet these themes are conspicuously absent from the definitions that ultimately formed the basis for policy on rape, spouse abuse, crime against the elderly, and child abuse. Instead the issues were defined almost solely in terms of the criminal aspect of victimization. Thus, rape was narrowed to a category of assault perpetrated by certain men against women; spouse abuse and child abuse were related to the dysfunctions of the "violent family"; crime against the elderly represented old people's susceptibility to and fear of attack, particularly from juveniles.

It is not that broader-based definitions were not proposed; all four issues attracted proponents of social critique. However, the structure of policymaking rendered such definitions marginal and only indirectly influential. Ultimately, the issue definition process reduced and flattened the complexities of victimization. Although the simplification of victims' issues initially aided recognition of the problems, it can be argued that in the end, these definitions deterred the development of more substantive and sustained policies.

Issue definitions were among the most vital influences on the development and implementation of victims' policies. But an equally critical influence on the policies' implementation was the short-term nature of public and policymakers' interest in the issues. Rape, child abuse, spouse abuse, and elderly crime were all subject to what Anthony Downs termed an "issue attention cycle."[13]

Initially, interest in each issue was treated to a period of tremendous public and legislative enthusiasm. Media coverage of an issue jumped, and federal, state, and local governments developed funding mechanisms and programs to grapple with the newfound problem. Within three to five years, however, interest in the specific problem diminished. In the 1970s, the attention of public and policymakers moved from rape to elderly crime to spouse abuse or family violence. Interest in the issues overlapped but was not simultaneous. Thus, local-level programs established when public concern was at its peak found it increasingly difficult over time to sustain interest in their work or maintain sponsors for their services. The opportunities for federal grants dwindled, and local public and private sponsors were often reluctant to replace the federal support. The difficulties posed by this cycle were exacerbated by the small financial commitments made by federal grantors even when issue attention was at its height. Federal spending consistently fell short of the amounts service providers in the field claimed was needed.

Issue attention cycles occur in all areas of policy. One can argue that the cycle is one of the ways the machinery of government manages dissent. In the case of victims' issues, service funds became a way to respond to interest group pressure and aggrieved social movements. The appropriation of federal funds on a research and demonstration basis or in small amounts was a relatively safe but politically attractive and feasible way of reacting to efforts by victims' advocates to gain federal funds for their programs. Further, once federal funds were authorized through legislation or by administrative decision, the advocates for these programs often turned their attention to other arenas and issues, thus reducing the pressure on Congress and federal officials for a more substantive response to the problems at hand.

In each case, though, the issue benefited from its brief spell in the limelight, gaining a certain ineradicable legitimacy. Total government spending never fell back to the spending level that had existed prior to federal investment in these victims' issues. During the 1980s, advocates for these victims' programs have been able to gain spending increases at the state, county, and municipal levels, as well as from the private sector, to compensate for the declines in federal funding. Child abuse programs are the best example of this phenomenon, primarily because of the political leverage that the reporting laws provided child welfare advocates: increases in reported cases generate political support for state funding increases. Also, despite a wave of cutbacks in the early 1980s, rape and battered women's services continue to receive support from new small-scale federal programs and from new state initiatives.

Only elderly crime was virtually wiped off of the federal policy agenda, though state agencies continue to fund programs to deal with the problem. And many victim witness and other generic victims' service programs offer counseling and other services to aged victims.

Thus, these issues did not become "private concerns" again as federal funding declined. Federal funding helped transform the politics surrounding these victims' issues, giving legitimacy and publicity to advocates of victims' service programs. Compared to the struggle for federal attention, victims' advocates have had an easier time shaking loose public funds from state and local sources for victims' service programs.

Despite the differences in grant programs and service projects addressing individual issues, several common themes also recurred in the implementation process.

First, conflicts arising in the early stages of policy formation resurfaced in implementation. Thus, conflicting interpretations of the issue, varying perspectives on appropriate measures to deal with the problem, and competition between interest groups were by no means resolved with the passage of legislation, the development of grant programs, or the issuance of agency directives. Debates that occurred at the federal level were duplicated by state and local policymakers, as well as by service providers. This was most apparent in the debate over whether victimization derived from the deviance of individual offenders and situations, or whether it was the result of deeply embedded societal attitudes, relationships, and inequities. The correctness of either view is immaterial. What is germane is that the advocacy was paralleled in local-level service delivery. The philosophical disagreements—most pronounced in the debates on rape and spouse abuse—gave rise to distinct service approaches that rarely intersected; programs operating with an alternative service approach maintained a distance from traditional services offered by medical, social service, mental health, and criminal justice agencies. The different service systems attracted different types of staff, financial, and community support, as well as clientele.[14]

Another conflict that recurred in the development and implementation of victims' policy was between a law enforcement and mental health perspective. Again this clash was basically related to which elements of victimization were emphasized. From a law enforcement perspective, most forms of victimization involve not only a crime against the individual but a crime against the state. Prosecution is thus undertaken by the state on behalf of the individual victim. The interest in the staff of law enforcement agencies in victims stemmed from a desire to strengthen the justice process as a whole, as well as a belief that sensitive, sympathetic services for victims might enhance victims' willingness to cooperate with the justice system in addition to helping the victim cope emotionally with his or her victimization.

By contrast, social services, hospitals, and mental health facilities approached victimization as an offense against an individual woman, child, or old person. The primary focus was on the individual's needs, however they were defined, and on resolving the psychological crisis precipitated by the victimization. Although the two outlooks were not absolutely polarized, there did exist a certain tension between them. It was the rare victims' service which successfully balanced the two; generally, programs concentrated on either one or the other. Moreover, certain questions, such as whether encouraging victims to report crimes was beneficial to the recovery process, became major precipitants of friction.

A second pattern which appeared in the implementation of victims' programs was that federal policy favored certain organizational settings over others. Typically, federal grants were awarded to established social service, law enforcement, mental health, and medical facilities. Far fewer grants were awarded for the creation of entirely new agencies or services or to support programs operating outside the conventional service system. Thus, alternative service programs were less well received by federal grantors, and feminist rape crisis centers were the least acceptable to funding agencies.

Within each category of victims' services, particular institutions or professional agencies were the predominant recipients of federal funds. Hospitals and criminal justice agencies were the main recipients of rape-related monies. Funds to address elderly crime were most frequently awarded to social services, aging agencies, police departments, and district attorneys' offices. Mental health, social service, and to a lesser extent criminal justice agencies were the most common grantees in the field of domestic violence. And child abuse funds were usually awarded to hospitals, public departments of social services, and private social work agencies. What determined which agencies or institutions became involved with particular victims' issues? The nature of the issue, as defined, was important. For example, crime against the elderly was defined as a criminal justice, rather than a mental health, problem; thus, it is not surprising that law enforcement agencies were most prominent in developing elderly crime programs. Professional commitment and interest was another factor. The professional groups that became involved with a particular issue because of personal or work-related experience were often determinative of later agency or institutional involvement. For example, the activism of pediatricians regarding child abuse helped draw child abuse funds to hospitals, while facilitating the development of hospital-based programs. Finally, the policy domain of the grantors that became most involved with particular issues was also significant. Grantors influence the tone of policy, and whether the funding agency was oriented toward mental health or criminal justice affected which agencies applied for or received funds. For instance, LEAA funding of spouse abuse programs was a strong impetus for prosecutors' offices to develop specialized units to assist battered women.

A third notable pattern in implementation was the influence of the institutional ethos or ideology of organizational settings on victims' programs. Mental health, medical, law enforcement, social service, and alternative service agencies each have distinct organizational cultures, structures, and objectives. The prevailing ethos of each institutional setting influenced their respective victims' service programs. While programs based in different agencies may have had many of the same service components, the thrust of service delivery differed. Law enforcement agencies stressed the criminal aspect of victimization and developed programs oriented toward the justice system. Programmatic goals often included improving rates in reporting, easing the process of criminal prosecution for victims and witnesses, and disseminating information on measures to avoid victimization.

Social service programs tended to employ an extension of traditional case management strategies. In addition to providing emotional support and information, the programs helped the victim secure support services such as financial aid, employment, compensation, medical care, and legal aid. The emphasis was on strengthening the victim's environment and restoring his or her emotional and material resources.

Medical facilities most frequently provided therapeutic services aimed at the physical and emotional needs of the victims. Doctors, nurses, emergency room personnel, and medical students were trained to be sensitive to the symptoms of victimization and to the emotional state of victims in crisis. Hospital-based programs were often marked by a primary emphasis on treating the symptoms of emotional trauma, with secondary emphasis placed upon remedying the situation that gave rise to the victimization.

Although mental health agencies were less active in developing victims' programs, the mental health perspective was influential. Victims' services emphasized counseling and helping the individual resolve the emotional crisis. Not surprisingly, mental health agencies were most involved in the issues of child and spouse abuse, since these problems lent themselves to the types of longer-term assistance most commonly practiced by mental health professionals.

However, distinctions between programs stemmed not only from professional aims but also from the ideological orientation of various organizations. As Delila and Menachem Amir wrote, "Ideology provides the basic premises of the organization, its raison d'être and the basis of explaining the phenomenon—its origin, processes and conditions—which the organization aims to act upon. Ideology also influences the working philosophy of the organization.[15]

In victims' programs, the major ideological line of division ran between alternative services and traditionally focused programs. The ideological distinctions pervaded every area of victims' programs: service delivery, organizational structure, explanations of victimization—all were conceptualized in vastly different terms by alternative services and by traditional services. This was partly because, as Amir and Amir noted, "In service organizations based on social critique of and change in the environment, the ideological aspect of the organization's life is constantly evoked and plays an important role in its structure, internal processes and relations with the outside world."[16]

In evaluating the implementation of federal policy, the distribution of federal grants inevitably becomes a focus of study. For funding, in a sense, is the conduct of policy, the link between federal and local activities. The level and distribution of funds is indicative of the degree of policy commitment; as such, funding is a quantifiable measure of the relative priority of different policy areas.

Importantly, the influence of federal funds was unrelated to the programmatic content of agencies' requests for proposals (RFPs). To be sure, federal grant programs either implicitly or explicitly encouraged the development of certain types of service programs and discouraged others. The absence of substantial funding for preventive programs for child abuse in the 1970s was the result of a policy choice consistently followed by federal grantors. The research orientation of NIMH's National Center for the Prevention and Control of Rape was written into the agency's authorization. But in most cases, federal RFPs were relatively flexible, and the types of programs grantors were interested in funding were in line with prevailing ideas of effective service delivery. Indeed, federal grant programs often simply subsidized methods of service delivery already being deployed at the local level.

The most profound influence of federal agencies on programmatic developments occurred in the distribution of funds. The competition between victims' programs for federal funds was resolved in a distinct pattern: programs operating under the auspices of established agencies or institutions were consistently favored over those developed by alternative service organizations. It has been suggested that grantors prefer to work with organizations that have clearly defined structure, points of accountability, and professional or academic credentials, all of which most alternative services lack.

But as the study conducted by the Center for Women's Policy Studies acknowledged, other types of alternative services—for runaways, drug and alcohol abuse, and mental health programs—have enjoyed significant federal support.[17] This point raises the question whether there was a peculiar element of nontraditional victims' programs that deterred federal support. One can speculate that it was not simply the service delivery or organizational structure of battered women's shelters and rape crisis center that was at issue, but rather the political, ideological definitions of rape and spouse abuse these programs employed. For viewing rape or spouse abuse as social phenomena potentially entering any man or woman's life eradicated the comfortable distance between victims and nonvictims, abusers and nonabusers.

A second influential aspect of the funding process concerns the types of grants made available to victims' programs. A large portion of victims' program money was spent on research and research-demonstration projects.

Most federal agencies relied on the use of demonstration monies to sponsor direct services. Demonstration grants were awarded to projects developing innovative and specific concepts of service delivery. Although the types of programs differed, the essential nature of demonstration grants did not. The grants were usually of limited duration—between one and three years. Ostensibly, these projects would be a low-cost method of discovering the most efficient, effective service model. In theory, if a particular project was deemed worthy, it would be replicated throughout the country. In reality, the evaluations of demonstration projects were rarely utilized and the potential of effective demonstration models infrequently realized. Moreover, the notable absence of policy influence of these projects almost forces one to conclude that these grants were a back-door method of providing short-term support to direct services. In many cases, programs depended on a succession of demonstration grants to continue providing their services.

Victims' services were also eligible for some nonspecific discretionary funds and block grant programs. Although both supported ongoing services, neither was without its drawbacks. Discretionary funds typically meant smaller, nonrenewable awards for limited periods. The funds from block grant and revenue-sharing programs such as CETA, Community Development Block Grants, and Titles XX and IV-B of the Social Security Act were distributed through state and local administrations. Programs' success in receiving awards, therefore, depended on state or local political priorities. Victims' issues did not enjoy the same status in all states, nor did the different types of victims' programs.

Grant programs such as CETA, LEAA, Title XX, and Community Development Block Grants were problematic in another respect. Because the program funds were subject to annual appropriations, with little certainty of how long the programs would last, and because the funding periods for CETA and LEAA were restricted, local governments preferred to subcontract services to agencies rather than develop new programs which they would be compelled to continue when federal funding expired.[18] This policy contributed to the endemic instability of victims' programs regardless of category.

Federal funding, whether through demonstration, discretionary, or block grants, was awarded with the expectation that local grantors would eventually assume responsibility for the project. However, many agencies encountered difficulties in developing local public and private sources of support. Indeed, those agencies most dependent on federal monies were frequently the least successful in obtaining local sponsors. In this regard, demonstration grants were often a liability: few communities could support programs at the level of demonstration grants, and many resented the supposition that local grantors could or would pick up a particular service. This situation was especially true of programs installed through federal rather than local initiatives.

Underscoring this point is the fate of victims' service programs during the 1980s. The victims' service with the heaviest reliance on federal support—elderly crime programs—has all but disappeared from the public policy agenda, save for a relative handful of programs funded through the Victims of Crime Act (VOCA) of 1984. Rape crisis centers, which relied heavily on federal dollars, have also foundered, although the number of centers is showing a slight increase as state governments contribute their own dollars for rape services. Battered women's shelters have weathered the federal cutbacks even better, primarily because shelter advocates had built up politically potent statewide coalitions during the 1970s even while they were seeking federal funding. And finally, child abuse programs, which have relied on state-level support since their inception, have come to dominate the child welfare agenda in states across the country. The strong local support for these programs has been crucial to the continued escalation in total government dollars from all sources on the child abuse problem. This support has been nurtured and stimulated by federal initiatives of the last 25 years which spurred state human service administrators to initiate child abuse reporting laws and professionalize and expand the level of state-funded public and private child protection services.

In the mid-1980s, federal victimization policy is at a new turning point. The Reagan administration took office in 1981 with a platform that included strong support for victims' rights. Shortly after Reagan assumed office, he declared a National Victims' Rights Week, to focus attention on the plight of crime victims. Eventually, the administration won passage of the Victims of Crime Act, which established a funding mechanism for the provision of victims' services at the local level.

The VOCA legislation was thus the culmination of more than two decades' worth of efforts to build attention and support for greater legal protections and service programs for victims. Moreover, VOCA represented the most significant victory to date for victims' advocates who prefer to view victims as a class of injured citizens with shared problems and experiences, rather than as separate categories of unfortunates, which was the implicit view that prevailed in the 1970s. Thus, it may be that future initiatives will be geared to victims as a group, rather than to discrete constituencies of victims.

Despite the resurgent interest in victims, the outlook for future victims' programs is very cloudy. The political alliance supporting victims' programs is very fragile, comprised of partners who lend their support for opposite reasons. On the one hand, liberals support government programs for victims out of an overall commitment to extend the welfare state to needy citizens. On the other hand, the fight for victims' rights is being led at the federal level by conservatives who support victims' rights because of its compatibility with their retributive criminal justice policies and because of their pronounced antistatist sentiments. These conservatives are also dedicated to curtailing the growth of the welfare state, particularly at the federal level, despite the recent VOCA legislation.

Conservative opposition to further expansion in the welfare state sets the stage for a possible repeat of the issue-attention cycle phenomenon with regard to VOCA. Indeed, the announced cutbacks in VOCA funding for FY 1987 by the Justice Department already suggest that a decline in funding is beginning to occur, as public attention shifts to other issues on the public policy agenda.

It is also possible that the movement for greater victims' services and legal protections will lose steam as law enforcement officials continue to adapt their programs to show greater sensitivity to the victim. In addition, many victims' programs could eventually merge with established health and social service programs; thus, the larger institution would oversee and manage a victims' program as one part of its operation. This shift in organizational locus already is underway among rape victim services.

Finally, the evolution of victims' services demonstrates many characteristics that distinguish American social policy from that of other industrialized nations: the tendency toward policy fragmentation; the difficulty of exerting a strong national presence; the sharing of federal, state, and local responsibility; and the preference for financially weak, nonprofit organizations funded by government to deliver services. Since the current era has witnessed a strengthened and renewed commitment to these aspects of American social policy, it is likely—political rhetoric aside—that victims' services will continue to be organizationally unstable and inadequate.

NOTES

1. A remarkable diversity of political perspectives converged on the issue of victims' status. On the one hand, the issue attracted advocates who tended toward conservative positions on other political issues, or who leaned toward a "law and order," punitive approach to criminal justice problems as a whole. On the other hand, victims' issues attracted groups and individuals who had been active in the women's, children's, and senior citizens' movements. Often these groups tended to take a more liberal approach to social issues, deriving their political positions from a civil rights framework. And issues like rape and spouse abuse drew advocates who were identified with a radical left perspective on other political questions, such as radical feminists.

2. See the introduction for a fuller discussion of the analytic framework of this policy analysis.

3. The dynamic interaction between federal policy and local politics has been the subject of several excellent treatises. See, for example, Jeffrey

L. Pressman, *Federal Programs and City Politics: The Dynamics of the Aid Process in Oakland* (Berkeley: University of California Press, 1975); Jeffrey L. Pressman and Aaron Wildavsky, *Implementation*, 3rd ed. (Berkeley: University of California Press, 1984); Martha Derthick, *New Towns, In Town* (Washington, D.C.: Brookings Institution, 1972).

4. Charles E. Lindblom, *The Policy-Making Process* (Englewood Cliffs, N.J.: Prentice-Hall, 1968), quoted in George E. Hale and Lief Palley, *Politics of Federal Grants* (Washington, D.C.: CQ Press, 1981), p. 34.

5. For a more detailed discussion of the importance of issue definition to the policy process, see Roger W. Cobb and Charles D. Elder, *Participation in American Politics: The Dynamics of Agenda-Building* (Baltimore: Johns Hopkins University Press, 1972), pp. 82–93; Barbara J. Nelson, *Making an Issue of Child Abuse: Political Agenda Setting for Social Problems* (Chicago: University of Chicago Press, 1984), esp. chap. 6.; John W. Kingdon, *Agendas, Alternatives, and Public Policies* (Boston: Little, Brown and Co., 1984), pp. 115–21.

6. Nelson, *Making an Issue of Child Abuse*, pp. 93–94.

7. See ibid., pp. 92–125.

8. Policymakers' hesitation regarding state intervention in victims' issues may also be related to a traditional mistrust of the state throughout American history. See Louis Hartz, *The Liberal Tradition in America* (New York: Harcourt Brace Jovanovich, 1955); Samuel P. Huntington, *Political Order in Changing Societies* (New Haven, Conn.: Yale University Press, 1968), chap. 2; Andrew Shonfield, *Modern Capitalism: The Changing Balance of Public and Private Power* (London: Oxford University Press, 1965), chap. 13.

9. See Jeffrey H. Reiman, "Aging as Victimization: Reflections on the American Way of (Ending) Life," in *Crime and The Elderly: Challenge and Response*, ed. by Jack Goldsmith and Sharon Goldsmith (Lexington, Mass.: Lexington Books, 1976), pp. 77–81.

10. For a good discussion of self-defense pleas, see Ann Jones, *Women Who Kill* (New York: Holt, Rinehart and Winston, 1980). Jones argues that many cases of domestic homicide in fact involve battered women who killed their husbands in self-defense.

11. Nick King, "Victims Victimized," *Boston Globe*, 10 May 1981, p. A22.

12. Consult, for example, David G. Gil, *Violence against Children: Physical Child Abuse in the United States* (Cambridge, Mass.: Harvard University Press, 1973); Fay Lomax Cook et al., *Setting and Reformulating Policy Agendas: The Case of Criminal Victimization of the Elderly* (New York: Oxford University Press, 1981); Susan Brownmiller, *Against Our Will: Men, Women and Rape* (New York: Simon and Schuster, 1975); Ann Jones, *Women Who Kill*.

13. See Anthony Downs, "Up and Down with Ecology—The 'Issue Attention Cycle,' " *The Public Interest* 28 (Summer 1972):34–50. Downs noted in reference to environmental issues that "a systematic 'issue attention cycle' seems to influence public attitudes and behavior concerning most key domestic problems. Each of these problems suddenly leaps into prominence, remains there for a short time, and then—though still largely unresolved—gradually fades from the center of public attention." Downs identified five steps of the cycle: (1) the preproblem stage; (2) alarmed discovery and euphoric enthusiasm (in which Downs believes the combination of alarm and confidence result in public pressure for solving the problem: "The implication is that every obstacle can be eliminated and every problem solved *without any fundamental reordering of society itself, if we only devote sufficient effort to it*"); (3) the realization of the cost of significant progress; (4) the gradual decline of intense public interest, during which discouragement, suppression, and boredom set in; and (5) the postproblem stage, about which Downs noted that despite the waning of public interest, the creation of institutions, programs, and policies ensures that the issues continue to receive a higher level of attention and general concern.

14. Our research indicates that the clients (and staff) attracted to feminist rape crisis centers were frequently young, white, middle-class women, whose own views were compatible with a feminist orientation. Programs offered through more traditional agencies tended to serve a more socioeconomically diverse group of women, although in many cases, the clientele of traditionally oriented rape victims' services reflected the larger catchment population of the host institution.

The distinction between alternative and traditional battered women's services runs along somewhat different lines. The differences in clientele relate, in part, to the fact that residential programs are run primarily by alternative service organizations, whereas nonresidential programs are mostly operated by traditional agencies. Thus, the clientele are in a sense self-selecting: women seeking to leave their abusers (at least temporarily) seek out shelter services; women who cannot or do not want to leave the situation seek nonresidential services. There does not seem to be any socioeconomic correlation as to whether a woman chooses a shelter or a counseling service (except insofar as the limited capacity of shelters leads many to turn away women who have sources of financial or emotional support).

15. Delila Amir and Menachem Amir, "Rape Crisis Centers: An Arena for Ideological Conflicts," *Victimology: An International Journal* 4, 2 (1979):248.

16. Ibid. See also James Gordon, "Grassroots Mental Health Services,"

Social Policy 9, 1 (May–June 1978):32–36. Gordon discusses the emergence and evolution of alternative mental health services (which included programs for drug addiction, alcoholism, runaways, and other social problems). Gordon's description of the philosophical origins of these alternative service programs is pertinent to alternative victims' programs:

> These activist workers believed that given time and space, ordinary people could help themselves and one another to deal with the vast majority of problems in living that confronted them. They questioned the appropriateness of professional services which labelled or stigmatized those who came for help. In their own work, they tried to blur or obliterate boundaries between staff and clients. Determined to remain responsive to their clients, these early workers continually advocated for the social changes that would make individual change more possible. (P. 32)

17. Lisa Brodyaga et al., *Rape and Its Victims: A Report for Citizens, Health Facilities and Criminal Justice Agencies* (Washington, D.C.: National Institute of Law Enforcement and Criminal Justice, 1975), p. 123.

18. Elizabeth O'Sullivan, "What Has Happened to Rape Crisis Centers? A Look at Their Structures, Members and Funding," *Victimology: An International Journal* 3, 1–2 (1978):57.

SELECTED BIBLIOGRAPHY

CHILD ABUSE

Alvy, Kerby T. "Preventing Child Abuse." *American Psychologist* 30, 9 (September 1975):921–28.

American Humane Association. *Child Protective Services in the United States.* Denver: American Humane Association, 1956.

———. *Child Protective Services: A National Survey, 1967.* Denver: American Humane Association, 1967.

———.*Child Protective Services, Entering the 80s.* Englewood, Colo.: American Humane Association, 1979.

Bourne, Richard, and Eli H. Newberger, ed. *Critical Perspectives on Child Abuse.* Lexington, Mass.: Lexington Books, 1979.

Cicchetti, Dante, and J. Lawrence Aber. "Abused Children—Abusive Parents: An Overstated Case?" *Harvard Educational Review* 50, 2 (May 1980): 244–54.

Cohn, Anne Harris. "Effective Treatment of Child Abuse and Neglect." *Social Work* 24, 6 (November 1979):513–19.

Community Research Applications. *Child Abuse and Neglect Programs: Practice and Theory.* Washington, D.C.: U.S. Department of Health, Education, and Welfare, National Institute of Mental Health, 1977.

Costa, Joseph J., and Gordon K. Nelson. *Child Abuse and Neglect: Legislation, Reporting and Prevention.* Lexington, Mass.: Lexington Books, 1978.

Gelles, Richard J. "The Social Construction of Child Abuse." *American Journal of Orthopsychiatry* 45, 3 (April 1975):363–71.

Gerber, George, Catherine J. Ross, and Edward J. Zigler, eds. *Child Abuse: An Agenda for Action*. New York: Oxford University Press, 1980.

Gil, David G. *Violence against Children: Physical Child Abuse in the United States*. Cambridge, Mass.: Harvard University Press, 1970.

Goldstein, Joseph, Anna Freud, and Albert J. Solnit. *Beyond the Best Interests of the Child*. New York: Free Press, 1973.

———. *Before the Best Interests of the Child*. New York: Free Press, 1979.

Grimet, Barbara R. "The Plaintive Plaintiffs: Victims of the Battered Child Syndrome." *Family Law Quarterly* 4, 3 (September 1970):296–317.

Holmes, Sally. "Parents Anonymous: A Treatment Method for Child Abuse." *Social Work* 23, 3 (May 1978):245–47.

Kalmer, Roberta, ed. *Child Abuse: Perspectives on Diagnosis, Treatment and Prevention*. Dubuque, Ia.: Kendell/Hunt Publishing Co., 1977.

Kempe, C. Henry. "The Battered-Child Syndrome." *Journal of American Medical Association* 181, 1 (July 7, 1962):17–24.

Kempe, C. Henry, and Ray E. Helfer, eds. *Helping the Battered Child and His Family*. Philadelphia: J. P. Lippincott, Co., 1972.

Kempe, Ruth, and C. Henry Kempe. *Child Abuse*. Cambridge, Mass.: Harvard University Press, 1978.

Kimmich, Madeleine H. *America's Children: Who Cares? Growing Needs and Declining Assistance in the Reagan Era*. Washington, D.C.: Urban Institute Press, 1985.

Light, Richard J. "Abused and Neglected Children in America: A Study of Alternative Policies." *Harvard Educational Review* 43, 4 (November 1973):556–98.

Maden, Marc F., and David F. Wrench. "Significant Findings in Child Abuse Research." *Victimology: An International Journal* 11, 2 (Summer 1977):196–224.

Nelson, Barbara J. *Making an Issue of Child Abuse: Political Agenda Setting for Social Problems*. Chicago: University of Chicago Press, 1984.

Paulsen, Monrad, Graham Parker, and Lynn Adelman. "Child Abuse Reporting Laws—Some Legislative History." *The George Washington Law Review* 34, 3 (March 1966):484–506.

Pfohl, Stephen J. "The Discovery of Child Abuse." *Social Problems* 24, 3 (February 1977):310–21.

Resnick, Patricia A., and Jerry J. Sweet. "Child Maltreatment Intervention Directions and Issues." *Journal of Social Issues* 35, 2 (Spring 1979):140–52.

Sussman, Alan, and Stephen J. Cohen. *Reporting Child Abuse and Neglect: Guidelines for Legislation*. Cambridge, Mass.: Ballinger Publishing Co., 1975.

U.S. National Center on Child Abuse and Neglect (NCCAN). *Child Abuse* and Neglect: The Problem and Its Management. Vol. 1: An Overview of the Problem. Vol. 2: Roles and Responsibilities of Professionals. Vol. 3: The Community Team—An Approach to Case Management and Treatment. Washington, D.C.: Department of Health, Education, and Welfare, 1976.

ELDERLY CRIME

Antunes, George, Fay Lomax Cook, Thomas D. Cook, and Wesley Skogan. "Patterns of Personal Crime against the Elderly: Findings from a National Survey." The Gerontologist 17, 4 (1977):321–27.

Butler, Robert N. Why Survive: Being Old in America. New York: Harper and Row, 1975.

Center, Lawrence J. Summary Report: Evaluation of the National Elderly Victimization Prevention and Assistance Program. Washington, D.C.: National Council of Senior Citizens, 1979.

Cook, Fay Lomax. Setting and Reformulating Policy Agendas: The Case of Criminal Victimization of the Elderly. New York: Oxford University Press, 1981.

Cook, Fay Lomax, and Thomas D. Cook. "Evaluating the Rhetoric of Crisis: A Case Study of Criminal Victimization of the Elderly." Social Service Review 50, 4 (December 1976):632–46.

Criminal Justice and Elderly Project, National Council of Senior Citizens. Criminal Justice and Elderly (CJE) Newsletter. Washington, D.C.: National Council of Senior Citizens, Summer 1978–Summer 1980.

D'Angelo, Stephen. "Senior Home Security Programs." Police Chief 44, 2 (February 1977):60–61.

Florida Bureau of Criminal Justice Assistance. Florida's Plan to Reduce Crime against the Elderly. Tallahassee, 1980.

Goldsmith, Jack, and Sharon S. Goldsmith, eds. Crime and the Elderly: Challenge and Response. Lexington, Mass.: Lexington Books, 1976.

Greenstein, Marcia. "An Invitation to Law Enforcement." Police Chief 44, 2 (February 1977):46–47.

Gross, Philip. "Crime, Safety and the Senior Citizen." Police Chief 44, 2 (February 1977):18–26.

Gubrium, Jaber F. "Victimization in Old Age: Available Evidence and Three Hypotheses." Crime and Delinquency 20, 3 (July 1974):245–50.

Hahn, Paul. Crimes against the Elderly: A Story in Victimology. Santa Cruz, Calif.: Davis Publishing Co., 1976.

Kutza, Elizabeth A. "Toward an Aging Policy." Social Policy 12, 1 (May–June 1981):39–43.

Malinchalk, Alan A. *Crime and Gerontology.* Englewood Cliffs, N.J.: Prentice-Hall, 1980.

Midwest Research Institute. *Crimes against Aging Americans.* Kansas City: Midwest Research Institute, 1974.

New York Crime Control Planning Board. *Protecting the Elderly from Criminal Victimization and Providing Services to the Elderly Victim of Crime: Third Annual Report to the Governor, the Legislature and the Office for the Aging.* New York: Division of Criminal Justice Services, 1979.

Neugarten, Bernice L. *Aging: Agenda for the Eighties.* Washington, D.C.: National Journal Issue Book, 1980.

Pennsylvania Commission on Crime and Delinquency. *Strategies to Reduce the Incidence and Impact of Crime that Victimizes the Elderly in Pennsylvania.* Harrisburg: Pennsylvania Commission of Crime and Delinquency, 1980.

Pratt, Henry J. *The Gray Lobby.* Chicago: University of Chicago Press, 1976.

Schack, Stephen, Grant Grissom, and Saul Barry Wax. *Police Service Delivery to the Elderly.* Washington, D.C.: University City Science Center, March 1980.

Stein, John Hollister. *Anti-Crime Programs for the Elderly: Combining Community Crime Prevention and Victim Services.* Washington, D.C.: National Council of Senior Citizens, 1979.

Young-Rifai, Marlene A. *Justice and Older Americans.* Lexington, Mass.: Lexington Books, 1976.

PUBLIC POLICY

Cobb, Roger W., and Charles D. Elder. *Participation in American Politics: The Dynamics of Agenda Building.* Baltimore: Johns Hopkins University Press, 1972.

Downs, Anthony. "Up and Down with Ecology—The 'Issue Attention Cycle.' " *The Public Interest* 28 (Summer 1972):38–50.

Gray, Virginia. "Innovation in the States: A Diffusion Study." *American Political Science Review* 67, 4 (December 1973):1174–85.

Heclo, Hugh. "Review Article: Policy Analysis." *British Journal of Political Science* 2 (1971):83–108.

Kingdon, John W. *Agendas, Alternatives and Public Policies.* Boston: Little, Brown and Co., 1984.

Lipsky, Michael. "Standing the Study of Public Policy Implementation on Its Head." In *American Politics and Public Policy,* ed. by Walter Dean Burnham and Martha Wagner Weinberg. Cambridge, Mass.: MIT Press, 1978.

Mazmanian, Daniel A., and Paul A. Sabatier. *Implementation and Public Policy*. Glenview, Ill.: Scott, Foresman and Co., 1983.

Nathan, Richard P., and Fred C. Doolittle and Associates. *The Consequences of Cuts: The Effects of the Reagan Domestic Program on State and Local Governments*. Princeton, N.J.: Princeton Urban and Regional Research Center, 1983.

Pressman, Jeffrey L., and Aaron Wildavsky. *Implementation*. 3rd ed. Berkeley: University of California Press, 1984.

Walker, Jack L. "The Diffusion of Innovation Among States." *American Political Science Review* 63, 3 (September 1969):880–99.

RAPE

Amir, Delila, and Menachem Amir. "Rape Crisis Centers: An Arena for Ideological Conflicts." *Victimology: An International Journal* 4, 2 (1979):247–57.

Amir, Menachem. *Patterns of Forcible Rape*. Chicago: University of Chicago Press, 1971.

Bienen, Leigh. "Rape III: National Developments in Rape Reform Legislation." *Women's Rights Law Reporter* 6, 3 (Spring 1980):171–217.

Brodyaga, Lisa, Margaret Gates, et al. *Rape and Its Victims: A Report for Citizens, Health Facilities and Criminal Justice Agencies*. Washington, D.C.: National Institute for Law Enforcement and Criminal Justice, 1975.

Brownmiller, Susan. *Against Our Will*. New York: Simon and Schuster, 1975.

Burgess, Ann W., and Lynda L. Holmstrum. *Rape: Victims of Crisis*. Bowie, Md.: Robert J. Brady, 1974.

Dworkin, Roger B. "The Resistance Standard in Rape Legislation." *Stanford Law Review* 18 (February 1966):680–89.

Forman, Bruce D., and J. Charles Wadsworth. "Delivery of Rape-Related Services in CMHCs: An Initial Study." *Journal of Community Psychology* 11, 3 (July 1983):236–40.

Fox, Sandra Sutherland, and Donald J. Scherl. "Crisis Intervention with Victims of Rape." *Social Work* 17, 1 (January 1972):37–42.

Herman, Lawrence. "What's Wrong with the Rape Reform Laws?" *The Civil Liberties Review* 3, 5 (December 1976–January 1977):60–73.

Holmstrum, Lynda L., and Ann W. Burgess. *The Victim of Rape: Institutional Reactions*. New York: John Wiley and Sons, 1978.

King, H. Elizabeth, and Carol Webb. "Rape Crisis Centers: Progress and Problems." *Journal of Social Issues* 37, 4 (Fall 1981):93–104.

Law Enforcement Assistance Administration. *Forcible Rape: An Analysis of Legal Issues.* Washington, D.C.: Government Printing Office, March 1978.

O'Sullivan, Elizabeth. "What Has Happened to Rape Crisis Centers: A Look at Their Structure, Members and Funding." *Victimology: An International Journal* 3, 1–2 (1978):45–62.

Rose, Vicki McNickle. "Rape as a Social Problem: A By-Product of the Feminist Movement." *Social Problems* 25, 1 (October 1977):75–89.

Russell, Diana H. *The Politics of Rape: The Victim's Perspective.* New York: Stein and Day, 1975.

Schultz, Leroy, ed. *Rape Victimology.* Springfield, Ill.: Charles C. Thomas, 1975.

Walker, M. J., and S. L. Brodsky, eds. *Sexual Assault: The Victim and the Rapist.* Lexington, Mass.: Lexington Books, 1976.

SPOUSE ABUSE

Ahrens, Lois. "Battered Women's Refuges: Feminist Cooperatives vs. Social Service Institutions." *Radical America* 14, 3 (May–June 1980):41–47.

Colorado Association for Aid to Battered Women. *A Monograph on Services to Battered Women.* Washington, D.C.: U.S. Department of Health and Human Services, 1979.

Davidson, Terry. *Conjugal Crime: Understanding and Changing the Wife Beating Pattern.* New York: Hawthorn Books, 1978.

Elshtain, Jean Bethke. "Politics and the Battered Woman." *Dissent* (Winter 1985):55–61.

Gelles, Richard J. *The Violent Home: A Study of the Physical Aggression between Husbands and Wives.* Beverly Hills, Calif.: Sage Publications, 1974.

Hamos, Julie E. *State Domestic Violence Laws and How to Pass Them: A Manual for Lobbyists.* Domestic Violence Monograph Series no. 2. Rockville, Md.: National Clearinghouse on Domestic Violence, 1980.

Jones, Ann. *Women Who Kill.* New York: Holt, Rinehart and Winston, 1980.

Jones, Valle. "Federal Legislation Concerning Spouse Abuse." *Victimology: An International Journal* 2, 3–4 (1977–78):623–27.

Martin, Del. *Battered Women.* San Francisco: Glide Productions, 1976.

Pfouts, Jane H., and Connie Renz. "The Future of Wife Abuse Programs." *Social Work* 26, 6 (November 1981):451–55.

Roberts, Alvin R., and Beverly J. Roberts. *Battered Women: A National*

Study and Service Guide. New York: Springer Publications Co., 1981.

Schechter, Susan. *Women and Male Violence: The Vision and Struggles of the Battered Women's Movement.* Boston: South End Press, 1982.

Scutt, Jocelyne. *Even in the Best Homes: Violence in the Family.* Ringwood, Victoria, Australia: Penguin Books, 1983.

Steinmetz, Suzanne K. *The Cycle of Violence: Assertive, Aggressive and Abusive Family Interaction.* New York: Praeger Publishers, 1977.

Straus, Murray A., Suzanne K. Steinmetz, and Richard J. Gelles. *Violence in the Family.* New York: Dodd, Mead and Co., 1974.

Straus, Murray A., Richard J. Gelles, and Suzanne K. Steinmetz. *Behind Closed Doors: Violence in the American Family.* Garden City, N.Y.: Anchor Books, 1981.

United States Commission on Civil Rights. *Battered Women: Issues of Public Policy.* A Consultation Sponsored by the United States Commission on Civil Rights. Washington, D.C.: U.S. Commission on Civil Rights, 1978.

Vapner, Gretchen. *The Shelter Experience: A Guide to Shelter Organization and Management for Groups Working Against Domestic Violence.* Domestic Violence Monograph Series no. 4. Rockville, Md.: National Clearinghouse on Domestic Violence, August 1980.

Walker, Lenore. "Battered Women and Learned Helplessness." *Victimology: An International Journal* 2, 3–4 (1977–78):525–33.

VICTIMS/VICTIMS' COMPENSATION

Baluss, Mary E. *Integrated Services for Victims of Crime: A County-Based Approach.* Washington, D.C.: National Association of Counties Research Foundation, 1975.

———. "Services for Victims of Crime: A Developing Opportunity." *Evaluation and Change*, Special Issue (1980):94–102.

Bard, Morton, and Dawn Sangrey. *The Crime Victim's Book.* New York: Basic Books, 1979.

Chappell, Duncan. "Providing for the Victim of Crime: Political Placebos or Progressive Programs." *Adelaide Law Review* 4 (1971–72):294–306.

Chappell, Duncan, and John Monahan, eds. *Violence and Criminal Justice.* Lexington, Mass.: Lexington Books, 1975.

Doerner, William G., Mary Knudten, Richard Knudten, and Anthony Meade. "An Analysis of Victim Compensation Programs as a Time-

Series Experiment." *Victimology: An International Journal* 1, 2 (Summer 1976):295–313.

Dussich, John P. J. "Victim Service Models and Their Efficacy." In *Victims and Society*, ed. by Emilio C. Viano, pp. 471–83. Washington, D.C.: Visage Press, 1976.

Edelhertz, Herbert, and Gilbert Geis. *Public Compensation to Victims of Crime.* New York: Praeger Publishers, 1974.

Ennis, Phillip. *Criminal Victimization in the United States. A Report on the National Survey.* President's Commission on Law Enforcement and Administration on Justice. Washington, D.C.: U.S. Government Printing Office, 1967.

Forer, Lois G. *Criminals and Victims: A Trial Judge Reflects on Crime and Punishment.* New York: W. W. Norton and Co., 1980.

Galaway, Burt, and Joe Hudson, eds. *Offender Restitution in Theory and Action.* Lexington, Mass.: Lexington Books, 1978.

Hudson, Joe, and Burt Galaway, eds. *Considering the Victim: Readings in Restitution and Victims' Compensation.* Springfield, Ill.: Charles C. Thomas, 1975.

————. *Restitution in Criminal Justice: A Critical Assessment of Sanctions.* Lexington, Mass.: Lexington Books, 1977.

Meade, Anthony, Mary C. Knudten, William Doerner, and Richard Knudten. "Discovery of a Forgotten Party: Trends in American Victim Compensation Legislation." *Victimology: An International Journal* 1, 3 (Fall 1976):421–33.

Mendelsohn, Beniamin. "The Origin of the Doctrine of Victimology." *Excerpta Criminologica* 3 (1963):239–41.

Polish, James. "Rehabilitation of Victims of Crime: An Overview." *UCLA Law Review* 21, 1 (October 1973):323–28.

Reiff, Robert. *The Invisible Victim: The Criminal Justice System's Forgotten Responsibility.* New York: Basic Books, 1979.

Schafer, Stephen. *The Victim and His Criminal: A Study in Functional Responsibility.* New York: Random House, 1968.

Symonds, Martin. "Victims of Violence: Psychological Effects and Aftereffects." *American Journal of Psychoanalysis* 35 (1975):19–26.

Viano, Emilio C. ed. *Victims and Society.* Washington, D.C.: Visage Press, 1976.

Yarborough, Ralph W. "The Battle for a Federal Violent Crimes Compensation Act: The Genesis of S.9." *Southern California Law Review* 43, 1 (1970):93–106.

Ziegenhagen, Eduard A. *Victims, Crime and Social Control.* New York: Praeger Publishers, 1977.

INDEX

ABOUT THE AUTHORS

STEVEN RATHGEB SMITH and SUSAN FREINKEL worked at the Kennedy School of Government, Harvard University, on a study of victimization policy funded by the National Institute of Mental Health; this study forms the basis of this book. Currently, Mr. Smith is an assistant professor, George Warren Brown School of Social Work, Washington University, St. Louis, Missouri. Ms. Freinkel is a journalist with *The Wichita Eagle-Beacon*, Wichita, Kansas.